Renaissance Thinking
IN THE CLASSROOM

*Interdisciplinary Learning,
Real-World Problems,
Intellectually Curious Students*

NATHAN D. LANG-RAAD

Solution Tree | Press

Copyright © 2025 by Solution Tree Press

Materials appearing here are copyrighted. With one exception, all rights are reserved. Readers may reproduce only those pages marked "Reproducible." Otherwise, no part of this book may be reproduced or transmitted in any form or by any means (electronic, photocopying, recording, or otherwise) without prior written permission of the publisher.

555 North Morton Street
Bloomington, IN 47404
800.733.6786 (toll free) / 812.336.7700
FAX: 812.336.7790

email: info@SolutionTree.com
SolutionTree.com

Visit **go.SolutionTree.com/instruction** to download the free reproducibles in this book.

Printed in the United States of America

Library of Congress Cataloging-in-Publication Data

Names: Lang-Raad, Nathan D., 1982- author.
Title: Renaissance thinking in the classroom : interdisciplinary learning,
   real-world problems, intellectually curious students / Nathan Lang-Raad.
Description: Bloomington, IN : Solution Tree Press, 2025. | Includes
   bibliographical references and index.
Identifiers: LCCN 2024030850 (print) | LCCN 2024030851 (ebook) | ISBN
   9781958590256 (paperback) | ISBN 9781958590263 (ebook)
Subjects: LCSH: Interdisciplinary approach in education. | Motivation in
   education. | Critical thinking--Study and teaching. | Problem
   solving--Study and teaching.
Classification: LCC LB2361 .L27 2025 (print) | LCC LB2361 (ebook) | DDC
   370.15--dc23/eng/20240821
LC record available at https://lccn.loc.gov/2024030850
LC ebook record available at https://lccn.loc.gov/2024030851

Solution Tree
Jeffrey C. Jones, CEO
Edmund M. Ackerman, President

Solution Tree Press
President and Publisher: Douglas M. Rife
Associate Publishers: Todd Brakke and Kendra Slayton
Editorial Director: Laurel Hecker
Art Director: Rian Anderson
Copy Chief: Jessi Finn
Production Editor: Kate St. Ives
Copy Editor: Mark Hain
Cover Designer: Rian Anderson
Text Designer: Julie Csizmadia
Acquisitions Editors: Carol Collins and Hilary Goff
Assistant Acquisitions Editor: Elijah Oates
Content Development Specialist: Amy Rubenstein
Associate Editor: Sarah Ludwig
Editorial Assistant: Anne Marie Watkins

Acknowledgments

Completing this book has been a journey of inspiration and unwavering support. I am deeply grateful to everyone who contributed to the creation of this work.

First and foremost, I want to thank my husband, Herbie Raad. Your constant encouragement, patience, and love have been my anchor.

I would like to extend my gratitude to the team at Solution Tree Press. To Douglas M. Rife, Todd Brakke, Kendra Slayton, and Laurel Hecker: Your guidance and belief in this project have been pivotal. My heartfelt thanks to Jessi Finn, Kate St. Ives, Mark Hain, Julie Csizmadia, Carol Collins, Hilary Goff, Elijah Oates, Amy Rubenstein, Sarah Ludwig, and Anne Marie Watkins for your exceptional work in bringing this book to life.

A special acknowledgment goes to Kate St. Ives, whose extraordinary dedication and meticulous attention to detail have been instrumental in shaping this book. Kate, your tireless efforts in refining the manuscript, your insightful suggestions, and your unwavering support have been nothing short of remarkable. Thank you for your patience, your expertise, and your commitment to this project. Your work has truly made a difference, and I am deeply grateful for your partnership.

To the reviewers who provided invaluable feedback, your perspectives have enriched this work immensely. Thank you to Doug Crowley, Kelly Hilliard, Teresa Kinley, Ian Landy, Louis Lim, and Jennifer Renegar for your thoughtful insights and contributions.

I also want to acknowledge the incredible educators and thought leaders I've worked with. Your dedication to transforming education and fostering creativity has been a beacon of inspiration.

Lastly, to the readers and educators who will use this book in their classrooms, your commitment to fostering a renaissance in thinking is what truly brings this work to life. Thank you for your dedication to your students and for being part of this transformative journey.

Solution Tree Press would like to thank the following reviewers:

Doug Crowley
Assistant Principal
DeForest Area High School
DeForest, Wisconsin

Kelly Hilliard
GATE Mathematics Instructor
 NBCT
Darrell C. Swope Middle School
Reno, Nevada

Teresa Kinley
Humanities Teacher
Calgary, Alberta, Canada

Ian Landy
Regional Principal of PIE
School District 47
Powell River, British Columbia,
 Canada

Louis Lim
Principal
Bur Oak Secondary School
Markham, Ontario, Canada

Jennifer Renegar
Data & Assessment Specialist
Republic School District
Republic, Missouri

Visit **go.SolutionTree.com/instruction** to download the free reproducibles in this book.

Table of Contents

Reproducibles are in italics.

About the Author	ix
Introduction	1
The Nine Habits of Thinking	5
The Challenge-Based Framework	7
Support Interdisciplinary Student Learning	12
How This Book Is Organized and How to Use It	13

Part 1

1 Foster the Nine Habits of Thinking in K–12 Learning	19
Work Together to Develop Interdisciplinary Learning Environments	20
Engage Your Students in Interdisciplinary Learning	23
Concluding Thoughts	27
Reflection Cycle Guide	28
Strengths Utilization Guide	29

	Habit 1: Cultivate Diverse Curiosity	31
2	Look to the Science of a Wandering Mind	32
	Develop Learning Dispositions and Motivation	35
	Implement and Differentiate an Easy Activity to Nurture Curiosity in K–12 Students	41
	Concluding Thoughts	43

	Habit 2: Take Risks	45
3	Understand That Decisions Are Risks	46
	Consider the Odds	48
	Implement and Differentiate an Easy Activity to Nurture Risk Taking in K–12 Students	53
	Concluding Thoughts	59

	Habit 3: Use Humor	61
4	Cultivate a Safe Environment for Humor	63
	Model How to Use Humor in Learning	65
	Implement and Differentiate an Easy Activity to Nurture Learning Through Humor in K–12 Students	68
	Concluding Thoughts	71

	Habit 4: Create and Innovate	73
5	Find the Intersection of Fantasy and Reality	74
	Learn From a NASA Innovation Story and the Challenge-Driven Innovation	78
	Implement and Differentiate an Easy Activity to Nurture Creative Thinking and Innovative Action in K–12 Students	83
	Concluding Thoughts	86

	Habit 5: Self-Regulate	89
6	Use Strategies to Promote the Development of Self-Regulation	90
	Evaluate Students' Self-Regulation and Offer Them Opportunities to Practice	95
	Implement and Differentiate an Easy Activity to Nurture Self-Regulation in K–12 Students	102
	Concluding Thoughts	103

	Habit 6: Transfer Learning	105
7	Embrace Failure	106
	Use Analogical Thinking	110
	Inform Transfer Learning Instruction With Constructivist Thinking	112
	Implement Effective Transfer Learning Strategies	115
	Implement and Differentiate an Easy Activity to Nurture Transfer Learning in K–12 Students	121
	Concluding Thoughts	122

8 Habit 7: Ask Questions 125
Let Inquiry Pave the Way 126
Supplement Procedural Questions 129
Implement and Differentiate an Easy Activity to Nurture Genuine Inquiry in K–12 Students ... 133
Concluding Thoughts 137

9 Habit 8: Evaluate Evidence 139
Teach Students the Meaning of Evidence 140
Employ the Scientific Method in Evaluating Evidence 142
Delve Into Data Sets and Arguments 143
Encourage Insightful Questions 145
Implement and Differentiate an Easy Activity to Nurture Evaluating Evidence in K–12 Students . 147
Concluding Thoughts 148

10 Habit 9: Embrace Lifelong Learning and Perseverance 151
Establish Objectives 152
Cultivate an Environment for Effort 153
Nurture Collaboration and Community 156
Implement and Differentiate an Easy Activity to Nurture Perseverance and Lifelong Learning in K–12 Students 159
Concluding Thoughts 161

Part II

11 Integrate the Challenge-Based Framework and the Habits of Thinking 165
The Anatomy of the Challenge-Based Framework 166
Challenge-Based Instruction and Habits Integration 173
Challenge-Based Framework Examples for Different Grade Bands 179
Concluding Thoughts 185
Challenge-Based Framework Template 186

12 Integrate Academic Standards 189
Balance Academic Standards and Challenges 190
Chunk Within Challenges to Create a Tapestry of Interwoven Learning 194
The Harmonious Intersection of Challenge and Standard 196
Concluding Thoughts 198

13 Integrate 21st Century Skills 199

Dissect the Intersection of 21st Century Skills and Habits of Thinking 200

Link 21st Century Skills to the Challenge-Based Framework 203

Differentiate Grade-Level Examples Across Core Disciplines 205

Concluding Thoughts 208

14 Engage Teacher Collaboration 209

Create a Canvas of Collaboration 210

Use Interdisciplinary Projects to Combine Curricula 218

Sustain Collaboration Through Regular Check-Ins 219

Share Digital Platforms to Amplify Collaborative Potential 222

Enrich Educator Experiences and Collaborative Insights Through Peer Observations 226

Catalyze Collaborative Teaching Excellence in Professional Development Workshops 228

Overcoming the Hurdles in Teacher Collaboration 229

Concluding Thoughts 230

15 Engage Student Collaboration 231

Find the Essence of Student Collaboration in the Challenge-Based Framework 232

Use the Nine Habits of Thinking to Fuel Effective Student Collaboration 232

Differentiate Strategies for Helping Students Collaborate 234

A Real-World Inspired Classroom Scenario 235

Challenges to Student Collaboration in the Challenge-Based Framework 236

Concluding Thoughts 237

Epilogue 239

References and Resources 241

Index 245

About the Author

Nathan D. Lang-Raad, EdD, is an educator, speaker, and author, as well as the founder and CEO of Raad Education, where he spearheads innovations in educational practice and theory.

Nathan's distinguished career encompasses roles as a teacher, elementary and high school administrator, and university adjunct professor. Notably, he has served as the Director of Elementary Curriculum and Instruction for Metropolitan Nashville Public Schools and as an education supervisor at NASA's Johnson Space Center. His previous positions include Chief Education Officer at WeVideo and Vice President of National Product Line at Savvas Learning.

A dedicated advocate for global sustainability, Nathan serves as the U.S. State Ambassador for the Climate Action Project, a collaborative initiative supported by the United Nations, World Wildlife Fund, NASA, and the Jane Goodall Institute. He is also an advisor for Take Action Global (TAG).

An accomplished author, Nathan has contributed significantly to education literature, writing extensively about instructional coaching, innovative teaching methods, and the integration of technology in classrooms. His publications include *Everyday Instructional Coaching: Seven Daily Drivers to Support Teacher Effectiveness*, *The New Art and Science* of Teaching Mathematics (coauthored with Robert J. Marzano), *WeVideo Every Day: 40 Strategies to Deepen Learning in Any Class*, *Mathematics Unit Planning in a PLC at Work©, Grades PreK–2* (coauthored with Sarah Schuhl, Timothy D. Kanold, Jennifer Deinhart, Matthew R. Larson, and Nanci N. Smith), *The Teachers of Oz: Leading With Wizdom, Heart, and Spirit* (coauthored with Herbie Raad), *The Boundless Classroom: Designing Purposeful Instruction for Any Learning Environment* (coauthored with James Witty), *Instructional Coaching Connection: Building Relationships to Better Support Teachers*, and *Never Stop Asking: Teaching Students to Be Better Critical Thinkers*.

Nathan earned a bachelor's degree in general science-chemistry from Harding University, a master's degree in administration and supervision from the University of Houston-Victoria, and a doctorate in learning organizations and strategic change from Lipscomb University.

Nathan lives with his husband, Herbie Raad, in scenic Maine, where he continues his pursuit of empowering educators and transforming learning landscapes.

To learn more about Nathan's pioneering work, follow @drlangraad on X, formerly known as Twitter.

To book Nathan D. Lang-Raad for professional development, contact pd@SolutionTree.com.

Introduction

You walk into a classroom where the air hums with curiosity. This is no ordinary room, and certainly not a relic of the passive, humdrum, rote-learning routine of your bygone school days. Here, students buzz with the excitement of tackling real-world problems, their discussions leaping across subjects with the agility of Olympic athletes. Welcome to the future of education, where boundaries between disciplines blur and the status quo transforms into the extraordinary.

In your traditional school setting, the instructional model is as compartmentalized as an outdated filing cabinet. Each subject is neatly tucked into its drawer, untouched by the context of the subjects tucked away next to it. Picture the scene: students scribbling notes while the teacher drones on about photosynthesis, oblivious to how this knowledge could intersect with, say, environmental science or even social policy. There's a palpable disconnect, a missed opportunity to cultivate the kind of interdisciplinary thinking that today's world demands.

Now, let's pivot back to the vision of learning alive with curiosity. Imagine a class that operates like a think tank, where the study of photosynthesis seamlessly integrates with climate science, engineering, and even economics. Here, students might emulate the efforts of Project Vesta (2004), for example, a real-world initiative aimed at sequestering atmospheric carbon dioxide through innovative seaweed farming. In this setting, the learners are not merely students; they are budding scientists, engineers, and policymakers, collaboratively exploring how to optimize seaweed growth and its impact on carbon capture.

This dynamic, interdisciplinary approach does more than teach facts; it fosters creativity, critical thinking, and problem-solving skills. These students aren't just absorbing information—they're applying it, questioning it, and expanding upon it. They understand that the world's problems are not isolated within the confines of single-subject boundaries. Rather, solutions emerge from the synthesis of diverse fields, echoing the intellectual courage and strength of polymaths from history, such as Ada Lovelace, George Washington Carver, and, of course, Leonardo da Vinci.

Why is this shift so crucial? Because the challenges we face today—climate change, artificial intelligence, socio-economic disparities—cannot be tackled from a one-dimensional perspective. The capacity to think across disciplines, to connect the dots in novel ways, is not just an educational advantage; it is a necessity. An interdisciplinary education model prepares students to navigate and influence a world that is inherently complex and interwoven.

Your role in this transformative landscape is to be more than a teacher; you are a facilitator of curiosity and a cultivator of connections. By integrating subjects and emphasizing real-world applications, you help students develop a holistic understanding and the intellectual agility needed to become innovators and leaders. This approach does not merely fill students' minds with isolated facts; it equips them with the tools to synthesize information, ask profound questions, and seek out inventive solutions.

In essence, the difference between the old and new models of education is the difference between a stagnant pond and a flowing river. One is contained, static, and ultimately limited. The other is dynamic, connected, and boundless. It's time to break down the barriers of traditional education and usher in an era where learning is as fluid and interconnected as the world it aims to understand.

Through my personal experience as a STEM educator, I have witnessed the power of interdisciplinary thinking in sparking curiosity and fostering innovation. These experiences have driven me to research and advocate for a reimagining of our educational system. In this book, I share insights, examples, and strategies with the goal of guiding K–12 educators toward an education renaissance that nurtures the next generation of leaders and problem solvers. The premise is straightforward: by dismantling the artificial barriers that separate traditional subjects and embracing a more holistic, interconnected approach to education, you can empower students to become the innovative thinkers and changemakers our world so desperately needs. This is not just a lofty ideal but a practical, necessary shift. Let's embark on this journey toward an educational renaissance, forging a more resilient, enlightened, and compassionate future in the process.

As we dive deeper into the urgent need for fundamental changes in education, it's crucial to acknowledge the complex challenges our world faces and the interdisciplinary skills students need to effectively address them. The 21st century presents a landscape riddled with intricate issues that traditional educational models often fail to prepare students for. In this book, I emphasize the necessity of an educational shift, showcasing real-world problems paired with the interdisciplinary skills required to tackle them, supported by specific research-backed examples. Here are a few pressing challenges and how students with interdisciplinary learning might address them.

- **Climate change:** Tackling the global climate crisis demands a multifaceted approach that combines expertise in environmental science, engineering, economics, and policymaking. Students equipped with interdisciplinary skills can develop innovative solutions, such as carbon capture and storage, renewable energy technologies, and sustainable urban planning. A study by Katja Brundiers and Arnim Wiek (2017) highlights the success of interdisciplinary collaborations in advancing climate change mitigation strategies through the development of urban sustainability projects.

- **Public health:** The COVID-19 pandemic has highlighted the need for interdisciplinary collaboration in addressing public health emergencies. Combining knowledge in areas such as virology, epidemiology, data science, and public policy, students can develop the mindsets to invest in their futures beyond school and better understand and respond to complex health crises. A notable example of using interdisciplinary skill sets to address such a crisis is the rapid development of vaccines, where interdisciplinary teams of scientists, medical professionals, and policymakers worked together to expedite vaccine creation and distribution (Lurie, Saville, Hatchett, & Halton, 2020). Students who develop interdisciplinary thinking skills can better merge disciplines in solitary work as well as productively contribute to interdisciplinary teams.

- **Artificial intelligence and ethics:** As artificial intelligence (AI) continues to permeate our lives, ethical considerations become increasingly important. Students who possess interdisciplinary skills in computer science, philosophy, psychology, and social sciences can navigate the moral complexities that arise in the development and deployment of AI technologies. A study by Iyad Rahwan and colleagues (2019) demonstrates the value of interdisciplinary collaboration in reducing biases and promoting fairness in AI systems, with research teams that included ethicists, engineers, and social scientists working together to develop more equitable algorithms.

These few examples (so many more are possible) underscore the growing importance of interdisciplinary skills in addressing the pressing challenges of our time. By fostering changes that embrace holistic thinking and acting, we can better prepare students to navigate and contribute to our rapidly evolving world. The research clearly indicates that education must shift considerably away from a linear structure in which different fields of study are taught in isolation toward one in which these fields are intertwined. Studies by Brundiers and Wiek (2013) highlight the success of interdisciplinary collaborations in advancing climate change mitigation strategies through urban sustainability projects. Additionally, a review by Veronica Boix Mansilla, William C. Miller, and Howard Gardner (2000) finds that students who engaged in interdisciplinary learning demonstrated improved critical thinking, problem solving, and collaborative skills. Furthermore, Megan Tschannen-Moran, Serena Salloum, and Roger Goddard (2014) reveal a positive correlation between teacher collaboration and student achievement.

In a time where a renaissance in education calls for a return to interdisciplinary learning—a hallmark of the original Renaissance—it's apt to look toward Leonardo da Vinci as an exemplar of this approach. The Renaissance, a period of great cultural and intellectual rebirth, celebrated the interconnectedness of disciplines, much like the modern educational landscape we aspire to create. Leonardo da Vinci is a powerful source of inspiration for the vision in this book. Leonardo was active as a painter, engineer, scientist, theorist, sculptor, and architect throughout the High Renaissance, the ultimate engaged learner—a true polymath, that is, a voracious, wide-ranging learner with extensive knowledge in multiple subjects and a willingness to combine subject-area knowledge in pursuit of learning and doing. While he was renowned for his in-depth knowledge of the arts and sciences, and his original contributions across both fields, he also built on past knowledge to advance numerous fields in unprecedented ways. He did this by crossing disciplinary boundaries in search of more knowledge and he possessed habits of thinking, paired with investigative actions, that carried him to his successes and helped him better understand the world around him.

One such habit of thinking was asking insightful questions. Leonardo kept a notebook in which he recorded everything he saw, felt, tried, and thought. The seven thousand pages of his notebook that survive today show us that he had more questions than answers, to the point where he never finished compiling his findings and revelations. He was more interested in asking questions than in providing answers. Every solution he discovered left him with additional questions, and with an expanded sense of what was possible. The notebooks, often referred to as his codices, contain thousands of pages filled with his observations, ideas, sketches, and questions, offering a rare glimpse into the inner workings of his brilliant mind. The Codex Atlanticus, for instance, is the largest compilation of Leonardo's writings, consisting of approximately 1,750 pages, and provides an invaluable resource for understanding his thought processes and relentless curiosity (Pedretti, 1978).

The goal of *Renaissance Thinking in the Classroom* is not to transform every student into a polymath or to exactly replicate Leonardo da Vinci's thoughts and actions, nor is it to overlook the diverse backgrounds and unique circumstances of today's students. Rather, the book's purpose is to empower educators—including teachers, instructional coaches, and school and district leaders—to foster within their students the essential traits of great Renaissance thinkers and other polymathic thinkers throughout historical eras to meet the social and environmental challenges they will face in their lives. These traits include nurturing curiosity, encouraging the pursuit of individual passions, cultivating a love for learning, inspiring creative thinking, and instilling persistence in tackling complex problems, all within the context of supportive and stimulating learning environments. School and district leaders indeed possess the potential to spearhead transformative changes that promote interdisciplinary learning in their institutions. By dedicating resources and creating structures to support a more integrated mode of education, these leaders can foster an environment where students are encouraged to think critically, draw connections, and approach problems holistically. A renaissance thinker in today's context would be characterized by intellectual curiosity, adaptability, cross-disciplinary proficiency, and a commitment to addressing societal challenges with empathy and determination. In essence, our world requires students who embody the spirit of the Renaissance—individuals who are not only adept in various fields of knowledge but also driven by a passion for innovation, collaboration, and social impact.

By championing renaissance thinking in K–12 learning, we can cultivate a generation of thinkers prepared to face the complexities of our rapidly evolving world and contribute to a brighter, more equitable future for all. My purpose is to contribute to this renaissance by rethinking and repositioning 21st century skills (creativity, collaboration, critical thinking, and communication) within an interdisciplinary approach to learning for K–12 classrooms. To achieve this, I present nine specific habits of thinking to integrate into K–12 student learning and introduce a challenge-based framework, focusing on the application of these methods across all grade levels. In the following sections, I outline the habits of thinking, the challenge-based framework, and how these two components together support individualized, interdisciplinary, in-depth learning. You will also find an overview of the contents of this book and how to use it.

The Nine Habits of Thinking

Habits of thinking are a collection of skills and attitudes that can help students become more successful problem solvers and creative thinkers. Some educators use the term habits of mind; I prefer habits of thinking to emphasize, as thinking is a verb, the actions taken in these habits. These skills and attitudes can be taught to students through a variety of educational settings. You've heard of and read about how creativity, critical thinking, intellectual curiosity, and the ability to solve problems are vital mental habits. For example, a study by educational experts Bernie Trilling and Charles Fadel (2009) emphasizes that creativity and critical thinking are essential for students to navigate and succeed in the complex, rapidly changing 21st century landscape. Similarly, research by Bharath Sriraman (2004) highlights the importance of fostering intellectual curiosity and problem-solving abilities to enhance students' engagement and academic achievement. Additionally, a study by Yuan Zhao, Sheng Lin, Jinlan Liu, Jingyi Zhang, and Qian Yu (2021) underscores the necessity of these skills in preparing students for future challenges and opportunities in a globalized world. Educators can facilitate a more curious and open-minded attitude toward learning by instructing students in certain mental habits.

Cultivating habits of thinking has long and varied origins in K–12 education. Researchers have extensively examined, written about, and published in various formats on habits of thinking, also using terms such as *21st century skills* or *habits of mind* (Costa & Kallick, 2009; Miller & Mansilla, 2004; Partnership for 21st Century Skills, 2024). This book consolidates the existing research and focuses on nine specific habits of thinking, demonstrating how to systematically embed them into a challenge-integrated framework.

The inspiration for the nine habits I develop in this book stems from multiple sources. First, Leonardo da Vinci exhibited many of these habits, or similar ones, throughout his life. His curiosity, ability to ask insightful questions, and willingness to take risks are prime examples of the habits I have formalized in this book. However, Leonardo da Vinci is far from the only thinker who influenced my conception of habits of thinking. For instance, Arthur L. Costa and Bena Kallick's (2009) *Habits of Mind* series explores sixteen dispositions for effective learning, focusing on the intellectual behaviors that support problem solving and decision making. I was also influenced by the Partnership for 21st Century Skills (2024) framework outlining essential skills for success in the modern world, emphasizing creativity, critical thinking, communication, and collaboration as crucial components. While these works differ in the specific habits they discuss, they overlap significantly in their underlying principles.

In addition, researcher and education writer Robert J. Marzano's ideas about creativity have greatly influenced my selection and application of the habits of thinking. His emphasis on open-ended questions, brainstorming, and exploration aligns with the habits I propose. For example, Marzano and colleagues' (1992) suggestion to provide students with opportunities to experiment with ideas connects to the habits of taking risks and cultivating diverse curiosity. According to Marzano and colleagues' (1992) *Dimensions of Learning*, teachers can teach creative thinking by doing the following.

- Providing students with opportunities to explore and experiment with ideas
- Encouraging students to think outside the box and come up with creative solutions to problems

- Asking open-ended questions that require students to think critically and come up with their own answers
- Modeling creative thinking by sharing their own ideas and strategies for problem solving
- Allowing students time to brainstorm, discuss, and reflect on their ideas in small groups or as a class
- Providing feedback that encourages creative thinking rather than simply providing the correct answer or solution
- Incorporating activities that require students to use their imagination, such as writing stories or creating art projects
- Introducing new concepts and materials that challenge students to think creatively in order to understand them better

By incorporating Marzano's strategies into my teaching, I was able to foster an environment where students felt empowered to think creatively, take risks, and collaborate with their peers to develop innovative ideas and solutions. For instance, when I taught high school science, I would often present real-world problems (for example, the impact of flooding on our community, because of the tropical plain we lived on) and encourage students to brainstorm creative solutions in small groups. I would walk around the classroom, asking thought-provoking questions and prompting students to think beyond conventional approaches. Additionally, I would share examples from my own experiences to model creative problem solving and highlight the importance of perseverance when tackling challenges. This approach not only enriched their learning experience but also helped to build essential skills for success in the 21st century.

Reflecting on these experiences, I realized that fostering creative thinking in the classroom is a dynamic process that evolves with each group of students and each unique challenge. This evolution in my teaching practice, inspired by the principles of creative inquiry, inevitably led me to appreciate the depth of Leonardo da Vinci's interdisciplinary approach and the nine habits that defined his genius.

The nine habits of thinking that inform this book's interdisciplinary learning model are as follows.

1. **Habit 1: Cultivate diverse curiosity**—Encourage students to explore various subjects and interests, fostering a well-rounded approach to learning. In a student learning context, this would involve engaging with different disciplines or topics, sparking a broader understanding of the world.

2. **Habit 2: Take risks**—Promote an environment where students feel comfortable pushing boundaries and trying new ideas. In practice, this would mean students attempting novel solutions to problems or embracing unfamiliar subjects.

3. **Habit 3: Use humor**—Incorporate wit and cleverness into learning experiences to stimulate critical thinking and create a more engaging atmosphere. This would involve using thought-provoking anecdotes or employing subtle humor to challenge students' perspectives and encourage deeper understanding of complex topics.

4. **Habit 4: Create and innovate**—Encourage students to think outside the box and develop original ideas. In a learning context, this would

involve brainstorming, designing projects, or finding innovative solutions to challenges.

5. **Habit 5: Self-regulate**—Teach students to manage their emotions, thoughts, and behaviors effectively in different situations. This would involve practicing mindfulness, cultivating self-awareness, setting goals, or reflecting on their learning experiences.

6. **Habit 6: Transfer learning**—Help students apply knowledge and skills from one context to another. This would involve connecting concepts from different subjects or using a skill learned in one area to solve a problem in another.

7. **Habit 7: Ask questions**—Cultivate a sense of curiosity and inquiry by encouraging students to ask questions and seek answers. This would involve promoting open-ended discussions or fostering a classroom culture that values questioning.

8. **Habit 8: Evaluate evidence**—Teach students to critically assess information and sources to form well-founded opinions and make informed decisions. This would involve analyzing data, comparing perspectives, or scrutinizing the reliability of sources.

9. **Habit 9: Embrace lifelong learning and perseverance**—Instill in students the importance of continuous learning and the resilience to overcome obstacles. This would involve promoting a growth mindset, celebrating persistence, or discussing the value of learning from mistakes.

It is my intent that these nine habits, inspired by and synthesizing a long tradition of insights about habits of thinking, offer a unique perspective. Further, I intend that my integration of the nine habits of thinking into a challenge-based learning framework will provide a fresh lens on learning, bridging the gap between past research and contemporary educational practices, ultimately guiding educators to inspire a new generation of renaissance thinkers.

The Challenge-Based Framework

As I took on the role of an administrator at a STEM school in Clarksville, Tennessee, I found myself facing a challenge: creating a STEM-integration approach that was clear, sustainable, scalable, and innovative. With various loose definitions of what STEM should look like in the classroom, and each educator drawing from their own personal experiences to define success, it became apparent that we needed a more cohesive approach.

In response to this need, I set out to develop a well-defined leadership structure around STEM education and to clearly articulate what high-quality STEM instruction, integration, and learning would look like. This journey led me to conceptualize the challenge-based framework. Drawing inspiration from my own experiences as an educator and administrator, as well as extensive research on interdisciplinary learning and habits of thinking, the challenge-based framework was born. This framework not only addressed the unique needs of our STEM school but was also adaptable and applicable to various educational contexts.

The *challenge-based framework* is predicated on the concept that all fields of study are inextricably linked to one another and ought to be taught together to give students a more well-rounded education. Students build skills that will benefit them in the future while also gaining a deeper understanding of each subject area when the curriculum is structured in this manner. This interdisciplinary teaching and learning approach bridges the gaps in traditional education, such as those created by the separation of disciplines and the lack of real-world context. It lays a robust foundation for integrated learning and addresses the need for cohesive STEM education by linking science, technology, engineering, and mathematics with other subject areas, encouraging holistic understanding and application.

The challenge-based framework is a structured, interdisciplinary approach to education that focuses on presenting students with real-world challenges. This framework encourages collaboration as students work together to solve these challenges, thereby fostering active learning and critical thinking. By navigating complex issues and developing viable solutions, students integrate a broad range of academic skills and habits of thinking. Anchoring learning in tangible tasks, the challenge-based framework deepens understanding of content areas while simultaneously developing practical and cognitive skills such as problem solving, creativity, and resilience.

While kit-based, recipe-driven STEM education has become popular in many schools, our team of educators at the STEM school in Clarksville wanted something more meaningful and impactful for our students that mirrored Leonardo da Vinci's approach to learning. We were passionate about providing students with opportunities to refine their work, find solutions to problems in their own communities, experiment with various technological approaches until they found one that worked, and apply mathematical practices to scientific (real-world) contexts. To achieve this, we recognized the need for a challenge-based framework in which students could engage with engineering approaches, such as inquiry-based problem solving.

The challenge-based framework consists of several key components, which collectively provide a comprehensive and effective approach to interdisciplinary learning. These components include the following.

- **Clear learning goals:** These goals define what students should know or be able to do by the end of the unit or lesson.
- **Essential questions:** Thought-provoking questions launch students into the challenge and help guide their inquiry.
- **Standards integration:** By aligning the unit or lesson with relevant content-specific and content-neutral standards, teachers acknowledge the interconnectedness of various fields of study.
- **Engineering design process:** This process asks students to structure the sequence of actions they will take to solve the problem, and incorporate iterative cycles of asking, imagining, planning, creating, and improving. In tandem, it also engages teachers in the cycles of asking, imagining, and so on, giving a space for closely related but unique, educator-led versions of each action.
  - *Ask*—Identify the problem and pose questions.
  - *Imagine*—Brainstorm potential solutions.
  - *Plan*—Develop a blueprint for implementation.
  - *Create*—Construct the solution.
  - *Improve*—Evaluate and refine the solution.

- **Habits of thinking:** Teachers foster, while students engage in, the essential habits of thinking throughout the learning process, inspired by Leonardo da Vinci's own habits.
  - Cultivate diverse curiosity.
  - Take risks.
  - Use humor.
  - Create and innovate.
  - Self-regulate.
  - Transfer learning.
  - Ask questions.
  - Evaluate evidence.
  - Embrace lifelong learning and perseverance.
- **Assessments:** Teachers determine how they will assess student learning throughout the process.
- **Reflection:** Teachers evaluate their successes and areas for improvement in future iterations of the lesson or unit.

The challenge-based framework begins with a clear student goal that defines what students should know or be able to do. The teacher then poses an essential question, launching students into the challenge and setting the stage for problem solving. Teachers plan to integrate content-specific and content-neutral standards, ensuring a well-rounded learning experience. Next, teachers and students collaboratively design the sequence of actions students will take to solve the problem, emphasizing the activation of critical dispositions and habits of thinking throughout the process. This teacher-student collaborative partnership is central to the challenge-based framework, ensuring that students are not passive recipients of knowledge but active participants in their learning journey. The teacher facilitates the process, providing structure and guidance, while the students contribute their ideas and perspectives, fostering a sense of ownership and engagement with the material. Assessment in the challenge-based framework focuses on students' products, processes, designs, and presentations, serving as artifacts for authentic and formative assessment.

To effectively implement the challenge-based framework, educators can use a detailed template as a guide for designing and executing interdisciplinary lessons. Figure I.1 (page 10) shows a completed example. This template outlines each component of the framework, providing a structured approach to ensure all aspects of the learning experience are addressed. By following this challenge-based framework template, educators can create rich learning experiences that not only deepen students' understanding of subject matter but also foster essential habits of thinking. This approach paves the way for a renaissance in education, equipping students with the interdisciplinary skills needed to become innovative thinkers and problem solvers in our rapidly changing world.

STUDENT GOAL:
Develop a sustainable urban garden that can provide fresh produce to the local community.

ESSENTIAL QUESTION:
How can we design and implement a sustainable urban garden that maximizes yield and minimizes environmental impact?

STANDARDS INTEGRATION:
Understanding plant biology and ecology. Mathematics—Calculating area, yield, and resource requirements. Social Studies—Examining the impact of urban agriculture on communities. Language Arts—Writing proposals and reports on the garden project.

ENGINEERING DESIGN PROCESS:

Teacher Actions and Support	Student Actions and Behavior
Ask: Introduce the concept of urban food deserts and discuss their impact. Provide resources and materials about urban gardening and sustainable agriculture. Facilitate a brainstorming session on potential garden designs.	*Ask:* Identify the problem of urban food deserts and pose relevant questions. Engage with provided resources to understand urban gardening principles. Participate actively in brainstorming sessions.
Imagine: Encourage students to research different types of urban gardens and innovative gardening techniques. Support students in developing initial sketches and ideas for their garden project. Organize guest speakers or virtual field trips to existing urban gardens.	*Imagine:* Conduct research on urban gardening techniques and solutions. Develop and share initial sketches and ideas with peers. Interact with guest speakers and explore real-world examples.
Plan: Guide students in creating detailed blueprints for their garden, including plant selection, layout, and resource management. Provide templates and tools for project planning and management. Review and provide feedback on student plans, ensuring feasibility and sustainability.	*Plan:* Create detailed blueprints for the urban garden project. Utilize provided templates and tools for planning. Incorporate feedback to refine and finalize plans.
Create: Assist students in procuring materials and setting up their garden. Monitor progress and offer troubleshooting support as needed. Facilitate regular check-ins and progress reports.	*Create:* Implement the garden design, setting up and planting according to the plan. Maintain the garden, documenting progress and challenges. Report regularly on the status of the project.
Improve: Encourage students to evaluate the performance of their garden and identify areas for improvement. Support iterative cycles of testing and refinement. Provide opportunities for students to present their findings and reflect on their learning process.	*Improve:* Evaluate the garden's performance and suggest improvements. Engage in iterative testing and refinement. Present findings and reflect on the project's impact and learning outcomes.

HABITS OF THINKING:

Teacher Actions and Support	Student Actions and Behavior
Habit 1: *Cultivate diverse curiosity* Provide diverse resources and encourage exploration.	**Habit 1:** *Cultivate diverse curiosity* Explore various aspects of the project with enthusiasm.
Habit 2: *Take risks* Create a safe environment for experimentation.	**Habit 2:** *Take risks* Try new approaches and learn from failures.
Habit 3: *Use humor* Use light-hearted anecdotes and playful activities to build rapport and reduce anxiety, encouraging a positive classroom culture.	**Habit 3:** *Use humor* Participate in activities with a sense of fun and openness, using humor to build connections with peers and reduce stress. Engage in collaborative tasks with a positive attitude, finding joy and laughter in the learning process while maintaining respect and focus.
Habit 4: *Create and innovate* Encourage unique solutions and creative problem solving.	**Habit 4:** *Create and innovate* Develop and implement original ideas.
Habit 5: *Self-regulate* Teach time management and self-monitoring techniques.	**Habit 5:** *Self-regulate* Manage time and monitor progress effectively.
Habit 6: *Transfer learning* Connect project activities to broader academic concepts.	**Habit 6:** *Transfer learning* Apply knowledge from different subjects to the project.
Habit 7: *Ask questions* Model inquiry-based thinking and question posing.	**Habit 7:** *Ask questions* Continuously inquire and seek deeper understanding.
Habit 8: *Evaluate evidence* Teach students to critically assess data and findings.	**Habit 8:** *Evaluate evidence* Critically analyze data and project outcomes.
Habit 9: *Embrace lifelong learning and perseverance* Encourage resilience and continuous improvement.	**Habit 9:** *Embrace lifelong learning and perseverance* Demonstrate resilience and a commitment to improvement.

ASSESSMENTS:

Final presentation: Students will present their urban garden project, including design, implementation process, and outcomes, to the class.

Written report: Students will submit a comprehensive report detailing the project's goals, methods, challenges, results, and reflections.

Peer assessment: Students will assess each other's contributions and teamwork through a a structured peer-review process.

Self-assessment: Students will complete a self-assessment reflecting on their learning and participation, and the project's impact.

TEACHER REFLECTION: WHAT DID I DO SUCCESSFULLY? WHAT WILL I DO DIFFERENTLY NEXT TIME?

Plan for resource procurement well in advance. Consider creating a partnership with local businesses or community organizations to secure materials.

Structured milestones: Implement more structured milestones and checkpoints throughout the project to help students manage their time and tasks better. Provide additional guidance and scaffolding for students who need more support in self-regulation.

Group dynamics: Address group dynamics early by incorporating team-building activities at the beginning of the project. Regularly monitor and support group interactions to ensure all students are contributing equally.

Figure I.1: Sample completed challenge-based framework template for urban garden project.

By implementing the challenge-based framework at the STEM school in Clarksville, our team of educators was able to significantly enhance student engagement and learning outcomes. Our staff, which included teachers from various disciplines such as science, mathematics, social studies, and language arts, collaborated closely to integrate this innovative approach into our curriculum. The challenge-based framework provided a scaffold for designing interdisciplinary lessons and activities that encouraged students to develop essential habits of thinking, better preparing them to tackle the complex challenges of our ever-changing world.

As the challenge-based framework took shape and began to transform our school, it became clear that this framework could serve as a powerful tool for educators in any setting who strive to create meaningful learning experiences that foster the development of well-rounded, innovative thinkers—thus contributing to a renaissance in education. As the challenge-based framework began to reshape the educational landscape of our school, tangible transformations became evident. One example was in our biology classrooms, where students used local water quality issues to learn about ecosystems, resulting in a collaborative project with a local environmental agency. Another transformation took place in the mathematics department, where traditional textbook problems were replaced with real-world financial challenges faced by local businesses, and students worked on creating viable solutions. These examples showcase how the framework not only revitalizes curriculum content but also connects students' learning with their community, making education more relevant and impactful.

Research supports the effectiveness of interdisciplinary learning in promoting these habits of thinking. For instance, a study by Boix Mansilla and colleagues (2000) finds that students who engaged in interdisciplinary learning demonstrated improved critical thinking, problem solving, and collaborative skills. Additionally, a review of literature by Grady J. Venville, John Wallace, Léonie J. Rennie, and John A. Malone (2002) indicates that interdisciplinary approaches to teaching foster deeper understanding and improve transfer of learning across different subject areas.

By integrating challenge-based frameworks into their teaching, educators can cultivate a way of learning in their students that will serve them well both within and beyond the classroom. This approach sets the stage for immersive learning, empowering students to become innovative thinkers and problem solvers, much like Leonardo da Vinci, and capable of addressing the complex challenges of today's world.

Support Interdisciplinary Student Learning

The integration of the nine habits of thinking and the challenge-based framework work synergistically to promote interdisciplinary student learning. By intentionally weaving these habits into the challenge-based framework, we ensure that students not only acquire academic knowledge but also develop essential skills for lifelong learning. For instance, teachers cultivate diverse curiosity by providing a variety of resources and encouraging exploration, while fostering creativity and innovation involves brainstorming sessions and rewarding creative solutions. This practical integration makes the habits relevant and impactful, as they are embedded in the learning process and directly applied to project work.

The nine habits of thinking serve as a foundation for students to develop essential life skills and intellectual abilities, while the challenge-based framework provides the structure and context for them to practice and refine these habits. As students work through the stages of the challenge-based framework, they apply and strengthen the habits in a variety of real-world scenarios. For instance, as students embark on a challenge-based project, they draw on their curiosity (habit 1) and risk taking (habit 2) as they explore new concepts and generate innovative ideas. Similarly, as they progress through the engineering design process, they exercise their creativity and innovation (habit 4), self-regulation (habit 5), and transfer learning (habit 6) as they iterate and refine their solutions.

The collaborative nature of the challenge-based framework also offers opportunities for students to develop their communication and teamwork skills, as they work together to address complex, interdisciplinary challenges. By fostering an environment that values humor (habit 3), students can learn to navigate setbacks and challenges with a positive mindset, enhancing their resilience and adaptability. Furthermore, the emphasis on asking questions (habit 7) and evaluating evidence (habit 8) within the challenge-based framework helps students cultivate critical thinking skills and a healthy skepticism, empowering them to become discerning consumers and creators of information.

Finally, the challenge-based framework encourages students to embrace lifelong learning and perseverance (habit 9), as they continuously reflect on their progress and seek opportunities for growth and improvement. By integrating the nine habits of thinking within the challenge-based framework, educators can create a powerful, interdisciplinary learning experience that equips students with the skills, mindsets, and dispositions necessary to thrive in an increasingly interconnected and complex world. If we teach students how to think in an interdisciplinary manner and how to see the links between fields of study, we can support them in being more creative and successful throughout their lives. In addition, we can help learners acquire the emotional resilience and self-reliance necessary for effective lifelong learners if we encourage them to explore their own interests and assist them in building many abilities. The habits of thinking outlined in this book can be readily integrated into a challenge-based framework to meet this end.

How This Book Is Organized and How to Use It

This book is divided into two parts and fifteen chapters. Part I contains the chapters focused on the habits of thinking. Chapter 1, "Foster the Nine Habits of Thinking in K–12 Learning," lays the foundation by exploring how teachers can work together to create environments conducive to interdisciplinary learning. Chapter 2, "Cultivate Diverse Curiosity," encourages students to explore a wide range of topics and ask meaningful questions. Chapter 3, "Take Risks," emphasizes the value of intellectual risks and learning from mistakes. Chapter 4, "Use Humor," explores how to integrate humor into learning to enhance engagement and build a positive classroom environment. Chapter 5, "Create and Innovate," focuses on nurturing creativity and innovation in students. Chapter 6, "Self-Regulate," discusses the importance of self-regulation and how students can develop this habit. Chapter 7, "Transfer Learning," explains how students can apply knowledge and skills across different contexts. Chapter 8, "Ask Questions" emphasizes the importance of asking questions to drive inquiry and learning. Chapter 9, "Evaluate Evidence," focuses on the habit of critically evaluating evidence and making informed decisions. Chapter 10, "Embrace Lifelong Learning and Perseverance," encourages students to adopt a mindset of continuous learning and resilience.

Throughout these chapters, you will also find feature boxes that present side-by-side examples of what using the chapter's habit might have looked like in the past, or in a different way, and what such work might look like in the exploration and learning of contemporary students of diverse backgrounds. Each habit chapter contains activities differentiated for various grade bands, ensuring that the content is appropriate and engaging for students at different developmental stages. This practical integration makes the habits relevant and impactful, as they are embedded in the learning process and directly applied to project work.

Part II contains the chapters focused on the challenge-based framework, which guides readers in implementing those acquired habits of thinking in learning scenarios. Chapter 11, "Integrate the Challenge-Based Framework and the Habits of Thinking," explores the challenge-based framework and shows you how to connect it to habits of thinking for comprehensive interdisciplinary learning. Chapter 12, "Integrate Academic Standards," focuses on aligning the diverse learning embraced by the framework with traditional academic standards. Chapter 13, "Integrate 21st Century Skills," shows you how to build in and deepen the framework through teaching digital literacy and a technological awareness to support a proactive interdisciplinary learner. Chapter 14, "Engage Teacher Collaboration" guides you in the crucial educator teamwork that supports a strong interdisciplinary learning environment. Chapter 15 "Engage Student Collaboration" makes the argument that collaborative skills are essential to due interdisciplinary learning in the contemporary world and shows you how to foster these skills. The book concludes with the epilogue. It also features numerous complimentary tools throughout.

This book is designed for educators of all levels, as well as instructional coaches and curriculum designers looking to integrate interdisciplinary thinking and challenge-based learning into their curricula. While the book follows a structured progression, I encourage you to interact with the content in a way that best suits your needs. You may choose to read it sequentially to understand the foundational habits of thinking before applying them through the challenge-based framework. Alternatively, you can navigate directly to specific chapters or sections that address your immediate teaching challenges or curricular goals. The side-by-side feature boxes offer comparative insights that you can reflect on or use as direct inspiration in your teaching practice. Whether you're seeking to overhaul your entire approach or to enhance particular aspects of your teaching, this book is a resource that adapts to the diversity of educators' needs, providing both a comprehensive guide and a reference for targeted strategies.

A WORD ABOUT TAKING INSPIRATION FOR CONTEMPORARY K–12 LEARNING FROM POLYMATHS THROUGH HISTORY

In the ever-evolving landscape of education, it's enlightening to take inspiration from past intellectuals who exemplified holistic and interdisciplinary learning. Feature boxes in chapters 1 through 10 show educators the transition from historical polymath practices to present-day classroom applications. They highlight how the exploration and learning work of a student today can mirror the approaches of historical polymaths, even though the context and specifics may differ.

Polymaths like Leonardo da Vinci, who mastered multiple fields of study, are shining examples. Benjamin Franklin, a polymath known for his contributions to science, politics, and the arts, demonstrated how diverse experiences and perspectives fuel innovation. Similarly, Ada Lovelace's pioneering work in mathematics and computing illustrates the profound impact of interdisciplinary thinking. Exposure to the diverse accomplishments of these figures underscores the importance of integrating multiple disciplines into our learning blocks, promoting a richer and more holistic approach to learning that prepares students to tackle complex challenges with creativity and critical thinking.

This diversity in experience and perspective is crucial for fostering a well-rounded and inclusive educational environment. However, drawing inspiration from these figures does not mean replicating their exact processes in today's classrooms. Instead, educators should extract the essence of a polymath's approach to learning, which often involves curiosity, cross-disciplinary connections, and innovative thinking. These can be incorporated into contemporary K–12 learning in a myriad of ways, depending on the specific habit of thinking being focused on. In doing so, educators can foster students who are not only knowledgeable in multiple disciplines but also capable of integrating their learnings to solve complex problems, just like the polymaths of history.

Part I

Part I sets the stage for a transformative journey through the mindscape of educational practice. It's here that you'll be introduced to the core principles that underpin the nine habits of thinking. Each chapter not only unpacks a single habit but also places it within the broader context of interdisciplinary learning. You're invited to explore historical exemplars, such as the works of Leonardo da Vinci (and other polymaths you'll be introduced to), alongside contemporary student scenarios, illustrating the timeless value of these habits. Part I serves as both a theoretical and practical foundation, preparing you to implement these habits in diverse learning environments.

Learning never exhausts the mind.

—LEONARDO DA VINCI

Chapter 1

Foster the Nine Habits of Thinking in K–12 Learning

A thriving educational environment is more than simply transferring knowledge from teacher to student. It is a dynamic space where teachers guide students in the development of robust skills, attitudes, and mental habits that propel them toward success within the classroom walls and beyond in their personal and professional lives, as well as in the broader world, where, one hopes, they become agents of positive change. Because the nine habits of thinking are a set of mental practices that collectively nurture intellectual curiosity, encourage creative problem solving, promote resilience, and lay the foundation for lifelong learning, they are critical to each student's repertoire of those robust skills.

As a prologue to the chapters that delve into each of the nine habits and the chapters in part II that encompass the challenge-based framework, this chapter focuses on building a foundation in K–12 educational settings in which the nine habits become inherent. It does so by discussing the need for an overall school environment that values interdisciplinary learning and affirming the importance of collaboration among school and district educators in the creation of interdisciplinary learning environments. This chapter also articulates how teachers, instructional coaches, administrators, and other stakeholders must share the responsibility of establishing an educational environment that is rich in discovery and exploration. It explores hurdles to implementing the habits, how to find strengths and resources to support the habits (even when they are not obvious), and tips for customizing the development of the habits in your school, with your students. The chapter concludes with two reproducible tools. The first guides teams of educators in using a reflection cycle to improve collaborative efforts at fostering interdisciplinary learning in their school or district (page 28). The second aids individual educators in finding and utilizing their individual strengths to support this collective work (page 29).

Now, let's embark on this journey of exploring, understanding, and creating the dynamic, engaging learning environments where students learn and use the nine habits of thinking in their interdisciplinary learning.

Work Together to Develop Interdisciplinary Learning Environments

A learning environment conducive to the nine habits of thinking and interdisciplinary exploration is founded in collective value of this kind of learning and in an environment where this value is seen, experienced, and felt. In a school that genuinely values this kind of learning, stakeholders would see an array of compelling evidence. They would see classrooms bustling with energetic discussions, where students actively question, connect concepts, and build on each other's ideas. Teachers in these classrooms would be facilitating learning, rather than merely disseminating information, cultivating an environment where students are active participants in their education. The walls of the school would feature posters and displays, but not only of completed projects or top grades. Instead, you would see a celebration of the process of learning: diagrams outlining the steps of problem solving, charts tracking the progress of long-term projects, or even "failure boards" that highlight attempts, challenges, and the lessons learned, reclaiming the notion of failure as one suggesting courage in trying and pathways to growth. The school would acknowledge that success is not merely the attainment of a correct answer but the result of exploration, risk taking, collaboration, and learning from mistakes. Beyond the classrooms, shared spaces in the school would promote interdisciplinary learning. There might be a makerspace stocked with a variety of resources—art supplies, building materials, tech tools—allowing students to tinker, create, and learn in hands-on ways. Perhaps there would be a garden where students can engage with concepts of biology, sustainability, and even nutrition firsthand. In this kind of school, the concept of interdisciplinary learning would extend beyond the curriculum. Assemblies, extracurricular activities, and school events would highlight the interconnectedness of disciplines, demonstrating to students that learning is not confined to separate, compartmentalized subjects.

Through these vivid depictions of learning, the school sends a strong message: the journey of education is about curiosity, creativity, collaboration, resilience, and lifelong learning. It is these habits of thinking that we aim to foster, and it's the environment that values and nurtures them that truly drives interdisciplinary learning. Students might experience an environment that values interdisciplinary learning through the physical setup of their classrooms. Such an environment might offer flexible seating arrangements in classrooms, for instance, to promote collaboration and facilitate discussions. Students might have the opportunity to engage with diverse material resources, including books, digital media, and other hands-on materials spanning various disciplines. Students may sense the values of their learning environment through the things they see, experience, hear, and partake in, such as conversations in which teachers ask students for their opinions on topics of importance rather than primarily asking recall-based questions or questions with a predetermined "right answer" in mind. Teachers might ask students whether art can play as significant a role in combating climate change as engineering, or the ways in which daily practices contribute to a concentrated effort.

The following list offers a compilation of ideas for fostering a school environment invested in the development of interdisciplinary thinking and learning.

- **Implement flexible seating arrangements:** This encourages collaboration and makes it easier for students to engage in group discussions and hands-on activities.
- **Provide diverse learning resources:** These could range from books across various disciplines to digital media, hands-on tools, and more.
- **Encourage active learning:** Teachers can do this by involving students in experiments, debates, projects, and more. The intent is to shift from a traditional lecture-based approach to a more hands-on, student-centered one.
- **Value curiosity and questioning:** Teachers can foster an environment where all questions are welcomed and curiosity is encouraged.
- **Foster creativity:** Teachers can do this by providing opportunities for students to think outside the box and come up with original solutions to problems.
- **Apply learning across contexts:** Encourage students to connect what they are learning in one subject with another subject.
- **Promote real-world learning:** Use real-world examples, problems, and projects to make learning relevant and meaningful.
- **Create interdisciplinary projects:** Assign projects that require students to integrate knowledge and skills from multiple disciplines.
- **Cultivate a growth mindset:** Reinforce the idea that students can develop skills and intelligence, and that effort is a key part of success.

Most important to remember, perhaps, is that creating an interdisciplinary learning environment is a shared responsibility that involves not only teachers but also instructional coaches, administrators, and every stakeholder in the educational ecosystem. Each stakeholder must invest and feel invested in students' learning process. Table 1.1 offers possibilities for ways three types of educators—teacher, instructional coach, and administrator—may invest in an interdisciplinary learning environment.

Table 1.1: Ways Educators May Invest in Interdisciplinary Learning Environments

TEACHERS INVEST	INSTRUCTIONAL COACHES INVEST	ADMINISTRATORS INVEST
<ul><li>Integrate multiple subjects in single lessons, encouraging students to see the connections between disciplines.</li><li>Promote the importance of self-directed learning, encouraging students to delve deeper into topics that pique their interest.</li><li>Utilize technology and digital tools to broaden the scope of learning materials and to facilitate collaboration among students.</li><li>Design projects that require knowledge from multiple subject areas.</li></ul>	<ul><li>Expand knowledge base by continually learning new education strategies and staying informed of innovations in education.</li><li>Offer innovative learning strategies to teachers. Help them learn how to use them and customize them for their students.</li><li>Offer continuing support to teachers as they navigate the complexities of interdisciplinary learning.</li><li>Engage in reflective conversation and planning with school and district colleagues across job positions.</li></ul>	<ul><li>Provide flexible scheduling options for teachers.</li><li>Facilitate co-planning and co-teaching between teachers from different disciplines.</li><li>Ensure professional development opportunities for teachers that enable them to build understanding and increase their ability to implement interdisciplinary learning.</li><li>Engage in reflective conversation and planning with school and district colleagues across job positions.</li></ul>

continued →

• Prompt student discussions that link various concepts together. • Engage in reflective conversation and planning with school and district colleagues across job positions.	• Support teachers in developing interdisciplinary lesson plans by integrating pedagogical practices and strategies from different disciplines. • Foster a culture of continuous learning and improvement among teachers through workshops, training sessions, and sharing best practices. • Advocate for the inclusion of interdisciplinary approaches in the school's curriculum.	• Prioritize interdisciplinary approaches in the school's strategic planning, curriculum design, and resource allocation. • Recognize and reward innovative teaching practices that promote interdisciplinary learning. • Create spaces and opportunities for teachers to collaborate, brainstorm, and share their interdisciplinary practices and experiences.

Note that while the ways educators in different roles may invest in and support interdisciplinary learning in K–12 schools often differ, some ways are the same regardless of the educator's job position, such as the need to engage in reflection and support planning with colleagues. Recognizing when to apply one's unique strengths and knowledge to support the interdisciplinary learning environment and when to draw on a collective strength based in shared values is critical to effective collaboration. To illustrate how the concept of collective strength might work in practice, let's consider a scenario. A school is implementing an interdisciplinary project that seeks to integrate principles of science, art, and social studies. Teachers, instructional coaches, and administrators will each play distinctive roles, leveraging their unique strengths in this process.

Initially, teachers might be responsible for designing the project, establishing learning objectives, and setting guidelines that correspond to their respective subjects. Each teacher would bring their own subject expertise to the table, resulting in a project that is rich in content from multiple disciplines. Instructional coaches, armed with their knowledge of educational strategies and resources, could provide professional development for teachers to assist them in designing and implementing this complex project. Administrators, with their broader view of the school's vision and resources, would facilitate these collaborative opportunities and ensure that the interdisciplinary project aligns with the broader curriculum.

As the project unfolds, ensuring that objectives are met and identifying areas for improvement are crucial. Stakeholders do this through a process of reflection, a shared endeavor among educators who systematically evaluate the efficacy of their initiatives. During these reflection sessions, teachers, administrators, and other stakeholders come together to ask critical questions, discuss outcomes, and decide on adjustments to enhance the learning experience. This collaborative approach to reflection deepens understanding of the impact of educational strategies and promotes a culture of continuous improvement. Key questions in a reflective session might include these.

1. What are we observing about students' engagement and learning during this project?
2. How do these observations align with our initial objectives and expectations?
3. What adjustments do we need to make in real time to enhance students' learning experiences?
4. What are our takeaways about students' engagement in learning from this project?
5. How will we incorporate what we learned in future projects?

While any team member has the opportunity to lead a reflection cycle, it is not typically a spontaneous action but rather a structured part of the project's timeline. These sessions are planned in advance and scheduled at key points, allowing for preparation and ensuring that all team members can contribute meaningfully to the discussion. This structured approach ensures that reflection is an integral and expected component of the project, encouraging full participation and engagement from the entire team. Reflection might take place at regular intervals throughout the project, such as after each significant milestone, and at the conclusion of the project.

By combining individual strengths, collaborative planning, and reflective practice, the school community can create a rich, robust, and dynamic interdisciplinary learning environment. This process, grounded in the collective strength of the education team, enables the school to continually learn, adapt, and improve, leading to a sustainable and successful implementation of the nine habits of thinking in their students.

Engage Your Students in Interdisciplinary Learning

Embarking on the journey toward interdisciplinary learning involves navigating complex landscapes, both exciting and challenging. This journey requires us to break down traditional silos of knowledge and weave together the threads that link various subjects. This approach not only enhances the learning experience, making it more engaging and meaningful, but it also cultivates students' vital habits of thinking, such as those we focus on in this book.

Imagine students coming together to create a sustainable community garden, a project that interweaves various academic disciplines with the development of critical life skills. Here, students apply their biological studies to real-life plant cultivation, blending scientific knowledge with practical skills. Simultaneously, a mathematics teacher guides these students in calculating the garden's yield and projecting the community benefits. Social studies classes can join in by researching the historical significance of community gardens and analyzing their impact on local economies and social structures. Students participating in a sustainable garden project at school might encounter various resource limitations and environmental constraints. For instance, they may face challenges such as a limited budget for purchasing plants, tools, and soil amendments. Additionally, environmental constraints could include dealing with poor soil quality or limited access to water. To address these issues, students can innovate by utilizing recycled materials for garden beds, implementing rainwater harvesting systems, and selecting drought-resistant plants. These challenges encourage students to leverage their individual strengths like creativity in design and strategic problem solving, essential skills for sustainable practices.

Customization is key in this process. Students must adapt their garden plans, for example, to suit specific community needs and local environmental conditions. This means choosing plants that thrive in the local climate, utilizing space effectively, and even tailoring educational materials to suit varied learning styles within the group. Students in a sustainable garden project faced the challenge of poor soil quality. To solve this, they created a composting system using kitchen scraps and garden waste to enrich the soil naturally, enhancing plant growth and sustainability.

Through a project like this, students discover the importance of assessing and utilizing their strengths, navigating hurdles intelligently, and customizing solutions to create a functional and sustainable garden. This approach not only prepares them for the immediate task but also equips them with a mindset and skill set for future challenges.

In the process of implementing interdisciplinary learning, educators will encounter hurdles, leverage strengths, and customize their approach to fit their unique educational context. This is not a one-size-fits-all journey; rather, it mirrors the diversity within each learning community.

> **CUSTOMIZING INTERDISCIPLINARY LEARNING FOR DIFFERENT COMMUNITIES**
>
> At an urban high school, Ms. Rivera and her colleagues decided to implement an interdisciplinary project focused on urban sustainability. Faced with challenges such as limited green space and high levels of pollution, they designed a rooftop garden to teach students about ecology, biology, and environmental science. Collaborating with local experts, they overcame initial logistic challenges by securing grants for materials and involving students in every step, from planning to execution. The project not only provided hands-on learning but also fostered a sense of community and environmental stewardship among students.
>
> In a suburban middle school, Mr. Thompson and his team aimed to create an interdisciplinary project around renewable energy. They faced challenges such as gaining buy-in from colleagues with different teaching styles and coordinating schedules for joint lessons. By organizing professional development sessions and creating a shared vision, they developed a project where students designed and built small solar-powered devices. The project integrated physics, engineering, and social studies, and was supported by local businesses that provided materials and expertise. This initiative helped students see the relevance of their studies to real-world problems and sparked their interest in STEM fields.
>
> At a rural elementary school, Ms. Green sought to implement an interdisciplinary project on sustainable agriculture. The primary challenge was the limited access to advanced technology and resources. To address this, Ms. Green partnered with a local farm to provide students with hands-on experiences in planting and harvesting crops. The project included lessons in science, mathematics, and social studies, where students learned about crop rotation, soil health, and the economic impact of farming. The collaboration with the local community enriched the project, providing students with a deeper understanding of sustainability and the importance of agriculture in their daily lives.

By consciously creating opportunities for collaboration and reflection, we not only teach the curriculum but equip our students with the skills and habits that will empower them to creatively and critically engage with an interconnected world.

In this section, we'll delve into how to address the hurdles that may arise while planning your projects, how to identify the strengths within your community of learners that can support this shift, and how to customize your approach to the specific needs, resources, and context of your school. Each of these aspects is fundamental to successfully creating an environment that supports interdisciplinary learning and fosters the development of the nine habits of thinking.

Address Hurdles

In every journey toward interdisciplinary learning, educators are bound to encounter a few hurdles along the way. These challenges, although they may seem daunting, can be managed with strategic thinking and a growth mindset.

One of the primary hurdles could be time constraints in the school day. With packed curriculum schedules and standardized tests, finding time for interdisciplinary learning may seem difficult. However, educators can tackle this by weaving interdisciplinary connections into existing curriculum or reimagining the use of class time to address existing standards through collaborative, cross-curricular projects.

Resistance to change can be another challenge. This might manifest as a student claiming to have no curiosity, a family hesitating to support new educational practices, or even colleagues who are resistant to the change. In these cases, it's essential to maintain open communication, discuss the benefits of interdisciplinary learning, and gradually ease into the transition.

To illustrate the power of interdisciplinary learning in overcoming economic disparities and resource limitations, consider students in a middle school who decided to address the challenge of energy conservation. They encountered the specific issue of high energy consumption in their school. To tackle this, they conducted an energy audit, identifying key areas where energy was being wasted. As a solution, they designed and implemented a plan to replace old light bulbs with energy-efficient LEDs and created an awareness campaign to promote energy-saving practices among students and staff. This project integrated lessons in science, mathematics, and social studies, demonstrating the practical application of their learning to real-world problems.

Additionally, imagine a classroom with limited access to physical science labs. Teachers might utilize virtual lab simulations to give students hands-on experience with scientific principles, combining technology with traditional learning. Or, in a community facing food scarcity, a collaborative project could involve students from economics, health, and environmental science classes developing sustainable solutions by integrating budgeting skills, nutritional knowledge, and ecological studies. Through such examples, educators creatively bridge gaps in resources, illustrating the essence of interdisciplinary learning—connecting academic concepts with real-world challenges and available resources to enrich the educational experience for all students.

Finally, the pressure to deliver quick results can be a hurdle. Some stakeholders, such as administrators or parents, may expect immediate improvement in grades or test scores. Here, it's crucial to communicate that the benefits of interdisciplinary learning—like enhanced critical thinking, creativity, and a love for learning—are long-term and may not immediately reflect in traditional measures of success.

Remember, every hurdle is an opportunity to learn, grow, and adapt. Just as we encourage our students to embrace lifelong learning and perseverance (habit 9), we must embody these qualities ourselves as we navigate the path toward interdisciplinary learning.

Identify Strengths

In building an interdisciplinary learning environment, it is equally important to identify the unique strengths that can be harnessed. These strengths may lie within the school staff, the students, their families, or the local community.

Educators often bring a wealth of specialized knowledge to the table. A science teacher might have a background in environmental studies, for example, which they could leverage in a project exploring the local ecosystem. As an administrator with previous experience in science, I used to hold content sessions for teachers around science topics. Similarly, an instructional coach might have expertise in technology integration or a specific instructional strategy that could enrich interdisciplinary learning experiences.

The local community can also offer invaluable resources and strengths. Local businesses, organizations, or individuals with unique skills and experiences could be involved in projects or as guest speakers. For instance, a decision about a local park's renovation might provide an opportunity for students to engage in a project encompassing social studies (civic responsibility), science (environmental impact), and art (designing a new layout).

A student's family member who is an engineer may guest speak during a mathematics or physics lesson, sharing real-world applications of the theories being discussed. This not only enriches the curriculum but also provides students with a tangible connection between their studies and potential career paths. Alternatively, a family with a rich storytelling tradition could offer a narrative workshop in a language arts class, showcasing the art of storytelling and its cultural significance.

Finally, students themselves bring unique strengths to the table. For example, a student who excels in creative thinking might lead a brainstorming session for a group project, encouraging peers to think outside the box. Meanwhile, a naturally inquisitive student could spearhead the research phase, guiding the team through critical questioning and investigative methods. By utilizing the diverse backgrounds and innate strengths of students and their families, educators create a multifaceted and engaging learning experience that recognizes and values the individual contributions of each participant.

The key is to identify these strengths and consider how they can best be utilized in promoting and supporting interdisciplinary learning. This requires open communication, collaboration, and an ongoing commitment to leveraging all available resources in service of student learning.

Customize Approach

Schools are as diverse as the students they serve, and a one-size-fits-all approach to interdisciplinary learning won't yield the desired results. Understanding your school's unique context and adapting your strategies accordingly are key to successful interdisciplinary teaching and learning.

Urban, suburban, and rural schools each have their unique characteristics and challenges. For instance, urban schools may have more access to museums, industries, and cultural events that they can leverage to promote interdisciplinary learning. Suburban schools, on the other hand, might have more resources or parent involvement that they can utilize. Rural schools, while often facing challenges like limited access to resources or fewer local cultural institutions, may have a strong sense of community and unique opportunities for outdoor and environmental learning that they can incorporate into interdisciplinary projects.

Each school also has a unique set of staff skills, interests, and experiences that can greatly enrich the learning environment. For example, a school with a robust arts program may integrate visual arts into history lessons, allowing students to understand historical periods through the art of the times. A school that has a robotics club might use it to enhance computer science education, letting students apply programming skills to build and operate robots, deepening their engagement with STEM subjects. These specialized programs and talents can help tailor the curriculum to maximize the resources available and provide students with an immersive, hands-on educational experience.

The interests, skills, and cultural backgrounds of students should also be taken into account when customizing an interdisciplinary learning approach. The curriculum should be responsive to the students' identities and lived experiences, fostering a sense of relevance and engagement. For instance, a social studies curriculum might incorporate a unit on world religions where students from different cultural backgrounds present on their family's traditions and beliefs, enhancing the learning experience with personal narratives. In a language arts class, students could choose books by authors from their own ethnic or cultural background for a book report, fostering a deeper personal connection to the material. In a mathematics class, the curriculum could include statistical analysis of data relevant to the demographics of the student body, such as studying immigration patterns that mirror their own families' histories. In a science class, students could investigate case studies of environmental issues affecting their own communities, such as studying the effects of pollution in nearby rivers. These examples show how incorporating students' interests and backgrounds into the curriculum can create a more inclusive and engaging learning environment.

In essence, customizing the approach to interdisciplinary learning involves recognizing and leveraging the unique strengths and opportunities of your specific context. This requires an understanding of your school's community, staff, and students, and a willingness to continually reflect, adapt, and innovate to best meet the learning needs of your students.

Concluding Thoughts

Chapter 1 lays the foundational bricks for building the educational pathways and edifices we aspire to create within our K–12 learning environments. Leonardo da Vinci's timeless wisdom, "Learning never exhausts the mind," echoes through the chapter as we delve into the habits of thinking that form the cornerstones of intellectual growth and curiosity.

Through the course of this chapter, we've explored how creating an interdisciplinary learning environment is a collaborative venture, requiring the combined efforts of all educators and stakeholders. We've discussed strategies for fostering such an environment, from utilizing reflection tools to cultivating classrooms that buzz with inquiry and exploration.

As you turn the page from this introductory chapter, carry with you the understanding that the journey of education is a tapestry-like map with diverse threads of knowledge, skills, and experiences. It's an odyssey that transforms students into agents of positive change, equipped with the nine habits of thinking to navigate the complexities of the world. Together, let's embark on this journey of discovery, embracing the challenges and strengths that come our way, and customizing our approach to light the path for every learner.

Reflection Cycle Guide

This tool is designed to help educators and students engage in a structured reflection cycle, facilitating continuous improvement in learning and teaching practices. Follow these steps to effectively use the reflection cycle.

1. **Set goals:** At the beginning of the project or learning activity, clearly define the goals you aim to achieve. These goals should be SMART: specific, measurable, attainable, relevant, and time bound (Conzemius & O'Neill, 2014; University of California, n.d.).
2. **Reflect on progress:** Schedule regular intervals to assess progress toward these goals. During these reflection sessions, consider what has been successful and what challenges have arisen. Document these reflections in a journal or digital log.
3. **Identify improvements:** Based on your reflections, identify specific areas where you can make improvements. This could involve adjusting strategies, seeking additional resources, or altering the project plan.
4. **Implement changes:** Apply the identified improvements and continue with the project. After implementing changes, repeat the reflection cycle to assess the effectiveness of these adjustments.

STEP 1: SET GOALS

Define your SMART goal for the project or activity.

Specific: _____

Measurable: _____

Attainable: _____

Relevant: _____

Time bound: _____

STEP 2: REFLECT ON PROGRESS

Schedule regular reflection sessions (for example, weekly). Document successes and challenges.

Successes: _____

Challenges: _____

STEP 3: IDENTIFY IMPROVEMENTS

Discuss and document potential improvements.

Improvement 1: _____

_____

Improvement 2: _____

_____

Improvement 3: _____

_____

STEP 4: IMPLEMENT CHANGES

Apply the changes and continue with the project.

Schedule the next reflection session to assess the impact of these changes.

Date of next reflection session: _____

Strengths Utilization Guide

This tool is designed to help educators identify and utilize their individual strengths in their teaching practice. By leveraging personal strengths, educators can enhance their effectiveness and positively impact student learning. Follow these steps to effectively use the strengths utilization guide.

1. **Identify strengths:** Reflect on your teaching experiences and identify your key strengths. These could be specific skills, knowledge areas, or personal attributes that contribute to your effectiveness as an educator. Use the guide to document your strengths.
2. **Assess strengths:** Consider seeking feedback from colleagues or using self-assessment tools to gain a comprehensive understanding of your strengths.
3. **Plan for utilization:** Develop a plan for how you will leverage these strengths in your teaching practice. This could involve incorporating specific strategies, seeking professional development opportunities, or collaborating with colleagues to enhance your strengths.
4. **Implement and reflect:** Apply your strengths in your teaching practice and reflect on the impact. Use the reflection cycle guide to continuously assess and improve your utilization of strengths.

STEP 1: IDENTIFY STRENGTHS

Reflect on your teaching experiences and list your key strengths.

Strength 1: _____

Strength 2: _____

Strength 3: _____

STEP 2: ASSESS STRENGTHS

Seek feedback from colleagues or use self-assessment tools.

Feedback received: _____

Self-assessment results: _____

STEP 3: PLAN FOR UTILIZATION

Develop a plan to leverage your strengths.

Strategy 1: _____

Strategy 2: _____

Professional development opportunities: _____

Collaboration plans: _____

STEP 4: IMPLEMENT AND REFLECT

Apply your strengths in your teaching practice. Reflect on the impact using the reflection cycle guide (page 28). Document reflections and plan for further improvement.

Reflections: _____

_____

Plan for further improvement: _____

_____

I have been impressed with the urgency of doing. Knowing is not enough; we must apply. Being willing is not enough; we must do.

—LEONARDO DA VINCI

Chapter 2

Habit 1: Cultivate Diverse Curiosity

As we begin chapter 2, let's immerse ourselves in the practice of fostering a broad and inclusive sense of wonder in our students. This foundational habit is about encouraging learners to explore a wide range of interests, ask questions across disciplines, and appreciate diverse perspectives, setting the stage for a lifetime of inquisitive learning. While digital assistants like Siri, Alexa, Google, and so on provide people with quick access to information by providing answers to the questions they ask, the experiential aspect of curiosity, also known as learning by doing, is a slower process, more difficult but more rewarding.

John Dewey, an American philosopher and educational reformer, emphasized the importance of experiential learning in his work. He argued that knowledge is gained through direct interaction with the environment, emphasizing that learning is not merely a process of consuming information but rather a process of active engagement and interaction (Dewey, 1938). Further empirical evidence from the field of cognitive psychology supports Dewey's assertions. For instance, a study by Nate Kornell and Robert A. Bjork (2007) finds that the act of trying to answer a question, even if the attempt is unsuccessful, can enhance subsequent learning. Similarly, research by Chi and Wylie (2014) shows that learning by doing is more effective than learning by observing or reading.

From the perspective of cognitive neuroscience, experiential learning can lead to stronger and more enduring memory traces. This is because experiential learning involves multiple neural pathways and taps into various cognitive skills like attention, reasoning, problem solving, and reflection (Zull, 2002). A study by Louis Deslauriers, Logan S. McCarty, Kelly Miller, Kristina Callaghan, and Greg Kestin (2019) demonstrates that students who engage in active learning experiences, as opposed to traditional lectures, show increased performance in science, engineering, and mathematics. This aligns with the cognitive neuroscience view that experiential learning, by involving active problem solving and critical thinking, results in deeper cognitive engagement and stronger memory consolidation.

Therefore, while digital assistants may offer quick and easy access to information, they do not support the rich, nuanced, and personally meaningful learning experiences that come from active, experiential engagement with the world. When I say curiosity in the experiential context, I don't just mean the craving for information. This is why I use the action verb *cultivate* as well as the adjective *diverse* as it relates to developing this habit of thinking with students. The goal in cultivating diverse curiosity in students is to encourage active questioning, developing, and seeking all kinds of answers to anything and everything. There are no limits to what people can ask and the solutions they can discover.

This chapter aids educators in helping students effectively confront their own quandaries and delve deeply into the thinking habit of cultivating diverse curiosity. It provides a comprehensive overview of what the habit is and what it might look like in action, doing so, in part, by exploring the nature of inquisitiveness in the section Look to the Science of a Wandering Mind and the development of personal agency in the Learning Dispositions and Motivation section. This chapter discusses the role risk taking plays in cultivating diverse curiosity, offering a method, *gradual release of responsibility*, for helping students develop the ability to take responsibility for the pursuit of their interests. The chapter also offers easy activities that promote the development of the habit, differentiated for elementary grades, middle school grades, and high school grades.

As teachers, it is our duty to not give students all the information or all the answers, but to encourage them and give them the tools to discover for themselves. We must find ways to pique students' interest in a wide range of topics and stimulate their natural inquisitiveness. It is possible to support students in developing the abilities necessary to become lifelong learners if we create an environment that encourages exploration and discovery. This chapter ultimately will show you how to encourage diverse curiosity in your students by giving them opportunities to explore their interests and become curious, critical thinkers.

Look to the Science of a Wandering Mind

Curiosity, and the ability to channel that curiosity in the active pursuit of knowledge, stems from innate inquisitiveness. All humans have wandering minds. If you've ever tried to meditate, you may have realized that many times you can only go a few seconds before your mind wanders to what you'll have for lunch that day or that email you still need to send. While you may find this annoying and think of yourself as distractable, psychologists think mind wandering is seldom a waste of time. Jonathan Smallwood and Jonathan W. Schooler (2015), who coauthored a significant review of the studies on mind wandering, acknowledge that there are still many unresolved questions in this field.

When considering mind wandering in students, it might be tempting to dismiss it as distractable behaviors or lack of focus or even as lack of care for learning. It is more useful, however, to recognize mind wandering as rich ground for learning and consider the underlying mechanisms in students' brains, such as spontaneous thought or the decoupling of attention from perception. These thought processes occur when our ideas diverge from how we see the outside world. These two processes happen when we daydream or let our minds roam.

When given a task, activity in large sections of the brain, referred to as the default mode network (DMN), decreases (Raichle et al., 2001). Neurologist Marcus Raichle and colleagues first proposed the DMN in 2001 at the Washington University School of Medicine when they noticed a consistent decrease in activity in certain brain regions during goal-oriented tasks. They also noticed these same regions were more active when the brain was in a "rest" state. This suggested that these regions form a network that is active when the brain is not focused on the outside world. The DMN has since been associated with mind wandering, self-referential thought, and thinking about others.

However, despite these insights, much about the DMN and the process of thought generation remains unknown. The DMN is a set of cortical regions in the brain that are active when the brain is in a resting state rather than working on a specific goal-oriented task. The DMN is thought to be involved in a variety of higher-order functions such as self-reflection, daydreaming, and autobiographical memory retrieval (Matheson, Kenett, Gerver, & Beaty, 2023). Smallwood and Schooler (2015) point out that the functioning of the DMN involves a combination of different cognitive processes. When our minds wander, these cognitive processes often come together, allowing us to generate spontaneous thoughts and imagine future scenarios (Matheson et al., 2023).

Early research into the DMN suggested that its activity didn't increase during tasks, implying that it mainly comes into play when we are at rest. However, this perception was based on studies that involved externally focused tasks, requiring the participant to interact with the environment. Subsequent research found that the DMN also activates during tasks that don't involve external interaction, such as contemplating the future or mind wandering. This finding broadens our understanding of the DMN, revealing its role not just in resting states, but also in various cognitive activities that involve internal focus.

The DMN is not just active during rest or self-reflective states; it also plays a critical role in specific cognitive tasks, such as decision making. Regions in the default mode network become more active while individuals are making decisions, such as in the case of letting people view a sequence of shapes like triangles or squares on a screen while sporadically surprising them and asking a question like, "In the last trial, whose side was the triangle on?" (Smallwood & Schooler, 2015). This finding contradicts a prevailing belief that the DMN is primarily associated with mind wandering. It highlights that the DMN's activity is not just limited to unfocused states, but also extends to tasks that require the use of memory-based information. Indeed, it seems that any cognitive activity that relies on memory information, including mind wandering, engages the DMN. Thus, Smallwood and Schooler (2015) propose that the DMN is integral to our capacity for cognitive tasks that draw on our memory, whether we are reflecting on the past, imagining the future, or simply letting our minds wander.

As the research into activity levels of the DMN indicate, thoughts appear to be heavily influenced by the past and the future. Mind wandering is learning. It is the brain attempting to make sense of the events that have occurred so that we can act more appropriately in the future. The ability to make sense of past events and draw lessons from the past to create a better present and future is the foundation of the human experience (Smallwood & Schooler, 2015). It is worth noting, however, that daydreaming or mind wandering can have varying impacts depending on the context. In some situations, these thought processes may be beneficial, promoting creativity and problem solving. In other circumstances, they might be neutral or even harmful, particularly if they lead to rumination or obsessive thoughts about situations that cannot be altered (Kane et al., 2007). In such cases, mindfulness techniques like meditation may be useful in grounding an individual in the present moment, thus mitigating the potential downsides of excessive mind wandering (Bishop et al., 2004).

My focus here is on the ways mind wandering can be beneficial to learning. As educators, we also need to know how to channel mind wandering and use it to cultivate diverse curiosity. The following list of strategies offers ways to support your students in channeling their mind wanderings. These strategies are primarily designed for students from fourth grade through high school. However, with a few adjustments, they could also be used with younger students. I'd highly recommend you consider using them for yourself as well!

- Help students become aware of when their minds are wandering and ask them to make a mental note of what they are concentrating on at such times. Because students may anticipate being punished for daydreaming, ensure you are making this a positive learning experience for them. Asking students to divert attention to the topics they're wandering around will assist them in determining areas of interest that they may investigate deeper and further explore. Personally, I like to open up a note keeping app (such as Evernote, Bear, or Google Keep) and just type in what I'm focusing on. Students can use the appropriate and approved app or write it down in their journal. This helps them remember to return to their thought later. Younger students could draw pictures of what they are daydreaming about.

- When students find their thoughts traveling to a different subject, encourage them to ask themselves about that subject. They will develop a deeper comprehension of the topic as a result, and this will pique their interest in it even further.

- Ask students to create a list of subjects or issues that they would like to explore more deeply and make time in your schedule for them to conduct research on those subjects or questions. I applaud the efforts of schools that implement 20 percent time or genius hour (where students are allocated a certain portion of their learning time to explore and study topics of their own choosing) as I think these are great opportunities for independent research. If they want to learn more about the subjects that pique their interest, help students make use of the online resources available to them, such as podcasts, blogs, and books.

- Encourage students to make connections with others who have interests similar to their own and then engage in thought-provoking conversations with them to get fresh viewpoints and a deeper understanding of the subjects that captivate them. These could be local subject matter experts or across the globe. Facilitate these interactions through online platforms or local community resources.

Remember that integrating these strategies into the class time will require planning. You might want to begin the school day with a "mind-wandering session" or allocate a specific day of the week for independent research. The key is to create a structured environment where mind wandering is seen not as a distraction, but as a tool for fostering curiosity and deeper learning.

Mind wandering can function as a built-in incubator for new ideas and connections, giving rise to creative insights and facilitating knowledge transfer across different domains. By acknowledging and channeling the power of a wandering mind, educators can foster an environment where students actively engage in their learning, explore diverse areas of interest, and deepen their understanding. Thus, the science of a wandering mind serves as a crucial foundation for instilling the habit of diverse curiosity in students, enriching their learning experiences and preparing them for a future marked by innovation and interdisciplinarity.

Develop Learning Dispositions and Motivation

Helping students learn to both engage in mind-wandering explorations and channel that wandering is an important part of teaching them ways to apply discipline to the cultivation of diverse curiosity. So, too, is the creation of an atmosphere that encourages students to investigate their own levels of agency and self-regulation. To create this atmosphere, it is critical to have an understanding of the unique factors that motivate each individual student and design a classroom setting that provides opportunities for students to investigate these factors. Teachers may accomplish this by providing students with pedagogies that are culturally relevant and culturally sustaining, by allowing students to take educational risks within safe environments, and by enabling students to reflect on their own educational experiences. *Culturally relevant pedagogy* refers to teaching that connects students' cultural references to the curriculum. For example, a history lesson could explore events from the diverse perspectives of the students' ancestors, making the material more relatable and meaningful. Culturally *sustaining* pedagogy goes a step further by not only connecting to but also actively supporting the cultural identities of students. It might involve students creating projects that delve into their cultural practices, preserving and valuing these traditions within the educational framework. In addition, it is essential to provide experiences that require students to persevere in the face of adversity and develop tenacity. Such perseverance isn't always straightforward. Initially, overcoming obstacles can sometimes feel daunting, seeming to limit intellectual growth as the learning process becomes more challenging. However, this short-term perception of hindered progress is deceptive. In reality, challenges contribute to long-term development, as students who learn to navigate through difficulties often acquire enhanced problem-solving skills, resilience, and a more profound understanding of the material. Overcoming hurdles is a vital part of the learning process, contributing to the development of students' problem-solving skills, self-efficacy, and ultimately, the ability to engage their curiosity in diverse and meaningful ways.

The learner's dispositions and investment in their own education both play significant roles in the success or failure of the learning process. Failure in this context would mean the inability to achieve learning objectives, lack of engagement, or an unproductive mindset that hinders the acquisition of new knowledge and skills. Students enhance their learning journey and engagement when they take charge of their education, feel competent in their abilities, and establish meaningful connections with the material and those around them. It's their sense of autonomy, mastery of the subject, and the relationships they build that propel them forward in their quest for knowledge. In fact, motivation has been shown to be a more reliable predictor of future success than intellectual capacity, as highlighted in a study by Bodil Marie Stavning Thomsen, Jette Kofoed, and Jonas Fritsch (2021). They concluded that students' motivated behaviors significantly influence their academic performance, regardless of their cognitive abilities. However, there isn't just one type of motivation, and people's reasons for engaging in behaviors might involve both internal and external motives (Howard, Gengler, & Jain, 1995), even if their behaviors appear to be the same. For instance, participants in a group bike ride are likely to reflect a variety of these types of internal motives, including the following.

- "This is something I have to do." (My physician advised me to do regular exercise, therefore I do.)
- "I am up to the challenge." (I have the ability to ride a bike for a total of forty miles.)
- "I wish to carry out these plans." (Both psychologically and physically, I enjoy the way that riding my bike makes me feel.)

Similarly, classrooms are packed with students who are driven by a diverse set of factors. Daniel J. Howard, Charles Gengler, and Ambuj Jain (1995) indicate that it is helpful to conceive of a learner's motivation as being informed by three factors: identity, agency, and self-regulation. Understanding who we are as individuals contributes significantly to our sense of identity. The manner in which the outside world responds to us provides crucial input on our qualities, also known as our characteristics. Students acquire knowledge about themselves in relation to their interactions with others, and they adapt their reactions so that they are congruent with those of their primary caregivers. When a small child sees a strange dog for the first time, he turns to the adult who is holding his hand to determine whether or not he should be terrified. He will be able to utilize this experience to create a story about himself, which will go something like this: "I saw a large dog, but mom said I was courageous because I didn't act terrified." Identity shapes the narrative of each student's educational journey, agency empowers them to take the helm, and self-regulation guides their path. These components are intertwined with motivation, driving students to engage deeply and persistently with their studies. Curiosity, diverse in its expression, is fueled by these factors, leading to a vibrant, self-sustained quest for knowledge. When students understand their personal narrative, feel in control of their learning process, and regulate their own progress, they unlock a potent mix of intrinsic motivation and an ever-expanding curiosity about the world around them.

A person's gender, race, sexual orientation, cultural background, and socioeconomic standing all contribute in their own unique way to the formation of a person's identity. However, societal messages and stereotypes can also pose barriers to learners. This is evidenced by the phenomenon of *stereotype threat*, where individuals underperform due to anxiety about confirming negative stereotypes about their social group. Research has shown that the detrimental effects of stereotype threat can equate to a loss of a year's worth of learning (Aronson & Dee, 2012). Students are putting themselves in danger when they perceive that a poor performance on their part will perpetuate a negative stereotype about an affiliated group when they are in an educational setting where they believe that this will occur. Their performance suffers as a direct result of their nervousness about how well they will do.

According to Michel Désert, Gabriela Gonçalves, and Jacques-Philippe Leyens (2013), students as young as first graders experience stereotype threat. However, classroom training that includes positive messaging about students' identity groups can counteract this effect and even lead to a "stereotype boost," improving their academic performance. This can have a positive impact on the classroom environment as well (Pittinsky, Shih, & Ambady, 2000). This proactive approach doesn't just impact individual students, it also fosters a more inclusive and supportive classroom environment, leading to a range of beneficial outcomes. It's important to note that while a stereotype boost can have positive effects, the ultimate educational goal should be to appreciate the unique individuality and potential of each student, moving beyond stereotypes altogether. The significance of students' cultural backgrounds in their learning experiences can't be overlooked. Therefore, integrating culturally relevant and culturally sustaining pedagogies is a crucial responsibility in the educational process. These approaches involve using students' cultural experiences, histories, and backgrounds as conduits for learning, fostering a sense of respect and appreciation for their own and others' cultural identities.

Learning with one's own free will can contribute to a strong connection between a person's feeling of agency and their personal identity. The feeling that one has the ability to make a difference in the world is referred to as agency. It is something that is socially created and is influenced by the web of interactions that are present in a student's life both at home and at school. It is fair to say that agency is at the core of the *gradual release of responsibility instructional framework* developed by San Diego State University scholars Douglas Fisher and Nancy Frey (2008) and discussed in their book *Improving Adolescent Literacy: Content Area Strategies at Work*. The framework ensures that students have frequent opportunities to take calculated learning risks as they continually try on new knowledge and skills that cultivate their curiosity. Fisher and Frey (2008) describe the stages of modeling, guided practice, collaborative practice, and independent practice in the context of the gradual release of responsibility framework. This framework emphasizes a shift in cognitive work from teacher to student through a structured process starting with modeling, then guided practice, then collaborative practice, and finally independent practice. This progression gradually builds student autonomy and competency.

1. **Modeling:** Here, you demonstrate the task at hand, setting the stage for learning. Your role is to exemplify curiosity and critical thinking—prompting students to ask questions that stretch their understanding and explore possibilities beyond the demonstrated method.

2. **Guided practice:** As students begin to engage with the material, your guidance ensures they apply the concepts accurately while still encouraging exploration. This is where you ask probing questions that prompt them to think critically about the task, nudging them toward autonomy.

3. **Collaborative practice:** This stage leverages peer interaction to further student learning. Encourage your students to voice their thoughts, question each other, and collaborate on solutions. Your guidance is key to cultivating a shared curiosity that drives deeper inquiry.

4. **Independent practice:** Finally, you pass the baton to the students to work independently. This phase solidifies their learning and self-regulation skills. Your role now is to inspire them to question their own methods and results, fostering a lifelong habit of curiosity and self-improvement.

In integrating these stages into your teaching, consider interspersing them with how-to content that directly supports each phase. For example, during modeling, break down the task into clear, actionable steps. In guided practice, offer frameworks or strategies for approaching problems. In collaborative practice, provide guidelines for effective teamwork, and in independent practice, teach strategies for self-evaluation.

By embedding these how-to elements within each phase, you bolster students' ability to take charge of their learning and develop the self-regulation skills necessary for academic success and beyond.

Students who are confident in their abilities and believe in their capacity to learn and grow are more likely to exhibit positive self-regulation behaviors. These behaviors may include setting and pursuing individual learning goals, monitoring their own progress, and adjusting their strategies as needed. For instance, a student who struggles with a particular concept in mathematics may decide to dedicate extra time to practicing problems, seek out additional resources, or ask for help from a teacher or peer. These self-regulated actions are indicative of a student who feels empowered in their learning process. As educators, it's our role to foster an environment that supports and encourages these dispositions. This involves recognizing and validating our students' identities, cultivating their sense of agency, and guiding them in developing effective self-regulation skills. By doing so, we not only enhance their motivation but also equip them with the skills and mindsets necessary for lifelong learning.

Students' ability to successfully assume responsibility depends on the teacher's ability to successfully release it. If a teacher overestimates the usefulness of telling students what to think and doesn't give them opportunities to test out different ways of thinking, they will be unable to develop the agency necessary to take control of their own education. This educator fosters a culture of dependence among the students and sends the message that education is a one-way street: I educate, and you get information. This makes learning a passive experience rather than one that needs activity and effort on the part of the learner. Is it any wonder, given these conditions, that many students fail to identify their own motivation as an essential component of learning?

Developing the capacity for self-regulation is central to cultivating diverse curiosity because it equips students with the tools they need to pursue their interests and passions in a sustained and deliberate way. A student who is curious about the natural world, for instance, can set a goal to learn more about a particular topic, like the life cycle of butterflies. They can plan to read books, watch documentaries, or perhaps even raise butterflies themselves to observe the process firsthand. Along the way, they monitor their understanding, seeking clarification or additional information when they encounter something they don't understand. They reflect on what they're learning, making connections to other knowledge and adjusting their mental models of how the world works. They persist in the face of challenges and see mistakes as opportunities for learning rather than signs of failure. In this way, self-regulation forms the backbone of the learning process, supporting students as they explore their curiosities and expand their understanding of the world. It's what enables them to take charge of their own learning, turning passive absorption of information into an active and engaging quest for knowledge. Therefore, cultivating diverse curiosity not only enriches the learning experience but also fosters the development of critical skills and dispositions that empower students to be lifelong learners. People who can self-regulate are able to focus their attention where they want it, organize their thoughts in a logical manner, and come to decisions about what they should do next. They are flexible thinkers, able to shift perspectives, and adapt strategies as needed. Crucially, self-regulated learners are capable of setting goals, making plans, and monitoring their progress toward those goals, adjusting their plans as necessary based on the feedback they receive.

The ability to reflect on one's own thought processes is known as metacognition, and it is an essential component of self-regulation. Once upon a time, it was thought that only adolescents and adults were capable of metacognitive thinking. We now know that children as young as three years old are capable of thinking back on a job and articulating the steps that they need to take in order to finish it. In addition, once the activity is complete, they can reflect on the steps that, if taken, would have made it simpler (Kornell, Hays, & Bjork, 2009). Students' metacognitive abilities improve when they have the opportunity to reflect on their own learning, which is a requirement throughout the entire gradual release of responsibility teaching framework, for instance. This prompts students to think more deeply about what they have learned.

Another trait that plays a significant role in the maturation of self-regulation is persistence in one's tasks. Like metacognition, the ability to persist through challenges in a task, even when doing so presents a developmental challenge, is observable in students at a startlingly young age. Students with a high level of tenacity are able to direct and refocus their attention as necessary. They come to the conclusion that continuing to work and think is in their best interest, in part because doing so has afforded them success in the past, and in part because others have acknowledged the efforts they have made to maintain their concentration on the learning. They are also aware of the restorative value of taking a short break before going back to a task that is causing them difficulty.

The development of persistence is tightly linked to the development of curiosity, especially when it comes to sustaining the investigation of areas of interest (Koutstaal, Kedrick, & Gonzalez-Brito, 2022). Curiosity naturally drives us to explore and understand the world around us, but it's persistence that allows us to dive deeper into complex topics and persevere in the face of obstacles or challenges.

When we're curious about something, we start asking questions and seeking answers. However, true understanding often doesn't come easily or quickly; it requires us to invest time, effort, and thought. This is where persistence comes in. If we give up at the first sign of difficulty, we miss out on the opportunity to truly satisfy our curiosity and learn something new. But if we persist, we can often gain a deeper understanding and a more nuanced perspective.

For instance, a student may be curious about how engines work. They might start by reading a basic explanation or watching a simple demonstration. But to truly understand the intricacies of engine operation, they'll need to delve into more complex concepts, like thermodynamics and fluid mechanics. This will undoubtedly present challenges and require effort to comprehend. But with persistence, the student can overcome these difficulties and gain a deep understanding of the subject, thereby satisfying their initial curiosity.

Moreover, persistence in the face of challenge also provides an opportunity for students to learn about themselves as learners. They discover what strategies work best for them, how to manage their emotions when faced with difficulty, and how to motivate themselves to keep going. These are all valuable skills that not only support the pursuit of curiosity but also contribute to their overall development as self-regulated learners.

RICHARD FEYNMAN'S CURIOSITY

Richard Feynman, a Nobel laureate and one of the most influential physicists of the 20th century, was renowned not only for his scientific accomplishments but also for his unbounded curiosity and playful approach to learning. Feynman demonstrated throughout his life that curiosity, when intertwined with scientific thinking, can lead to profound understanding and groundbreaking discoveries. Feynman famously stated, "I don't know anything, but I do know that everything is interesting if you go into it deeply enough."

A friend once asked Feynman why a rubber ball filled with warm water bounced higher than the same ball filled with cold water. Rather than dismissing the question as trivial or searching for an answer in a textbook, Feynman embraced the problem with genuine excitement, seeing it as an opportunity to exercise his curiosity. He didn't know the answer immediately, but he began to form hypotheses and design experiments to test them. Through dedicated observation, experimentation, and revision of his hypotheses, Feynman finally arrived at a satisfactory explanation.

Consider a student named Emily, intrigued by the intersection of technology and nature. One day, while using her tablet outside, she notices an iridescent glow on her screen caused by sunlight. Rather than dismissing the phenomenon as a simple glare, Emily gets curious. She begins to experiment with different light sources, angles, and screen settings, observing the changes in the colorful display. She reads up on the physics of light reflection, diffraction, and digital screen technology. Like Feynman, Emily is driven by curiosity to explore a complex scientific concept through hands-on experimentation.

The curiosity-driven pursuits of Feynman and Emily share several similarities. Both were ignited by everyday observations and led to deep explorations of scientific phenomena. Both Feynman and Emily extended their curiosity beyond what they already knew, took initiative in their learning, and relied heavily on hands-on experimentation.

However, their experiences differ in context and available resources. Feynman, as an established physicist, had access to a community of fellow scientists for intellectual exchange and sophisticated equipment for his experiments. In contrast, Emily has to navigate her curiosity with the resources at her disposal, which includes her school's resources, the internet, and potential guidance from her teachers or parents.

Despite these differences, both examples emphasize the timeless essence of curiosity-driven learning. The joy of curiosity, the process of exploration, and the satisfaction of discovery are equally shared by a world-renowned physicist and a high school student. These stories underscore the relevance of cultivating a curiosity-driven learning environment in today's classrooms, where students are encouraged to question, explore, and discover.

Implement and Differentiate an Easy Activity to Nurture Curiosity in K–12 Students

Whether you teach a large class of rambunctious kindergartners or a small subject matter–focused group of tenth-grade students, you can implement easy, low-investment activities with your students that nurture their intrinsic curiosity while encouraging them to pursue things they are curious about, thereby building their sense of identity, agency, and self-regulation.

Here is an example. Say you have a student who is interested in nature—though that interest could be replaced with anything else: economics, history, or something more narrowly focused—industrialization on Lake Michigan, the physical design of the Brooklyn Bridge, how a new business affects housing equity in a city, and so on (more narrowly focused interests are more likely to emerge as the student gains confidence in investigating their interests). For the sake of this example, I'll focus on a more general interest in nature. Students in different grade bands will respond differently to activities based on their cognitive, social, and emotional development. Therefore, when implementing an activity like a nature exploration, you must differentiate the approach to make it appropriate, engaging, and educational for students of various age groups.

Elementary School Students

Younger students are generally characterized by their boundless curiosity, imagination, and inquisitiveness. They often enjoy hands-on experiences and concrete examples. When exploring a topic like nature, it's essential to engage them in activities that cater to these traits.

- **Nature walk:** To guide a nature walk effectively, consider integrating observational skills with analytical thinking. Start by directing students' attention to patterns in nature, such as the arrangement of leaves on a stem or the symmetry in a spider's web. Encourage them to ask questions and make predictions about why these patterns occur. For example, when noticing a bird building a nest, you might prompt students to compare the bird's actions to their own experiences of creating spaces for themselves, drawing parallels between animal behavior and human practices. Ask them how the materials the bird chooses for its nest serve a similar purpose to the materials used in human homes. Moreover, guide them to consider the *why* and *how* of animal behaviors—why a bird selects a particular tree for nesting, or how the shape of a leaf might affect its ability to collect sunlight. These comparisons and questions not only enhance students' observational skills but also deepen their understanding of the interconnectedness of living organisms and their environments.

- **Leaf rubbing art:** During the nature walk, gather a variety of leaves, observing with students the diverse shapes and textures you encounter. In the classroom, translate these observations into leaf rubbing art. Help students place a leaf under paper and gently shade over it with a crayon. The unique patterns of each leaf emerge. This activity not only harnesses creativity but also serves as a springboard for scientific exploration. Examine the rubbings students have created and ask them to consider why the leaves differ. You might prompt students by asking what the serrated edges on one leaf, the broad surface of another, or the dense network of veins on a third reveal about their respective roles in the plant's life. Hypothesize with students about the ecological purpose behind these differences. Is it about water conservation, sunlight absorption, or perhaps something else? This reflection turns art into a portal for scientific inquiry, deepening students' understanding of the natural world.

Middle School Students

Middle school students are typically more independent and are beginning to develop their own interests and hobbies. They are capable of complex thinking and are starting to understand abstract concepts.

- **Nature journaling:** Encourage students to maintain a nature journal where they can note their observations, questions, and reflections about the natural world. They can also include drawings or photographs.
- **Bird watching:** Teach students to identify local bird species. They can record sightings in their nature journal, noting the species, behaviors, and other interesting characteristics.

High School Students

High school students are usually capable of more sophisticated thinking and complex problem solving, and can understand more abstract concepts. They are also more capable of self-directed learning.

- **Nature photography project**: Allow students to undertake a nature photography project, capturing the diversity and beauty of local flora and fauna. In an urban school environment, students can focus on the unique aspects of urban nature. Utilize local parks, community gardens, and green spaces as rich sources of nature where students can explore and document the local ecosystem. Street trees and planted areas around buildings offer opportunities to study and photograph urban flora, creating a project where students document different tree species and flowers found on city streets. Urban areas are home to various wildlife species such as birds, squirrels, and insects, encouraging students to observe and photograph these animals in their natural urban habitats. Even within school grounds, there are opportunities to explore nature, such as in courtyards, rooftop gardens, and landscaped areas, allowing students to document seasonal changes in plants and observe insect life. Collaborating with local environmental organizations or city planning departments can provide additional resources and knowledge, enriching the project further by inviting guest speakers to talk about urban biodiversity and conservation efforts. By focusing on the unique ecological niches, students can gain a deeper appreciation for the natural world around them, fostering environmental awareness and encouraging them to look at their surroundings with a new perspective. They can then research the species they've photographed and present their findings to the class.
- **Community environmental project:** Encourage students to start a project that addresses a local environmental issue, such as recycling, conservation, or public awareness campaigns. First, provide clear and consistent positive reinforcement to build students' confidence and motivation. Recognize their efforts and progress regularly to foster a growth mindset. Encourage curiosity by prompting students to ask questions and explore topics beyond the surface

level, which helps them connect different disciplines creatively. Additionally, create a supportive environment where students feel safe to take intellectual risks and experiment with new ideas without fear of failure. Provide specific and constructive feedback that guides their learning process and encourages continuous improvement. Facilitate collaborative learning opportunities where students can share their thoughts, question each other, and work together on solutions, enhancing peer interactions and collective problem-solving skills.

By tailoring the activities to suit the students' developmental stages, we can ensure that they remain engaged, motivated, and curious. The essence remains the same—a focus on exploring and understanding nature—but the activities differ to meet the educational and developmental needs of the students.

Concluding Thoughts

In this chapter, we have embarked on a comprehensive exploration of the role of curiosity in interdisciplinary learning, focusing on its varied aspects and how to cultivate it within the K–12 educational setting. We have delved into the science of the wandering mind and its fundamental role in fostering an environment of curiosity. Understanding the connection between our brain's default mode network and our ability to foster diverse curiosity underscores the organic interconnectedness of disciplines, a cornerstone of interdisciplinary learning.

We have further explored the value of harnessing students' mind-wandering tendencies as a tool for encouraging learning by curiosity. Through this, we've drawn inspiration from the pioneering physicist Richard Feynman, whose insatiable curiosity exemplified the potential of mind wandering as a powerful catalyst for learning. By guiding students to channel their mind wanderings, we can foster an environment where curiosity thrives.

Critical to nurturing curiosity is the understanding of learning dispositions and motivation, with particular emphasis on identity, agency, and self-regulation. We have seen how the interplay of these factors impacts a student's engagement with the learning process. The development of self-regulation skills, the fostering of a sense of agency, and the reinforcement of a learner's identity are instrumental in fueling the pursuit of curiosity.

Addressing hurdles and identifying strengths while customizing learning approaches are other integral aspects of cultivating diverse curiosity. As we acknowledge the unique challenges educators and learners face, we become better equipped to strategize, overcome barriers, and utilize strengths for optimal learning outcomes.

Ultimately, our role as educators in the promotion of diverse curiosity is pivotal in facilitating interdisciplinary learning. As we encourage students to step out of their comfort zones, make connections across disciplines, and engage in self-reflective practices, we support them in becoming not only lifelong learners, but also active contributors to a multifaceted, interconnected world. Through this, we recognize that nurturing curiosity is not merely about imparting knowledge but is fundamentally about sparking the joy of discovery that underpins true lifelong learning.

The greatest risk is not taking one.

—LEONARDO DA VINCI

Chapter 3

Habit 2: Take Risks

Life requires constant decision making from all of us. We hope to make choices based on the clearest, most complete picture of a situation. In this sense, we might see taking risks as the readiness to accept and act on findings that are founded on facts, even if such conclusions are challenging or disturbing. While intuition may be a useful instrument in advancing scientific knowledge, we should never consider intuition as the last word in the absence of testing and proof—that is, in the absence of the substantiated facts. Trusting in the notion of authority without evidence is not the same as trusting in the scientific process. Therefore, it's more reliable to heed the advice of professionals who have thoroughly examined and tested their findings.

Imagine that you are in the kitchen making dinner. You decide to use a dull knife to chop up some veggies. You think dull knives are safer than sharp knives, but this is a myth. Because dull blades take more force to cut through food, there is a greater chance of the knife slipping out of your hand and harming you. Sharp knives, on the other hand, reduce the likelihood of this happening, as they easily glide through the food. With your sharp knife, you take your time and make sure that your fingertips are well away from the blade at all times.

Everyone enjoys a tasty dinner, and no one is harmed in the process. We may not think twice about this, because people often evaluate the merit of an action based on their own outcomes or experiences, without thoroughly examining a wide range of experiences or potential outcomes. For instance, if one day you cut yourself while chopping vegetables, you might consider changing your behavior, basing your decision solely on that single outcome. This type of decision making, rooted in personal experiences rather than broader analysis, is pervasive in our lives. It's why some people run red lights or speed while driving, because their personal experiences haven't yet included any negative consequences, despite the broader statistical risks associated with these behaviors.

In this chapter, you will learn strategies that you can use to foster an environment that encourages students to take calculated, informed risks. The goal is not to promote risk taking for its own sake, but to help students become more discerning in their decision-making processes. These strategies cultivate students' capacity to analyze information, weigh potential outcomes, and make decisions that expand their learning and personal growth. Through this, students will be able to realize their full potential, not just in academic pursuits, but in their broader life experiences as well. I will discuss the significance of cultivating a healthy sense of risk taking, understanding how to examine evidence to inform risk taking, and putting this evidence to objective test, as well as the necessity of having the guts to make choices when outcomes are unclear.

Educators must inspire students to embrace calculated risks and navigate the unfamiliar. This is central to fostering an interdisciplinary learning mindset, which requires stepping beyond the traditional boundaries of individual subjects. This exploration into unknown intersections of knowledge inherently involves taking risks. By learning to take considered risks, students build the courage to venture into new areas of study, make unique connections between disparate subjects, and develop innovative solutions to complex problems.

The ability to take such informed risks is not just about enhancing academic learning, but is vital in preparing students for the complex, interconnected world they will encounter beyond the classroom. Students may learn how to make educated decisions that will help them achieve their objectives by receiving feedback and reflecting on their decisions. Taking chances might be daunting, but students can learn how to be more confident taking risks while also having the most accurate picture of what is a likely or unlikely outcome rather than basing their assessment of that outcome on preconceived notions based on minimal or flawed evidence, on feelings about something, or purely on personal experience, which may be quite limited. When students are equipped with strategies to embrace calculated risks and develop an interdisciplinary mindset, they are better positioned to make informed decisions that align with their learning goals. This newfound self-assurance can ultimately guide them on a path toward success, both academically and beyond.

Understand That Decisions Are Risks

By recognizing that each decision involves weighing potential outcomes, educators can help students develop a mindset that values informed risk taking as a vital component of learning. In practical terms, this paradigm shift encourages students to view their choices as investments in their future selves. This perspective is particularly relevant in the context of interdisciplinary learning, where students often face complex, multifaceted problems that require innovative solutions. By teaching students to embrace risk and uncertainty, we equip them with the confidence to explore new ideas and make bold decisions, thereby enhancing their overall learning experience. For example, when students undertake a project like designing a sustainable garden at school, they must consider various factors such as resource limitations and environmental constraints. This real-world problem requires them to make informed decisions, weigh the risks, and predict potential outcomes, fostering a deeper understanding of the interconnectedness of different disciplines. By doing so, they not only learn about sustainability but also develop critical thinking and problem-solving skills that are essential for their future success.

By integrating this understanding of decision making as a risk-taking process into the curriculum, educators can cultivate a learning environment that encourages students to take calculated risks, make informed choices, and learn from their outcomes. This approach not only prepares students for academic challenges but also for real-world situations, where the ability to navigate uncertainty and make strategic decisions is crucial. Leadership experts Victor H. Vroom and Arthur G. Jago (2007) describe how every choice we make, whether personal or professional, is effectively a wager on the future. According to them, decisions are driven by the anticipation of potential outcomes, each representing a distinct future scenario, thereby supporting the concept that decision making is inherently a risk-taking process. Experiencing the consequences of our choices can be frightening and uncomfortable. Even thinking about the large number of unknowns involved in any choice, and about the possibility of consequences, can be uncomfortable. Some may choose to give up when confronted with this fear rather than expose themselves to the potential risks associated with making a decision.

By leveraging the natural curiosity of your students to foster probabilistic thinking, you cultivate both their analytical skills and their willingness to take risks. Encouraging students to explore possibilities and make decisions based on probabilities helps them to build resilience and develop a growth mindset. Instead of developing the habit of avoiding risks, students learn to view challenges as opportunities for learning and growth.

In your classroom, you can create an environment where students feel empowered to take intellectual risks. This involves providing them with opportunities to make predictions, test hypotheses, and analyze outcomes. By doing so, you help them to see failure as a valuable part of the learning process rather than something to be feared. This approach not only enhances their problem-solving abilities but also increases their confidence in tackling complex tasks.

Your role is to guide students through this process, offering support and feedback that encourage them to reflect on their experiences and learn from them. By consistently applying this method, you foster an atmosphere where students are motivated to take risks, innovate, and deepen their understanding of the subject matter. This practical approach ensures that your students develop the critical thinking skills necessary to navigate uncertainties and challenges both in and out of the classroom. Start with simple, relatable scenarios where outcomes are uncertain, like predicting the weather or the chance of a coin landing on heads. From there, guide students in classroom experiments where they can make predictions, observe outcomes, and reflect on the probability of different results. For example, when teaching probability, instead of just using numbers, use a clear jar filled with various colored beads. Students can hypothesize the likelihood of drawing a certain color before testing their hypothesis. After several draws, discuss how the outcomes compared to their predictions and what they learned about probability through the exercise. When discussing historical events or scientific phenomena, encourage students to consider what could have happened under different conditions. This practice can build critical thinking skills as students learn that while some outcomes are more likely than others, few are ever guaranteed. These strategies not only ground abstract concepts in the tangible world of your students but also provide them with tools to navigate the inherent uncertainties of life.

Consider the Odds

The sentiment expressed by Voltaire (1919, originally written 1767), that "Doubt is not a pleasant condition, but certainty is absurd," underlines the importance of adopting a mindset open to questioning, exploration, and adaptability in our pursuit of knowledge. In this context, it serves as a reminder of the limitations we face in seeking certainty and the value of approaching learning with an investigative and adaptable mindset. Historically, human understanding has been fraught with misconceptions due to our inherent imperfections and the limited access we have to all pertinent information. This highlights the vital role of critical thinking and skepticism in our journey of learning and discovery. Even in situations where we can only work with the accessible facts, applying an investigative methodology is key to navigating the uncertainties and potential pitfalls inherent in limited information.

As a poignant reminder that our understanding is limited not only by the facts we have at hand but also by our interpretation and application of these facts, research by psychologists reveals that many conclusions drawn from well-known psychological tests were based on flawed assumptions or misinterpretations.

- The Stanford-Binet intelligence test was formerly regarded as a reliable measure of intellect. It has since been shown, however, that the exam is biased against certain groups and does not represent a person's real potential (Ritchie & Tucker-Drob, 2018).
- James Wood, Teresa Nezworski, and Howard Garb (2023) reveal the subjectivity and inaccuracy of the Rorschach inkblot test.
- The Myers-Briggs Type Indicator was formerly thought to correctly classify people into various personality types, but research shows that this theory lacks the scientific validity and dependability to support its claims (McCrae & Costa, 1997).
- The polygraph exam was long considered an efficient instrument for detecting falsehoods, but research now indicates that the test is inaccurate and that some test subjects can readily manipulate the exam (National Research Council, 2003).

In the context of K–12 education, these insights underline the importance of teaching students not only to gather information but also to critically evaluate, interpret, and apply this information. As educators, it is our role to equip students with the skills they need to navigate the complexities and uncertainties of the learning process. This includes teaching them to embrace the value of taking calculated risks, to approach learning with an investigative mindset, and to view mistakes as opportunities for growth and learning. By doing so, we help them to become resilient, adaptable learners capable of navigating the ever-changing landscape of knowledge and understanding.

Cognitive biases play a significant role in how we make decisions and perceive our world. Rather than seeking absolute certainty, we benefit from evaluating the likelihoods and embracing the unknown. When you teach students about cognitive biases, you're equipping them to recognize how their perceptions can cloud judgment. Demonstrating the fallibility of tools we once believed infallible—the intelligence tests, personality indicators, and lie detectors—helps students to see the importance of questioning and critical evaluation. Encourage students to apply skepticism by considering the odds in everyday decisions, thus honing their ability to weigh probabilities against potential outcomes. Fostering a classroom environment that values inquiry over rote answers prepares students for real-world scenarios where information is incomplete and certainty is elusive. Through this, you cultivate a learning landscape that values calculated risks and embraces the exploratory nature of knowledge acquisition. These are essentially mental shortcuts or patterns of thought that can lead us to form beliefs or make decisions that are not based on sound reasoning or hard evidence. Often, cognitive biases cause us to ignore data that conflict with our worldviews and to rationalize evidence in ways that favor our existing beliefs rather than being truly objective. This is a crucial concept to understand in the context of encouraging students to take calculated risks and make informed decisions.

Cognitive biases can significantly complicate problem-solving and decision-making processes in an educational context.

As educators, it's essential to help students recognize these cognitive biases and challenge their unhelpful beliefs, promoting a more balanced and accurate self-perception that can foster learning and growth. The following list offers a few examples of biases and the dangers of relying on them.

- *Confirmation bias* is the propensity to look for, analyze, and recall information in a way that confirms one's prior ideas. This can be a positive or negative cognitive bias, depending on the circumstances. The effect of confirmation bias can indeed range from benign to harmful, depending on the situation and the belief in question. For instance, if a person mistakenly believes that eating a particular fruit every day significantly boosts their immune system, this bias may be relatively benign. While the belief might not be entirely accurate, the act of eating a piece of fruit daily is unlikely to cause significant harm. On the other hand, if a person refuses to accept the scientific consensus on climate change due to their pre-existing beliefs, this confirmation bias could contribute to harmful behaviors and policies that exacerbate environmental damage. A person who believes that global warming is a hoax may only seek material that confirms this opinion, rejecting any data that would challenge the belief.

  It's essential for students to understand that all of us are susceptible to confirmation bias, and that it's crucial to critically evaluate our beliefs and be open to evidence that challenges them. This can foster a more informed, objective understanding of the world and promote healthier decision-making habits.

- *Anchoring bias* is a cognitive bias where people rely too heavily, or "anchor," on the first piece of information they hear when making decisions. This bias happens because shifting away from this anchor point and considering other information requires additional cognitive effort. So, in a sense, we often take the path of least mental effort by sticking to our initial piece of information, even when presented with new data that might change our perspective or decision. For example, a person who is on the market for a new vehicle may allow themselves to be swayed by the first vehicle they see, even if it is not the most suitable option for their needs.

  This bias can limit our ability to fully explore or consider other relevant factors in a decision-making process. In the context of education, it's important to teach students to be aware of such biases, to think critically, and to consider multiple perspectives before drawing conclusions.

- *Availability bias* is the tendency to overestimate the likelihood of events that have greater availability in memory, likely because of how recently an event occurred or how emotionally charged it was. For example, if a person has just heard about someone else being involved in a vehicle accident, they may have an inflated perception of the possibility that they will be involved in one themselves.

- The *bandwagon effect* is the tendency to act in or believe a certain way because a large number of other people act in or believe the same way. The term *herd mentality* is another name for this phenomenon. For example, a person deciding to purchase a specific sort of phone just because many of their friends also own that model, even if it may not be the most suitable option for them, is showing the bandwagon effect.
- *Hindsight bias* is the tendency to look back on events in the past and see them as being more predictable than they actually were before they took place. For example, after an election, people may argue that they knew who was going to win all along, despite the fact that they had no means of forecasting the outcome before the election.

Let's consider confirmation bias—the tendency to seek out, interpret, and remember information that aligns with our existing beliefs while ignoring or discounting evidence that contradicts them. Suppose a student has formed a belief that they are inherently bad at mathematics based on a few poor test scores. This belief might lead the student to pay more attention to instances where they struggle with mathematics problems (confirming their belief) and overlook instances where they successfully solve mathematics problems or grasp new concepts (contradicting their belief). Over time, this bias can exacerbate their feelings of inadequacy in mathematics, discouraging the student from putting in the effort to improve, thus making the problem of low mathematics performance more difficult to solve.

The following activities serve dual purposes. First, they help students recognize and confront the five common cognitive biases, and second, they guide them through a process of calculated risk taking where they need to weigh their options carefully, consider potential outcomes, and make informed decisions.

- Introduce the concept of cognitive bias.
  - **Elementary school:** Use simple and concrete examples, like preferring a certain type of snack because it's the only one they've tried.
  - **Middle school:** Discuss more complex biases like bandwagon effect, using examples like fashion trends.
  - **High school:** Introduce biases such as confirmation bias with real-world implications, like research practices.
- Show students examples of bias in action.
  - **Elementary school:** Use stories or role-play scenarios where a character always chooses the same color crayon and misses out on the fun of using others.
  - **Middle school:** Present scenarios like a science fair where students only visit projects that look interesting from afar, potentially missing out on the best ones.
  - **High school:** Analyze historical events or current news stories for evidence of bias affecting outcomes.
- Have group discussions about bias.
  - **Elementary school:** Facilitate discussions with guided questions to help students understand how trying all crayon colors could change the outcome of their drawings.

- **Middle school:** Encourage students to consider how exploring all science fair projects might change their understanding of the best project.
- **High school:** Debate how recognizing bias in historical decisions could have led to different outcomes.
- Facilitate a class presentation.
  - **Elementary school:** Groups could use drawings or simple presentations to share what they learned about biases.
  - **Middle school:** Work with students to create posters or digital presentations detailing their scenarios and discussions.
  - **High school:** Encourage a more formal presentation style, possibly incorporating multimedia elements to illustrate how outcomes might differ without biases.

These activities on recognizing and presenting biases provide a foundation for understanding critical thinking in everyday scenarios. Building on this, the next activity integrates the skills of recognizing consequences and assessing probabilities, further enhancing students' decision-making abilities in various contexts. The following activity seamlessly weaves together the skills of recognizing consequences and assessing probabilities. It begins by presenting students with a hypothetical scenario tailored to their developmental level. For elementary students, this might be choosing a role in a group project; for middle schoolers, selecting a topic for a research assignment; and for high school students, deciding on a course of action for a community service project.

1. **The setup:** Present students with a hypothetical scenario where they need to make a decision. The scenarios can be academic (choosing a topic for a project), social (navigating a complex social situation), or practical (deciding how to spend a windfall). Adjust the complexity of the scenario to suit the age and maturity level of your students.
2. **Decision-making process:** Ask students to list all the possible options in this scenario, and the potential outcomes for each option. Encourage them to consider both short-term and long-term effects.
3. **Confronting biases:** Have students identify whether and where any of the five cognitive biases might be influencing their decision-making process. What factors are they giving too much or too little weight? Are they favoring information that confirms their existing beliefs?
4. **Making the call:** Once students have considered all the options, outcomes, and potential biases, ask them to make a decision. This should be a considered, calculated choice, based on the best information available to them.
5. **Reflection:** After making the decision, students should reflect on the process. What was challenging about it? How did identifying and confronting cognitive biases affect their decision? Would they do anything differently next time?

Remember, the objective of these exercises is to foster awareness of cognitive biases and cultivate a mindful approach to decision making. These activities are not intended to eliminate cognitive biases entirely, which is an unrealistic goal, but to provide students with the tools to recognize and mitigate these biases in their own thinking.

Making decisions invariably involves grappling with a level of risk, especially when the information at our disposal is uncertain or incomplete. The act of making predictions about outcomes, essentially wagering on probabilities and potential implications, can lead us toward making more informed and balanced decisions in the face of such uncertainties. However, the real impact of these decisions lies in their ability to shape our perspectives and influence our behaviors significantly.

Forming opinions or making decisions may appear straightforward when we're not directly involved or personally affected and the consequences seem insignificant. But when the stakes are high and we are personally invested, the decision-making process becomes more intricate and consequential. In these scenarios, it's essential to utilize all available information and recognize potential cognitive biases to guide our decisions.

In the context of education, it's critical to incorporate lessons about risks and decision making into the learning process. Lessons like the one described above, which help students understand and navigate the complexities of risks and decision making, should be embedded throughout the curriculum. These lessons not only involve understanding the mechanics of decision making but also personalizing this process for students of varying abilities and grade levels in the implementation and differentiation section. For instance, younger students might engage with simple decision-making scenarios, while older students could tackle more complex risk assessments. This scaffolded approach ensures that all students develop these critical life skills in a manner that is appropriate for their level of understanding and maturity. We must empower students to comprehend the implications of their choices, especially in ambiguous situations. By making these risks more tangible for students, we can illuminate the direct connection between their decisions and the resultant outcomes.

MAE JEMISON BREAKS BARRIERS

Dr. Mae Jemison is a true polymath: an engineer, physician, and NASA astronaut, she broke barriers as the first African American woman to travel into space in 1992. Additionally, she's a dancer and linguist, showcasing her diverse talents and interests. Her pioneering journey to space, along with her wide-ranging skills, demonstrate her embrace of taking risks, her enduring curiosity, and her pursuit of interdisciplinary knowledge.

Growing up, Jemison was fascinated by space exploration. However, she recognized the lack of female astronauts and, in particular, the absence of women of color. Undeterred by societal norms and the risks involved, she chose to chase her dream. Excelling in her studies, she became a medical doctor, later applying to NASA's astronaut program. Her acceptance and subsequent journey to space aboard Space Shuttle Endeavour marked a groundbreaking moment in diversifying the world of space exploration.

Picture a high school student named Alicia, who is passionate about combating climate change. Despite noticing that her community isn't heavily engaged in sustainability efforts, Alicia chooses not to shy away from the challenge. Echoing Jemison's spirit, she sees this as an opportunity to make a difference. She decides to start an environmental club at her school, despite the risks of failure or lack of interest. Organizing clean-up drives, educating her peers about recycling, and planting trees in her neighborhood are some of the activities she undertakes.

> Both Mae Jemison and Alicia exhibit risk taking in the face of challenges. Jemison pursued space travel, a significant risk, especially for a woman of color during her time, while Alicia chose to address a global issue at a local level, in spite of the daunting scale. Despite the differences in their domains, both exhibited risk taking, resilience, and an insatiable curiosity. These stories serve as examples that calculated risk taking, coupled with resilience, can lead to substantial learning experiences and impactful contributions, whether they occur in the confines of a classroom or on an international stage.

Implement and Differentiate an Easy Activity to Nurture Risk Taking in K–12 Students

As you delve into the intricacies of cognitive bias, you become better equipped to navigate through uncertainty. Probability acts as a bridge from recognizing these biases to applying that awareness in making reasoned evaluations and decisions. Whether it's predicting the weather, deciding on investment strategies, or playing a game, understanding probability helps us evaluate risk and make informed choices. Teaching students about probability not only enriches their mathematical understanding but also helps them develop critical thinking skills necessary for everyday life.

The following lessons, differentiated for elementary, middle, and high school students, introduce the concept of probability and connect it to real-world situations involving risk taking. By engaging in these activities, students will gain a deeper understanding of how probability can influence their decision-making and risk-taking behaviors.

Elementary School Students

The objective of this activity is to help elementary students understand the basic concept of probability and how it connects to the risk taking in making simple choices. The materials you will need include a jar filled with different colored balls (or similar objects), paper, and pencils.

- **Activity:** Begin by explaining the concept of probability using simple language and examples that are relevant to your students' daily life.

  You might say, "Probability is about figuring out how likely something is to happen. For example, if you toss a coin, there's a 50/50 chance it will land on heads or on tails." Next, do the following.

  a. *Demonstrate*—Show the jar filled with different colored balls to the students. Explain that each color represents a different possible outcome. For example, if there are ten red balls, five blue balls, and five green balls, each color has a different likelihood of being picked.

  b. *Make predictions*—Have each student write down their prediction of which color ball they think they will draw from the jar. They should also write down why they made that prediction, considering the number of each colored ball in the jar.

c. *Draw balls*—Each student takes a turn drawing a ball from the jar without looking. After drawing, they note the color of the ball and put it back into the jar. Repeat this several times so students can observe patterns.

d. *Discuss and reflect*—Discuss the results as a class. Ask questions like, "Was your prediction correct? How often did each color get picked? Why do you think that is?" This will help students understand the concept of probability through hands-on experience.

e. *Connect to risk taking*—Elaborate on the concept of risk by connecting it to their everyday experiences. You might say, "Think about the last time you had to choose between two new snacks. Choosing the one that most of your friends liked might have seemed less risky because it was probably tasty. That's using what you know to make an informed guess, much like predicting the color of the ball." Encourage them to consider how, just like in the jar activity, they can use what they know to weigh the odds when trying something new or making decisions, such as participating in a school contest or answering a question in class. Emphasize that understanding the likelihood of different outcomes can empower them to take calculated risks and make more confident decisions.

Other activity ideas for elementary students, differentiated by subject area, include the following.

- **Science:**
  - *Experiment design*—By predicting and then observing plant growth under varying sunlight conditions, students learn to assess the probability of outcomes based on given factors, highlighting how informed hypotheses can mitigate risks in science.
  - *Factor investigation*—Investigating how surfaces affect a toy car's speed teaches students to evaluate how altering variables can change outcomes, illustrating the risk-reward balance in experimentation.
- **English language arts:**
  - *Storytelling*—Crafting stories with alternate endings allows students to explore the concept of choice and consequence, thus recognizing how narrative risks can lead to varying probabilities in story outcomes.
  - *Character perspective*—Choosing a character's perspective involves assessing the risks of narrative depth and breadth, akin to weighing the odds of understanding from different viewpoints.
- **Social studies:**
  - *Historical research*—Selecting a historical figure to research and present involves assessing the risk of engagement and depth of information, much like considering the odds of successful conveyance of their significance.
  - *Economic systems*—Exploring different economic systems enables students to understand historical risks and probabilities in societies, akin to analyzing which systems had better odds of thriving.

- **Mathematics:**
    - *Spending plan*—Creating a budget for pet care requires students to use probabilistic reasoning to minimize risks, such as running out of funds, by making prudent spending choices.
    - *Simple investments*—Illustrating the growth of savings through simple interest introduces the concept of investing as a calculated risk, highlighting the probabilities of financial gain over time.

Middle School Students

In this activity, middle school students learn how to calculate probability and how it connects to risk taking. The materials you will need include dice, paper, and pencils.

- **Activity:** The first step is to explain the idea of probability and how it relates to the act of taking risks. Describe the concept of probability as a measurement of the likelihood that a certain occurrence will take place; start with asking about the likelihood of well-known fears like getting struck by lightning or eaten by a shark. Ask the students to list instances of events that have a given probability (for instance, the chance of getting a six when you roll a die is one out of every six). Next, have students work in pairs or smaller groups to determine the likelihood of a variety of occurrences by calculating the probability of each event (for example, rolling two dice and getting a sum of seven). Ask them to explain the connection between this and taking risks (for example, if you roll two dice, there is a higher chance that you will get a seven than any other number, so it is less risky).

    a. *Assign*—Assign each student a pair of dice and have them perform an assignment in which they record the outcomes of their rolls on paper. Ask them to determine the likelihood of each event using the given information (for example, what is the probability of rolling two sixes?).

    b. *Discuss*—Have a class discussion about how an understanding of probabilities can assist us in making decisions regarding the level of risk we are willing to take (for example, if we know that there is only a one-in-six chance of something happening, then we can decide whether or not it is worth taking the risk).

    c. *Reflect*—Before the class is through, have each student write down one thing they've learned from the activity on taking risks and dealing with probability.

Other activity ideas for middle school students, differentiated by subject area, include the following.

- **Mathematics:**
    - *Budgeting*—Creating a budget for an event or analyzing the outcome of probability scenarios allow students to apply mathematical concepts to real-life situations. They learn to manage financial risks within a budget and use probability to anticipate and influence practical outcomes, like planning an event or predicting game strategies.
- **Science:**
    - *Experiments*—In science experiments, students directly engage with the scientific method, enhancing their understanding of risk by making

and testing predictions. The act of hypothesizing about acids, bases, and pH levels, or the growth conditions for yeast, teaches them to assess the likelihood of various outcomes, offering a tangible grasp of risk taking and the importance of probability in drawing conclusions from data.

- **English language arts:**
  - *Craft stories*—These activities involve creative risk taking, as students craft stories with varied endings or central themes. They learn to evaluate the impact of their narrative choices, understanding that each creative decision carries different probabilities of reader engagement and satisfaction.

- **Social studies:**
  - *Present*—Researching and presenting on political ideologies or ancient civilizations enable students to analyze the risks associated with historical decision making and the probabilities of different ideologies or civilizations leading to various outcomes.

High School Students

Students' objective will be to use probability calculations to inform risk-taking decisions. The materials you'll need include a standard deck of cards, paper, and pencils.

- **Activity:** Begin by discussing the concept of probability and its real-world applications, including how it can inform risk-taking decisions.

  a. *Separate*—Divide students into small groups and provide each group with a deck of cards. Present them with various scenarios and have them calculate the probability of each scenario occurring. Ask, for example, "What's the probability of drawing a heart from a full deck of cards?"

  b. *Present*—Have each group present their calculations and explain how they arrived at their answers.

  c. *Guide*—Facilitate a class discussion about how understanding probabilities can inform risk taking in a variety of contexts, from games of chance to making financial investments.

  d. *Reflect*—Encourage students to reflect on their own lives and identify situations where they might use an understanding of probability to inform their decisions and risk-taking behavior. To initiate reflection among high school students, you could pose thought-provoking questions that connect the concept of probability with their personal experiences. You might say, "Think about a time when you had to make a choice without knowing all the outcomes. How could understanding probability have helped you?" or "Consider when you've taken a guess on a test question. How might knowledge of probability influence how you approach those kinds of questions in the future?" Encourage students to think about situations where they take risks, like participating in sports or choosing subjects for next semester, and discuss how assessing probabilities could lead to more informed decision making.

Other activity ideas for high school students, differentiated by subject area, include the following.

- **Mathematics:**
  - *Personal budgets*—Creating personal budgets or managing a stock portfolio requires students to apply mathematical concepts to real-life situations, including learning to manage financial risks and to use probability to inform sound economic decisions.
- **Science:**
  - *Population impacts*—Designing studies about population impacts or reaction rates asks students to predict outcomes based on certain conditions, teaching them to consider how likely different scenarios are to occur and to make decisions based on those probabilities—key aspects of risk taking.
- **English language arts:**
  - *Character perspectives*—Choosing a character perspective or setting for a story requires students to evaluate the potential of their narrative choices, akin to assessing risks and outcomes, thereby understanding the role probability plays in crafting a compelling story.
- **Social studies:**
  - *Researching historical figures*—Activities like researching historical figures or economic systems allow students to consider the risks associated with historical decisions and the probabilities of different systems leading to successful outcomes.

Incorporating activities that highlight the concept of risk and outcome across various subjects can support students in understanding this critical aspect of decision making in a broader context. Such activities provide practical, real-world applications of classroom learning and offer opportunities to analyze situations, weigh potential outcomes, and make informed decisions. By engaging in these activities, students can develop a heightened sense of awareness about the inherent risks and potential outcomes associated with various actions, thereby sharpening their decision-making skills. This is particularly beneficial as it not only enhances subject-specific knowledge but also fosters skills like critical thinking, analysis, and problem solving, which are crucial in navigating the complexities of the world beyond the classroom. These are easy-to-implement, low-investment activities at each grade band.

You might think I am hyperfocusing on risk versus the courage to take bold risks for the sake of innovating. Risk and courage, though distinct, are intertwined concepts in the context of learning and innovating. Risk refers to the potential for a chosen action or activity to lead to a loss or undesirable outcome. In an academic setting, risk might present itself when a student opts to tackle a challenging project or choose a complex topic for an assignment, understanding that the endeavor could potentially result in a lower grade or the failure to meet certain objectives.

On the other hand, courage, particularly intellectual courage, is the capacity to pursue and engage with ideas or tasks that may seem daunting, challenging, or contrary to one's initial beliefs. It's the daring attitude that emboldens learners to step out of their comfort zones, question the status quo, and venture into the realms of uncertainty and complexity for the sake of deepening their understanding and fostering innovation.

In this sense, taking bold risks means having the courage to engage with difficult, intricate, or unconventional tasks, topics, or ideas, even in the face of potential failure or setback. It involves an element of bravery and an openness to experiences that challenge one's cognitive capacities and preconceived notions.

The activities in this chapter foster this intellectual courage in students by allowing them to engage with probability, uncertainty, and decision making in a controlled, supportive environment. They teach students how to assess risks in a thoughtful and informed manner. By understanding the nature and degree of a risk, students can make more considered decisions about whether a potential risk is worth taking, and what they might gain from the experience, regardless of the outcome.

In doing so, these activities support the development of intellectual courage by equipping students with the skills and confidence to take on academic challenges, to question, to innovate, and to learn from both their successes and their failures. This sense of informed caution, far from stifling courage, can empower students with the confidence they need to engage bravely with their learning and to innovate in the face of uncertainty. For students to become more inventive, it is vital for them to understand how to take risks, recognize biases, and calculate probabilities. Students may learn how to make educated judgments and how to balance the possible benefits and dangers of any given circumstance by receiving instruction on risk taking. They will become more self-assured as a result, which will allow them to take measured chances that may result in new solutions. In addition, educating students about biases helps them become aware of their own preconceptions and the ways in which those preconceptions might influence their choices. They will be better able to make objective judgments because of this, which may result in more innovative solutions. Teaching about probability and its connection to risk taking equips them with the tools necessary to comprehend the possibility of particular events transpiring. Students can use this information to guide their processes of decision making and developing creative ideas that have a better possibility of being implemented successfully.

Teaching students about risk taking, biases, and probability is a vital step in helping them become more inventive thinkers. Innovation is the key to success in today's environment, and teaching students about these topics is an important step. Students can gain the abilities necessary to make informed judgments that could lead to innovative solutions if they comprehend these principles and use that knowledge to their advantage. In addition, students will get the self-assurance they need to take measured risks that may lead to inventive results if they are exposed to these ideas during their education.

HONOR STUDENTS' ACHIEVEMENTS

When students successfully take risks, honor their achievements but also encourage them to view their failures as learning opportunities. This will allow them to grow from their mistakes and develop more confidence in their ability to take chances in the future. For example, imagine you asked your students to present a product pitch to the class, and one particular student expressed being very nervous about speaking in front of the whole class. After he finished presenting, you affirmed his courage verbally and then followed it up with a letter. Use this risk-taking letter as a template to help students reflect on taking risks.

Dear [student name],

You have my utmost support for venturing into uncharted territory and making an effort to learn something new. Putting oneself in uncomfortable situations can be nerve-racking, but taking calculated risks is necessary for personal development and growth. Because I want to support you through this process, I have designed a reflection tool that will assist you in reflecting on your experience.

> Please take a moment to respond to these questions.
> 1. What risk did you take today?
> 2. How did it make you feel?
> 3. What insights did you get from going through that experience?
> 4. In light of this experience, what would you do differently the next time?
> 5. If you could provide one piece of advice to someone who is considering taking a risk comparable to yours, what would it be?
>
> I am always here to listen and offer support. It is a joy to watch you shine!
>
> Warmest regards, [your name]

Concluding Thoughts

As we bring the threads of this chapter together, it is imperative to recognize that the journey of learning is not a set of isolated paths but a confluence of many, intertwining and influencing one another. When students learn to identify and adjust for cognitive biases, they are sharpening their analytical skills, a process that fosters clearer judgment and more purposeful learning. This critical self-awareness is the foundation on which they can assess the probability of outcomes, whether in scientific experiments, literary analyses, or historical interpretations.

These skills—when holistically integrated—equip students to undertake interdisciplinary studies with a keen sense of inquiry and the ability to discern nuanced connections among disparate disciplines. Through the purposeful design and implementation of grade-appropriate activities, students are not just learning content—they are practicing a form of intellectual agility. This agility is vital for understanding the ripple effects of decisions in one field on another, enabling students to make choices that are informed by a broad spectrum of knowledge and its potential impacts.

Moreover, these interconnected skills allow students to navigate through the multifaceted nature of academic disciplines. By understanding cognitive biases, students are better prepared to question assumptions and approach complex problems with a balanced viewpoint. Probability teaches them to evaluate risk and reward, thereby enabling them to make informed decisions. The culmination of these skills is crucial for students to thrive in environments where interdisciplinary collaboration is paramount.

In the broader scope of interdisciplinary studies, the capacity to take calculated risks, informed by an understanding of cognitive biases and probability, serves as a pivotal skill set. It provides students with a versatile tool kit to engage in innovative problem solving and create synergies across diverse academic fields. It prepares them to question, to connect, and to innovate, which is precisely what the future landscape of education and the workforce demands.

In sum, the comprehensive approach discussed in this chapter does more than prepare students to succeed academically; it prepares them to excel in a world where boundaries between subjects are increasingly fluid. By fostering intellectual courage and a multidimensional thought process, we empower our students to become not just consumers of knowledge, but also creators and innovators. This is the essence of interdisciplinary learning: drawing on a spectrum of perspectives to forge new insights and solutions. It is how students evolve into lifelong learners and contributors who can confidently approach and transform the complex tapestry of the modern world.

Art is never finished, only abandoned.

—LEONARDO DA VINCI

Chapter 4

Habit 3: Use Humor

Educators often prioritize instilling students with transferable abilities such as cooperation, creativity, curiosity, resilience, critical thinking, empathy, and sophisticated communication. These skills, while invaluable, primarily focus on academic and career success. Yet, it's crucial to remember that the purpose of education isn't solely to produce capable employees, but well-rounded individuals. As such, I assert that schools should also focus on helping students develop robust interpersonal and intrapersonal skills. While the aforementioned transferable abilities include interpersonal skills such as cooperation, empathy, and communication, I believe the scope should be broadened to include skills such as emotional intelligence, conflict resolution, and active listening.

Interpersonal skills don't merely enhance our ability to work in teams but also empower us to build healthier relationships and foster a better understanding of others. Similarly, intrapersonal skills allow us to have better self-awareness, self-regulation, and introspection. It is within this context that we should consider humor a valuable skill in the educational realm. Not only does it make learning enjoyable, but it also cultivates resilience, creativity, and emotional well-being, all of which are crucial for a student's holistic development. A large number of young people, who appear to have nothing but a bright and hopeful journey ahead of them, are suffering everything from general malaise about their futures to major depression. For instance, the World Health Organization (2021) estimates that globally, depression is one of the leading causes of illness and disability among adolescents, and suicide is the third leading cause of death in fifteen- to nineteen-year-olds. This alarming scenario leads me to question whether the coveted 21st century skill set might be lacking a vital element: a sense of humor.

The capacity to employ humor plays a crucial role not only in fostering social and emotional intelligence but also in building relationships and managing challenging situations, making it an essential life skill. Humor also has a significant role in interdisciplinary learning. By bringing levity to complex topics, humor can make diverse subjects more accessible and engaging. It encourages creative thinking by presenting alternative perspectives and making connections between disparate ideas, thereby promoting an interdisciplinary mindset.

Studies underscore the value of humor in educational settings. For instance, San Bolkan, Darrin Griffin, and Alan Goodboy (2018) demonstrate that instructor humor is positively associated with student learning, satisfaction, and participation in class. Furthermore, humor has been found to reduce stress and increase resilience, fostering a better environment for learning and exploration (Savage, Lujan, Thipparthi, & DiCarlo, 2017). Therefore, cultivating a sense of humor in students can significantly contribute to their overall learning experience.

Indeed, a healthy sense of humor does more than just facilitate self-understanding and connect us with others; it adds zest to our lives, enabling us to find joy in a world that often seems nonsensical. It infuses our existence with laughter, companionship, and a sparkle that lightens our burdens.

Please don't take what I've said here as an endorsement for making humor a required subject alongside science and social studies. What I'm advocating is that we should all take a minute to acknowledge the power of humor and the ways in which it brings joy and light into our lives. It is important to keep in mind that humor is a skill that we can cultivate through time and improve on with experience. Using humor to make ourselves and others feel better in challenging circumstances is a skill that we can hone with practice until it eventually becomes second nature.

What I'm most advocating, however, is for educators to encourage students to find their inner sense of comedy. Overscheduled students are so intent on excelling in everything they do that they've forgotten (or were never told) that sports, music, dance, and theater are all things we ought to do primarily for enjoyment, not to add to résumés. When students are perpetually focused on achievement, the space for laughter, for merriment, for simple enjoyment shrinks. In our noble quest to equip students for successful adulthood, we educators may unintentionally rob them of the opportunity to experience unadulterated joy and happiness, key components of a well-rounded education.

Now, you might ask, why do joy and happiness hold such significance in the educational context? Research indicates that our capacity to learn is enhanced when the learning process incites joy (Reschly, Huebner, Appleton, & Antaramian, 2008; St-Amand, Smith, & Goulet, 2024). The joy inherent in exploration can serve as a catalyst to unlock our minds, making us more open to assimilating new information (Fredrickson, 2001). Furthermore, when young learners forge an association between joy and the process of learning, it cultivates a positive relationship with education, which can continue to benefit them throughout their adult lives (Pekrun, Goetz, Titz, & Perry, 2002).

As we strive to foster an interdisciplinary mindset, the role of humor proves pivotal. Students who derive enjoyment from their learning process are more inclined to create connections across different disciplines and appreciate the interwoven nature of knowledge. Humor has the power to dissolve barriers, not just between individuals, but also between traditionally isolated fields of study (Dunbar, Banas, Rodriguez, Liu, & Abra, 2012).

It can be difficult to teach students the skill of using humor because it requires striking a delicate balance between providing them with direction and allowing them to discover their own sense of humor. This chapter attempts to help educators strike that delicate balance by exploring methods for instructing students in the art of humor, such as cultivating a safe learning environment, modeling appropriate use of humor, and providing opportunities for students to learn through humor.

Cultivate a Safe Environment for Humor

The cornerstone of teaching students the art of humor rests on the creation of a safe learning environment. This requires an open discussion about the nature of humor and the setting of clear expectations for appropriate behavior and language, while maintaining a space where students can express themselves freely. Teachers should underscore that students should never use humor to cause harm or belittle others, and that everyone is entitled to comfort within the classroom setting.

In order to think about how humor works and what constitutes safe humor in the classroom, it can be helpful to consider the hypothesis explained by comedy scholars A. Peter McGraw, Caleb Warren, and Christina Kan (2015) called the *benign violation theory*. According to this theory, something is humorous when it is both seen as harmless and when it breaches a norm or expectation. Humor, as the argument goes, develops when one observes the transgression of a social standard or expectation while also realizing that the transgression is neither destructive nor even very significant. The cognitive dissonance caused by this contradiction is resolved by laughing at the absurdity of the circumstance.

Since everyone has their own set of expectations and conventions, benign violation theory explains why some things will make some people laugh while others won't. It's also an explanation for why the same joke might be hilarious in one setting but not in another: the joke itself constitutes a breach of a norm or expectation, but it's the setting that ultimately determines whether or not that violation is seen as harmless. This idea clarifies the reasons why puns and wordplay are so popular and appreciated by audiences of different backgrounds. These jokes focus on subverting our normal conceptions of how language operates, yet in a harmless and humorous way. They provide an amusing opportunity to experiment with and learn about linguistic conventions.

According to the hypothesis, humor also serves an adaptive purpose by facilitating the resolution of disagreements and misunderstandings (Martin, 2019). It can defuse tension, bridge gaps, and foster a more cohesive social environment. This underscores the importance of humor in an educational setting, where diverse individuals come together for learning. When we laugh at something, we can see a violation or discrepancy, admit it, and deal with it, all while realizing it is not a life-or-death situation. In times of doubt or confusion, this gives us the confidence that comes from feeling in charge and knowledgeable.

As educators, understanding the benign violation theory helps us create a classroom atmosphere where humor is used productively and respectfully. We can guide students to use humor that acknowledges and transgresses norms or expectations but remains benign, fostering an environment of creative and critical thinking without causing harm. This concept becomes an effective tool in nurturing students' ability to express themselves, engage with learning content more enthusiastically, and embrace their individuality in a respectful manner.

Moreover, teachers should guide their classes in exploring the diverse forms of humor, assisting students to develop the sensitivity to discern what's amusing and inoffensive. Here, the crux is not to validate potentially offensive content as a mere form of humor but to foster a nuanced understanding of humor that respects individual boundaries and cultural differences. Navigating this fine line requires a deliberate effort from teachers to foster an environment of mutual respect, alongside an open-minded exploration of humor.

Let's consider how to infuse humor into the learning process in a way that is considerate of the different developmental stages of students. As students mature, their understanding of humor evolves, and the ways we engage them in conversations about humor should reflect this progression. Figure 4.1 provides age-appropriate tips and activities to facilitate discussions about humor in the classroom setting. The goal is not only to help students appreciate and utilize humor, but also to understand its intricacies, implications, and cultural sensitivities. Remember, humor can be a bridge to deeper understanding, creative thinking, and mutual respect when used wisely.

GRADE BAND	TIPS AND ACTIVITIES FOR ENGAGING STUDENTS IN CONVERSATIONS ABOUT HUMOR
Elementary	• Encourage students to share jokes that they find funny and have a class discussion on why they are amusing. This initiates an early dialogue about humor. • Use storybooks or cartoons that incorporate humor to demonstrate the joy of laughter and its role in storytelling. • Discuss respect and kindness using age-appropriate language, emphasizing that humor should never be used to hurt others. • Role-play scenarios where a joke might hurt someone's feelings to foster empathy and understanding.
Middle School	• Start conversations about different types of humor—sarcasm, puns, slapstick, and so on—and discuss when and where they might be appropriate. • Encourage students to engage with their family members or individuals from different age groups about what they find funny and why. These conversations can illuminate how humor has changed and remained the same, providing a deeper understanding of the societal and temporal dynamics of comedy. • Guide students to consider the impact of technological advances on humor, as the way we consume comedic content has evolved significantly with the rise of digital media. The dialogue between different generations about humor can offer a fascinating glimpse into the social history and changing technologies that shape our shared laughter. • Discuss humor in the context of cultural and societal norms, exploring how humor can vary across cultures. • Role-play scenarios where humor might be misinterpreted, emphasizing the importance of context and empathy in humor. • Encourage students to share their favorite appropriate comedic videos or humorous books, initiating a discussion about why they find them amusing.
High School	• Delve into humor in literature, film, and media to examine how it can serve various purposes—satire, critique, comic relief, and so on. • Discuss the potential of humor to bridge social and cultural differences, but also to perpetuate harmful stereotypes. • Encourage students to develop and share their own comedic sketches, stand-up routines, or satirical essays, fostering their creativity and understanding of humor. • Discuss humor in the context of social dynamics and power structures, exploring its potential to both challenge and reinforce these structures.

Figure 4.1: The role of humor in education.

In all these activities, the emphasis should be on understanding humor as a powerful communication tool, which when used respectfully, can foster connections, stimulate creativity, and promote joy. Your role as the teacher is to guide students in exploring humor in a thoughtful and respectful way, understanding its potentials and pitfalls, and developing their own sense of humor in the process.

When it comes to making use of comedy in the classroom, teachers should emphasize using comedy to engage with students and make learning a more enjoyable experience. In addition, teachers should encourage students to employ self-deprecating humor so that they can demonstrate to other students that it is acceptable to laugh at oneself sometimes. To connect humor with learning, you might do the following.

- You could begin class by presenting a joke or hilarious anecdote connected to the subject matter you will cover that class.
- You might invite students to think of their own jokes or hilarious stories linked to the class topic.
- When conveying challenging subjects, you may incorporate funny analogies or metaphors.
- To further clarify a subject, you can employ visually funny examples, such as cartoons.
- You may choose to encourage students to make humorous comments about their own errors or misconceptions to assist the students in learning from their mistakes without feeling embarrassed or ashamed of themselves.

Importantly, while humor has its place, it is critical that it is always employed with sensitivity to the diversity of experiences and backgrounds in the classroom. By maintaining respect for all individuals, humor can be an inclusive tool that uplifts rather than alienates. As educators, you are in a unique position to leverage humor to inspire, connect, and educate. I encourage you to continue honing your comedic timing and content, always with an eye toward fostering a respectful, inclusive, and joyous learning journey for all students.

In concluding this section, it's paramount to affirm that humor is not merely a diversion but an essential pedagogical strategy that creates an engaging and dynamic learning atmosphere. An atmosphere infused with humor encourages students to participate actively, think creatively, and foster a positive relationship with the learning material.

Model How to Use Humor in Learning

Implementing learning through humor with students begins with modeling humor in the classroom. This powerful pedagogical tool provides students with tangible examples of how they can integrate humor into different facets of learning and communication. Modeling sets a tone for the acceptable use of humor and provides examples of humor that are respectful, inclusive, and relevant. It also offers an opportunity to expose students to different forms of humor and teach them about humor's various cultural and historical contexts.

Let's explore a specific method of humor that teachers can model. *Paraprosdokian* is a figure of speech in which the concluding portion of a statement or phrase is shocking or unanticipated in such a way that it compels the reader or listener to rethink or reinterpret the preceding portion of the sentence or phrase. An example is the statement, "I've had a perfectly wonderful evening, but this wasn't it." Initially, the listener is led to believe the speaker is expressing satisfaction with the evening. However, the conclusion of the statement takes an unexpected turn, indicating the opposite sentiment and forcing the listener to reinterpret the first part of the sentence.

By presenting this form of humor, you not only engage students with the linguistic playfulness of paraprosdokians but also stimulate their critical thinking as they analyze the structure and meaning of the statement. It invites them to consider the power of word placement and timing in humor, and how a simple twist can alter the entire perception of a narrative. This also serves as a launch pad for discussions about the nuances of language and communication, highlighting the importance of context and expectation in shaping meaning. Paraprosdokians are frequently used for comedic or rhetorical effects, which is why they are a useful strategy to help students cultivate a sense of humor, wit, and creativity. A paraprosdokian is a valuable tool for fostering humor in the classroom, and its structure lends itself well to a modeling approach. Teachers can use this technique to introduce humor into their instruction, providing live examples of how to deliver a punchline that subverts expectations. This can be particularly beneficial in teaching subjects like language arts, but it can also be incorporated into other subjects to make learning more engaging.

Importantly, as teachers model this type of humor, they also set examples of clever and respectful humor that can enhance the social-emotional climate of the classroom. As an example, I'll focus on incorporating paraprosdokians into teaching to help students with their writing, speaking, and collaborating with their peers, and to encourage students to creatively apply amusing or surprising figurative language to their work. Using paraprosdokians can also be tailored to different age groups or grade bands.

- **For elementary school students:** Start by introducing the concept of surprise in storytelling. A simple exercise could be to provide a story with a missing ending and have students suggest different funny or surprising endings. You could also use well-known fairy tales and ask students to create a surprising twist at the end.

- **For middle school students:** Introduce the term *paraprosdokian* and illustrate it with age-appropriate examples from literature or popular media. Have students practice creating their own paraprosdokians, perhaps in pairs or small groups, to promote collaboration and peer learning. Creative writing assignments and speech projects are some of the contexts that lend themselves to creating paraprosdokians.

- **For high school students:** High school students can delve deeper into the use of paraprosdokians in literature, stand-up comedy, and rhetoric. Teachers can facilitate discussions around why this device is effective and how it serves different purposes in humor and persuasion. Assignments might include writing a persuasive speech or an op-ed piece that incorporates paraprosdokian or analyzing its use in a comedic monologue or a political speech. Students can share their work with the class, fostering a culture of humor and intellectual curiosity.

Throughout all these levels, the aim is to cultivate a sense of humor that's intertwined with critical and creative thinking, and to foster an understanding of the nuances of language and the impact of unexpected turns in communication. This language device will also equip students to better understand how to construct amusing phrases and add a layer of cleverness to their daily conversations. In addition, giving students experience in the use of paraprosdokian can assist in making them feel more at ease when it comes to taking creative risks and thinking outside the box when it comes to their writing.

The first step in teaching students how to utilize paraprosdokian is to provide an explanation of what it is and how to use it thoughtfully. Start off by presenting some instances of paraprosdokians, such as "I'm not lazy, I simply don't care," or "I used to believe that I was indecisive, but now I'm not so sure." Here a few more.

- **"War does not determine who is right—only who is left."** This play on words subverts the expectation by exploiting the dual meanings of "right" and "left," leading the listener to reconsider the initial part of the sentence.
- **"You can always count on the Americans to do the right thing—after they have tried everything else."** This witticism, often attributed to Winston Churchill, subverts an assumed compliment into a critique, prompting a reconsideration of American tenacity.
- **"If I could just say a few words . . . I'd be a better public speaker."** Here, the expectation is subverted by twisting the phrase to imply that brevity is the speaker's weakness, whereas it usually suggests the start of a longer speech.

Explain that each of these phrases consists of two distinct parts: the first portion creates an expectation for the reader or listener, and the second half surprises them by going against that assumption. This not only has the effect of making the reader or listener laugh, but it also pushes them to think more carefully about what was stated.

Students can begin practicing the use of paraprosdokian in their own writing and speaking when they have gained an understanding of what the device is and how it operates. To begin, have them brainstorm (individually, small groups, or whole group) phrases they could make into paraprosdokians. Inspire them to think of examples of situations in which expectations are formed, and then those expectations are defied. Once they have some concepts, have them record their phrases, and then have a conversation with them about why they work as paraprosdokians. They will thus have a better understanding of how to construct powerful sentences by making use of this figurative language.

Students can begin incorporating paraprosdokian into bigger writing assignments such as stories or essays once they have gained experience with the language on its own and practiced using it independently. Inspire them to keep an eye out for situations in which they might leverage this figurative language device to infuse their work with a sense of comedy or give it a more profound significance. Furthermore, by encouraging students to use paraprosdokian not merely for comedic effect but to enhance their arguments or narratives, teachers are effectively demonstrating how humor can serve a dual purpose—to entertain and to illuminate. This balance is crucial in various aspects of life, from professional presentations to interpersonal communications.

This practice also underlines the idea that humor is not an isolated aspect of communication, but a tool that can make learning more engaging, deepen understanding, and foster a more vibrant and open classroom environment. Students will observe how to weave humor into serious contexts, creating a memorable learning experience that stimulates both their intellectual curiosity and creativity.

BENJAMIN FRANKLIN USES HUMOR TO CHALLENGE SOCIETAL NORMS

Benjamin Franklin, one of America's founding fathers, was a true polymath. His interests and contributions spanned a range of fields, including politics, science, and literature. Known for his wit and humor, Franklin often used these tools to shed light on societal issues or to make his writings more engaging. His life and work provide compelling examples of the power of humor in interdisciplinary learning.

Franklin created a fictional character, Mrs. Silence Dogood, a witty middle-aged widow who made incisive observations about society. This humorous approach not only got his work published but also allowed Franklin to critique societal norms in an engaging and accessible way. He took a similar approach with *Poor Richard's Almanack*, a yearly publication filled with humorous and insightful aphorisms. His ability to weave humor into his work made it memorable and impactful.

Consider a middle school student, Maya, who enjoys writing and has a keen sense of humor. She's tasked with a writing assignment about a current event. Drawing inspiration from Benjamin Franklin, Maya decides to create a fictional character to narrate the events in a satirical way. For example, when discussing environmental sustainability, Maya uses her character to highlight the importance of reducing plastic waste. She humorously portrays a scene where her character struggles with a mountain of plastic bags, drawing attention to the everyday impact of plastic pollution and encouraging her audience to consider more sustainable alternatives. She cleverly uses humor to highlight the issues she cares about. Maya's unique approach not only makes her assignment engaging but also allows her to offer insightful commentary on the event.

Both Benjamin Franklin and Maya leveraged humor to make their work more engaging and impactful. Franklin used satire to comment on societal norms, while Maya used it to offer unique insights on a current event. In both cases, humor is a tool for engaging their audience and encouraging critical thinking. These examples underscore the value of humor as an interdisciplinary tool, capable of enhancing learning and fostering creative and critical thinking. Whether in the 18th century political sphere or a 21st century classroom, humor remains a powerful asset in the learning process.

Implement and Differentiate an Easy Activity to Nurture Learning Through Humor in K-12 Students

Opportunities for students to practice humor could include activities such as improv games or writing exercises in which students think of their own jokes or come up with their own amusing stories. In addition, educators could task students with projects in which they research various subgenres of humor and present their results. Participation in these activities provides the opportunity for students to develop their own sense of humor in a risk-free setting.

It may seem like a challenge to incorporate these humor-based activities into an already packed school schedule, but there are creative ways to integrate humor practices into the existing curriculum. For instance, language arts teachers can weave humor into writing exercises, storytelling, or oral presentations. In science or mathematics, teachers can use humorous examples or scenarios to illustrate concepts or solve problems. Even history or social studies teachers can explore the historical uses of humor or the humor styles in different cultures. Educators may even find time for dedicated humor activities in transition periods between subjects, during homeroom periods, or even as part of extracurricular clubs or activities. The aim here is not to add an additional subject into the curriculum, but to imbue existing lessons and activities with elements of humor, thereby promoting an interdisciplinary learning mindset.

Practicing humor should be seen not as an extra task, but rather as an investment in students' comprehensive development. The following sections show examples of activities to help cultivate comedy and a sense of humor in the classroom, differentiated by grade band. Implementing humor into core subjects allows for an engaging and enjoyable learning experience, fostering a sense of community in the classroom while simultaneously reinforcing academic content.

Elementary School Students

In elementary school, introducing humor into learning is more than just an exercise in engagement—it's a key component in fostering a joyous and inclusive classroom environment. These activities, specifically designed for young learners, leverage the natural playfulness and creativity of this age group. By incorporating humor, we tap into the students' innate sense of wonder, making abstract concepts more concrete and memorable.

When employing humor with elementary school students, it's essential to ensure that it is age-appropriate, nondisparaging, and inclusive. Children at this developmental stage are beginning to understand more complex forms of humor beyond slapstick, including puns and wordplay, which can be used effectively in educational contexts.

By carefully selecting humor that is constructive and empathetic, we create a learning space that is not only educational but also emotionally safe and welcoming, allowing children to express themselves and grow with laughter.

- **Mathematics:**
    - *Comics*—Students can illustrate a mathematical concept using a comic strip, perhaps explaining the concept of addition or subtraction using funny characters or scenarios.
    - *Funny mathematics problems*—Create mathematics problems where the objects involved are humorous or silly, such as "If Tommy had 15 rubber ducks and gave 5 to Susie, how many would he have left?"
- **Science:**
    - *Silly experiments*—Conduct an experiment using funny materials or by giving the procedure a humorous twist.
    - *Funny animal facts*—Ask students to research and present funny facts about animals.
- **English language arts:**
    - *Joke books*—Allow students to create their own joke book using simple puns and language play.
    - *Silly story prompts*—Students can write and share short stories based on humorous prompts.
- **Social studies:**
    - *Funny moments in history*—Ask students to illustrate a comic strip depicting a humorous (but historically accurate) moment from a time period they are studying.

- *Silly maps*—Students can draw a silly map of their town, adding humorous landmarks.

Middle School Students

Middle school is a pivotal time for students as they navigate the transition from childhood to adolescence. It is a period marked by a quest for identity, increased cognitive abilities, and a burgeoning appreciation for more sophisticated forms of humor, such as satire and parody. This developmental stage offers fertile ground for integrating humor into the curriculum in ways that resonate with students' growing intellectual and emotional capacities.

Activities that merge humor with educational content should be crafted to align with middle school students' heightened ability to understand abstract concepts, appreciate wordplay, and engage with more complex narratives. It's important to emphasize the use of humor that is sensitive to individual differences and cultural contexts, avoiding stereotypes and ensuring that humor adds to the learning experience without causing discomfort or misunderstanding. With these considerations in mind, humor can be a powerful tool in creating an engaging and dynamic middle school classroom.

- **Mathematics:**
  - *Mathematical puns*—Students can create and share mathematical puns related to the topics being studied in class.
  - *Humorous problem solving*—Students can write a story about a character who must solve a funny problem using mathematical concepts.
- **Science:**
  - *Parody of a scientific method*—Students can write a parody of a scientific experiment by replacing the steps with funny actions while still maintaining the sequence and logic of the scientific method.
  - *Science jokes*—Students can research or create science jokes or puns related to the topics they are studying.
- **English language arts:**
  - *Literary parodies*—Students can create parodies of well-known literary works by adding comedic elements.
  - *Humorous book reviews*—Students can write a humorous review of a book they've read.
- **Social studies:**
  - *Historical parodies*—Students can create parodies of historical events, taking care to be respectful while adding elements of humor.
  - *Comic strip history*—Students can create a comic strip to explain a historical event using humor.

High School Students

High school is a formative period where students refine their critical thinking skills and develop a deeper understanding of the world around them. Humor, at this stage, can be an effective pedagogical tool that not only engages students but also helps them to process complex ideas and consider alternate perspectives.

- **Mathematics:**
  - **Mathematics-based comic strip**—Students can create a comic strip that explains a complex mathematical theory or concept using humor.
  - *Mathematical mock debate*—Organize a mock debate on a ridiculous premise, where students must use mathematical evidence to support their arguments.
- **Science:**
  - *Scientific satire*—Students can write a satirical article on a misunderstood or misrepresented scientific concept.
  - *Science myth debunking*—Students create a humorous presentation debunking popular science myths.
- **English language arts:**
  - *Satirical essays*—Students can write a satirical essay on a current event or social issue.
  - *Comedic play scripts*—Students can write a comedic script exploring themes from literature they are studying.
- **Social studies:**
  - *Historical mock trials*—Conduct mock trials for historical figures using humorous but plausible scenarios.
  - *Parody political campaigns*—Students can run a parody political campaign for a historical figure, adding elements of humor in their speeches and campaign materials.

When integrating humor into high school education, it is essential to consider students' maturity, ensuring that the humor is sophisticated and thought provoking rather than simplistic. It should encourage inclusivity, empathy, and respect for diverse perspectives. By doing so, humor can become a bridge that connects students with the curriculum in a manner that is both enlightening and enjoyable.

Concluding Thoughts

It is essential for teachers to instill a sense of humor in their students early on in their academic careers. It aids in the development of social skills, helps individuals deal with stress, and facilitates the formation of connections. Additionally, it stimulates creative thinking and analytical pondering. Students can cultivate a positive sense of humor in a way that serves them well throughout their life if they receive the appropriate instruction and assistance. By nurturing a sense of humor, we foster resilience, creativity, and the ability to approach problems from unique angles.

Integrating humor in education promotes an environment where learning is not just an academic exercise but a pleasurable, engaging experience. This shift toward a more joyful learning landscape supports the formation of an interdisciplinary mindset. With humor, we encourage students to see connections where others might see boundaries, which is a critical attribute of interdisciplinary thinking.

It should not be hard for you to look at the stains on walls, or the ashes of a fire, or the clouds or mud, and if you consider them well you will find marvelous new ideas, because the mind is stimulated to new inventions by obscure things.

—LEONARDO DA VINCI

Chapter 5

Habit 4: Create and Innovate

In every corner of a classroom lies the potential for discovery. The obscure, the overlooked, the seemingly mundane—they all harbor the seeds of innovation, waiting for the right mind to nurture them. By fostering a space where students can question, explore, and wonder, educators are not just imparting knowledge but lighting the torches of future visionaries. And as we journey through the annals of history, from the Renaissance to the digital age, this spirit of inquiry remains the beacon guiding humanity's quest for knowledge. As we prepare to delve deeper into the intricacies of education in the coming chapters, remember this: every great thinker, from Leonardo da Vinci to Albert Einstein, was once a curious child, looking at the world with wide-eyed wonder.

In the tempestuous waters of the 21st century, creativity and innovation stand out as twin lighthouses guiding our educational vessels. Creativity, at its core, is the capability to dream, to envision, and to ideate. It's the wellspring from which all original ideas emanate. It's the audacity to ask, "What if?" and imagine realms that have not yet come into being. Innovation takes these ephemeral dreams and makes them tangible. It's the process of implementing creative ideas into practical, actionable solutions or novel methodologies. While creativity is boundless imagination, innovation is its realization in the material world. The reason we discuss these concepts in tandem is their symbiotic relationship. Without creativity, innovation lacks its muse; devoid of innovation, creativity remains in the abstract. For an interdisciplinary approach to learning, students need to be both dreamers and doers. They need the imaginative prowess to conjure solutions and the innovative spirit to bring them to life.

In this chapter, we'll work to understand how creativity and innovation are relevant today in the realm of interdisciplinary K–12 learning. At the crossroads of fantasy and reality lies a fertile realm where the most profound insights and groundbreaking ideas germinate. We first consider how the harmony between the imagined and the actual shapes the essence of creativity and, more importantly, the processes of creating and innovating for students. Then, we investigate a real-life innovation story and explore classroom activities that nurture creative thinking and innovative action.

Find the Intersection of Fantasy and Reality

Fantasy offers unbridled freedom, a boundless expanse where the limitations of the physical world don't apply. For students, it's the canvas of imagination, where dragons coexist with robots, where the laws of physics can be bent, and where novel solutions to age-old problems spontaneously arise. Fantasy nurtures the "what if," stimulating young minds to envision a world outside the confines of textbooks and classrooms. It's the nebulous mist from which the spark of creativity emerges.

But imagination, without an anchor in the real world, remains a fleeting wisp. This is where reality steps in. It provides the context, the boundaries, the challenges that need overcoming. For students, reality translates their imaginative flights into projects, experiments, and actionable solutions. Boundaries, in the context of creativity and learning, are akin to the banks of a river. While the river's flow represents the boundless current of imagination, it is the banks that give direction to this flow, channeling it toward a particular destination. In the educational journey, boundaries play a pivotal role in giving shape, substance, and meaning to a student's imagination.

These boundaries come in various forms: the structured methodologies of scientific research, the grammatical rules of a new language, or the principles of mathematical logic. They are not obstacles to be begrudgingly overcome; rather, they are the solid framework on which the suspension bridge of innovation is anchored. By understanding and pushing against these boundaries, students learn not just to dream, but to do—to transform the "what if" into the "what can be."

Reality checks brought about by these boundaries help students discern the feasible from the fantastical, not to limit their thinking, but to enhance the quality of their creative outputs. They ensure that the ideas conceived in the classroom can take flight in the outside world. By navigating the limitations and frameworks of reality, students find the fertile ground for the seeds of their imagination to take root and blossom into contributions that can reshape their own lives and society.

As an example, addressing the global need for sustainable energy requires interdisciplinary knowledge from environmental science, engineering, economics, and social sciences. Students can engage in projects to design and implement small-scale renewable energy solutions in their community, such as solar panels or wind turbines. Research by Amory Lovins, Diana Ürge-Vorsatz, Luis Mundaca, Daniel Kammen, and Jacob Glassman (2019) highlights successful community-driven renewable energy initiatives that combine technical knowledge with social engagement to foster sustainable practices. Similarly, developing sustainable and functional urban spaces demands a multidisciplinary approach, incorporating urban design, civil engineering, environmental science, and sociology. A study by Kevin Leyden, Abraham Goldberg, and Philip Michelbach (2011) demonstrates the benefits of community-based urban planning initiatives that improve public spaces by integrating input from diverse stakeholders, resulting in more livable and inclusive cities.

Students can simulate this by redesigning a public park or a community area, applying their interdisciplinary skills to create models and proposals that address real community needs. Furthermore, combating food insecurity and promoting sustainable agricultural practices require expertise in biology, environmental science, economics, and social sciences. Projects where students design and implement urban farming solutions can illustrate this integration. Research by Miguel Altieri and Clara Nicholls (2020) on agroecology practices shows how combining scientific knowledge with local farming practices can enhance food security and environmental sustainability.

In this way, the inward focus of the imagination is given outward expression. The students' conceptual understanding matures as they realize that every limitation is an opportunity for a creative workaround, every challenge a call for an innovative solution, and every boundary a guideline that shapes their path to meaningful and practical creations. In this way, the inward focus of the imagination is given outward expression. The students' conceptual understanding matures as they realize that every limitation is an opportunity for a creative workaround, every challenge a call for an innovative solution, and every boundary a guideline that shapes their path to meaningful and practical creations.

The commonly held belief has been that there are creative types and analytical types. However, the world's most prolific innovators often return to the confluence of art and science, imagination and reason. Leonardo da Vinci epitomized this balance, as he never saw these domains as disparate. For him, imagination kindled the flames of curiosity, while rationality offered the tools to explore that curiosity (Pedretti, 1964). The integration of art and science, imagination and reason, can be seen in the lives and works of many historical figures who followed in the footsteps of Leonardo da Vinci.

- **Thomas Alva Edison:** Known for his prolific inventing process, Edison held 1,093 U.S. patents. He was both a skilled scientist and a shrewd businessman who could market his inventions—traits that require both logical thinking and creative insight.

- **Nikola Tesla:** A visionary inventor and engineer, Tesla and his work on alternating current electricity systems and wireless communication technology were ahead of their time. He was a dreamer with a poetic vision for the future, which he supported with rigorous scientific experimentation and innovation.

- **Marie Curie:** The first woman to win a Nobel Prize, Curie was not only a physicist and chemist but also someone deeply involved in the humanistic side of science. Her meticulous scientific methods combined with her profound empathy led to groundbreaking discoveries in radioactivity that also considered the human implications of science.

- **Rachel Carson:** A marine biologist and conservationist, Carson combined her scientific background with evocative writing to communicate the wonders of the natural world and the necessity of preserving it, most notably in her 1962 book *Silent Spring*.

- **Steve Jobs:** As a cofounder of Apple Inc., Jobs was known for his emphasis on design aesthetics and intuitive usability as much as technological innovation.

He believed in the intersection of technology and the humanities, which is evident in Apple products that are both functional and artistically designed.

These individuals exemplify the symbiotic relationship between the creative and analytical mindsets. They show that when science and art converge, the potential for innovation is boundless. The interplay of these two faculties can offer invaluable insights into how we might approach education and the cultivation of young minds in contemporary settings.

The interplay of art and science, imagination and reason, in education offers several insights into the cultivation of young minds.

- **Interdisciplinary learning:** Education can move beyond compartmentalization into traditional subjects by encouraging students to draw connections between disciplines. This approach mirrors the real-world scenarios where art informs design in technology, or mathematical concepts manifest in architectural beauty.

- **Process over product:** Focusing on the creative process rather than the final product can help students appreciate learning as a journey. This approach encourages experimentation, risk taking, and the understanding that "failures" are often just steps toward success.

- **Critical and creative thinking:** Educators can foster environments where students think critically to question and analyze, and think creatively to innovate and solve problems. Students can learn to use reason to navigate through their imaginative ideas, bringing them to fruition in concrete forms.

- **Customized learning paths:** Recognizing that each student may exhibit a unique blend of creativity and analytical skills, teachers can tailor lessons to address individual learning styles. This personal approach helps nurture students' innate strengths while also developing their lesser-used faculties.

These insights suggest that a more holistic approach to education, one that harmonizes the creative with the analytical, can lead to the development of more well-rounded individuals capable of innovation and flexible thinking.

By acknowledging and incorporating both imaginative and rational faculties, educators can expand students' horizons and encourage them to see connections where none seemingly exist, fostering a holistic worldview. This interconnected way of thinking and learning prepares students for a world that's not neatly divided but is a rich tapestry of interconnected domains.

Leonardo da Vinci's perspective blurred the lines between domains, recognizing the interconnectedness of all phenomena. He viewed space as an unbroken chain of occurrences, where every event was part of an intricate dance of cause and effect. His work exemplifies the harmony between analytical observations and imaginative extrapolations, offering a model for K–12 education to encourage seeing the links between different areas of knowledge. Here's how to apply this philosophical approach in classroom practice.

- **Cross-disciplinary projects:** Students can work on projects that require knowledge from various disciplines, mirroring the interconnectedness of the world. For example, a science fair project might also include elements of writing and art, teaching students that boundaries between subjects are permeable and complementary.

- **Systems thinking:** In both philosophy and practice, students can engage with systems thinking—the concept that different parts of a system are so intertwined that a change in one affects the others. This is evident in ecological studies, social sciences, and technology, and helps students grasp the complexity and dynamics of real-world systems.

- **Critical observation and creative application:** Teachers can guide students to use careful observation in their studies, as Leonardo did with his anatomical drawings, and then use their imagination to apply these observations creatively, as seen in his artwork. This cultivates both a respect for empirical evidence and a freedom to innovate.

- **Emotional intelligence:** Just as Leonardo captured human emotion in his art, students can learn to recognize and express emotions in their work, leading to richer learning experiences and fostering empathy.

- **Teaching interconnected concepts:** Educators can teach cause and effect, action and reaction, not only in science but also in humanities and the arts, to illustrate the ripple effects of historical events, technological advancements, and personal choices.

By embracing such a holistic view of learning, educators can inspire students to develop a love for learning that is intuitive, interconnected, and infused with wonder. This approach can help students see learning not as segmented tasks or isolated facts, but as a continuous journey of discovery that is both rigorous and imaginative.

Imagine teaching students that their creativity is like the early stages of a plant's life, like the seed and the soil, where potential lies dormant. In classrooms, this creative phase is when brainstorming happens, where the wild and wonderful "what ifs" flourish without concern for practicality. It's where a history lesson sparks a screenplay in a young writer's mind, or a mathematics problem hints at a new game for a budding app developer.

Innovation is the next phase—the growth of the plant toward the sunlight, turning creative ideas into tangible outcomes. In education, this is when students create prototypes of their inventions in a makerspace, write the first draft of that screenplay in English class, or code a basic version of their game in computer science.

Students journey from "Aha!" to "It's alive! " through guidance, tools, and encouragement to transform their fertile imaginations into real-world projects and skills. By understanding this journey from inspiration to realization, students learn resilience, the value of iteration, and the satisfaction of seeing their ideas take shape. They also come to appreciate the need for both dreaming and doing—that one feeds the other and that both are essential steps on the path of learning and creating.

Our classrooms aren't like Leonardo's studio, though. How do we foster creativity and innovation in learning environments that are hyperfocused on standards, covering content, and structured routines? I'll share with you a parallel and a lesson learned about NASA. Despite its seemingly rigid and structured character, NASA has been a hotbed of innovation, and there are significant takeaways from its approach that are relevant to student learning in K–12 classrooms.

Learn From a NASA Innovation Story and the Challenge-Driven Innovation

In 2007, I transitioned from my role as a high school chemistry and physics teacher to join the Next Gen team at NASA. Despite looming challenges, like the Space Shuttle's retirement, our team's goal was clear: bring fresh ideas to NASA, enhance cross-generation communication, and most importantly, make space accessible to the general public.

What transpired next was NASA's adoption of the *challenge-driven innovation* (CDI) methodology. CDI is akin to problem-based learning, where the teacher presents a challenge or problem and the students collectively explore and develop the solution. The difference? In educational contexts, student inquiry problems are typically hypothetical or based on historical scenarios. They serve as effective tools for learning concepts but may not directly translate to current real-world applications. Conversely, NASA's adoption of CDI involves tackling actual, pressing issues that affect space missions and the broader goals of space exploration. These challenges are grounded in reality and demand solutions that are viable in current and future space endeavors. For example, issues like preserving the quality of food in space or predicting solar activity are not exercises in theoretical problem solving but are actual, practical problems that NASA needs to address to advance its mission objectives.

Initially, NASA's transition to CDI was driven by a necessity to find unconventional solutions to the complex challenges of space exploration. By adopting this methodology, NASA began soliciting ideas and solutions not just from within its walls, but from a global community of scientists, engineers, and even laypeople who possessed diverse expertise and fresh perspectives. This pivot to harness collective intelligence became a cornerstone of NASA's innovation strategy. It started with clear communication of the specific challenges and an open invitation for solutions. This approach was underpinned by the creation of platforms that facilitated crowdsourcing ideas, such as the NASA Tournament Lab and various challenges posed through the InnoCentive platform. These platforms enabled a broader participation by reducing barriers to entry, allowing passionate individuals and teams to contribute their insights and solutions, thus fostering a community around problem solving.

The impact of this strategic move was multifold. First, it led to the discovery of novel solutions that may have otherwise remained unearthed within the traditional confines of the agency. For instance, in the challenge to preserve the quality of food in space, the collective brainpower led to innovative food packaging and preservation techniques that had applications both in space and on Earth. Second, it provided a cost-effective approach to research and development by tapping into the existing research and bypassing the initial stages of conceptualization. Third, it created an ecosystem where innovation thrived; solutions were not just theoretical but ready to be tested and implemented, propelling NASA's missions forward with renewed vigor.

Moreover, this open innovation model had the serendipitous effect of enhancing NASA's public image, showcasing the agency's willingness to engage with the public in meaningful ways. It demonstrated that leveraging collective intelligence could lead not only to scientific and technological breakthroughs but also to an enhanced public understanding and appreciation of NASA's work. This transparent and inclusive approach served as a beacon, showcasing how public entities can drive progress while nurturing public trust and interest.

In essence, NASA's CDI journey from inception to success illustrates how opening the gates to a wider pool of talent and embracing a culture of shared knowledge can lead to unprecedented advancements. For educators and students, this narrative underscores the importance of collaboration, the strength found in diverse perspectives, and the boundless potential of harnessing collective problem-solving capabilities in any learning environment.

- **The power of collaboration:** Just as NASA brings together experts from various fields—astrophysicists, engineers, biologists, and even artists—to solve complex problems, schools can adopt an interdisciplinary approach. By breaking down silos between subjects and encouraging teachers from different disciplines to collaborate on lesson plans, students get a holistic understanding. This not only aligns with standards but also fosters creativity as students learn to apply knowledge from one subject to another.

- **Out-of-the-box thinking:** NASA faces challenges that often don't have textbook solutions. Hence, it encourages its teams to brainstorm and think beyond the norm. Similarly, while K–12 education might be rooted in standards, there should be room for students to explore solutions outside of the traditional framework. Activities like open-ended projects, where students define the problem and the solution, can be a step in this direction.

- **Failure as a learning tool:** A part of NASA's success lies in its acceptance of failure as a stepping-stone. Each failure is dissected, studied, and used as a lesson for future missions. Schools can adopt this mindset by creating environments where students aren't penalized for mistakes but are instead encouraged to understand the reasons behind them and learn.

- **Structured flexibility:** Structured flexibility is an approach that combines a clear, organized framework with elements of adaptability and student autonomy. It means having a well-defined structure or set of guidelines while allowing for flexibility within that structure to accommodate individual needs, preferences, and creativity.

    Structured flexibility can be the key to fostering engaging and effective learning environments. Just as NASA has protocols but is also open to innovative solutions when challenges arise, curricula can have a clear framework but also pockets of flexibility. These pockets can be moments where students are given the autonomy to choose projects, topics, or methods of study. This approach not only ensures that essential standards and goals are met but also allows students to explore their interests, develop critical thinking skills, and take ownership of their learning.

- **Continuous learning:** NASA thrives on continuous learning. As new technologies and theories emerge, they are integrated into projects. Schools can adopt a similar approach. Instead of a static curriculum, there can be a dynamic element integrating emerging trends, technologies, or methodologies, ensuring that students are prepared for the evolving world outside.

In essence, while K–12 education operates within a framework of standards and routines, it is entirely possible to foster creativity and innovation within this structure. Taking cues from NASA's approach, schools can strike a balance between structured learning and innovative thinking, producing not just well-informed students but also thinkers and creators ready for the challenges of the future.

Drawing parallels to the K–12 education environment, there's a primary underlying lesson here. Our schools often operate in a siloed fashion, much like many governmental entities. If NASA, a behemoth organization, could pivot and reimagine its innovation approach, what stops our classrooms from doing the same? Embracing an open and collaborative methodology, akin to the challenge-driven innovation, can lead to diverse perspectives, efficient problem solving, and a culture of inclusivity and creativity.

However, while NASA's story is inspiring and offers a blueprint, the K–12 setting is uniquely different, requiring adaptations. The real challenge is how educators can take the spirit of NASA's model—openness, collaboration, and challenge-driven learning—and mold it into a framework that fits the classroom, stimulating young minds to think beyond the textbook and innovate. Imagine a scenario where educators present students with multifaceted problems. Instead of feeling overwhelmed, students learn the power of *deconstruction*—to disassemble a problem into its constituent parts and out of the dissection isolate small questions. Not only are they refining their analytical skills but they're also paving the way for innovative thinking as they tap into a myriad of solution avenues they might not have perceived initially.

At NASA, deconstruction played a critical role in addressing complex problems. This method allowed the agency to tackle multifaceted issues by breaking them down into more manageable parts and examining each one in depth. Returning to the challenge of preserving the quality of food in space, NASA deconstructed this problem by examining individual aspects such as nutritional content, packaging materials, and food's shelf life under space-travel conditions. By doing so, they could address each aspect systematically, leading to comprehensive solutions that collectively solved the broader problem.

In educational settings, this skill of deconstruction is vital for students' intellectual growth. For younger students, it involves simple tasks that require them to distinguish between the different aspects of a problem or object, like identifying the components of a plant in biology. As students progress to higher grade levels, they take on more complex deconstruction tasks, such as analyzing the factors leading to a historical event or dissecting the layers of meaning in a piece of literature.

Thus, whether it's in the vast corridors of NASA or the compact confines of a classroom, the art of deconstruction stands paramount. It is an essential bridge that links challenges to creativity and innovation. Emphasizing this strategy from the outset ensures that whether students are looking at algebraic equations or real-world scenarios, they approach problems with an innovative mindset, ready to dissect, understand, and innovate.

Educators can foster the skill of deconstruction by presenting problems that require students to identify and assess individual variables before synthesizing them into a coherent whole. Teaching students to deconstruct not only problems but also established methods and theories can encourage them to think critically and innovatively, a practice that is crucial for future academic and professional success. Let's explore how educators can introduce and differentiate deconstruction for various grade bands.

For early elementary grades (K–2), when introducing the concept of story deconstruction, vary the stories used to prevent students from forming solutions based solely on memory and to encourage a deeper understanding of the problem-solving process. Here's how you might approach it.

- **Visual story breakdown:** Begin with a simple story that contains a problem and resolution. After reading, use visual aids like storyboards to help students identify the problem, the characters involved, and the solution.
- **Hands-on group activities:** Encourage students to brainstorm alternative solutions to the problem in a new story you read to them. This activity pushes them to think creatively and understand that there can be multiple solutions to a single problem, fostering divergent thinking.
- **Guided questions:** Apply the guided questions to the story used for the hands-on group activity. This ensures that students are analyzing the specific components of the problem they are actively trying to solve, which solidifies their understanding and application of the problem-solving process.

In the later elementary grades (3–5), use real-world analogy strategies such as analogies with toys and basic mind mapping.

- **Analogies with toys:**
  - Present building blocks and explain that they represent the city infrastructure. Have students construct a model city with their blocks.
  - Introduce a problem, such as traffic congestion, and ask students to identify where in their city the problem is occurring.
  - Encourage students to think critically about how changes to the infrastructure could alleviate the traffic, asking guiding questions such as, "What happens if we add another road here?" or "How might creating a no-parking zone affect traffic flow?"
  - Facilitate a discussion on the implications of each change, promoting understanding of cause and effect.
- **Basic mind mapping:**
  - Begin by presenting a central problem on the board or on paper. This could be a real-world issue like pollution, or a conceptual challenge like improving team collaboration.
  - Guide students to identify the main causes of the problem by asking probing questions, such as, "What do you think leads to this issue?" or "Can you think of events or actions that might contribute to this problem?"
  - Once students identify causes, ask them to think of potential solutions and how they could implement these solutions.
  - Encourage them to draw branches from the central problem to each cause and solution, visually representing the complexity of the problem and the interconnectedness of its potential solutions. To effectively guide this process, provide examples of mind maps, offer feedback on their connections, and facilitate group discussions to help students refine their ideas.

Middle school (6–8) students can use real-world scenarios and role play.

- **Real-world scenarios:** Present students with more complex, real-world problems, such as environmental issues. Encourage them to break the problem down into its root causes using tools like flowcharts or cause-and-effect diagrams.

- **Role play:** Let students role-play different stakeholders in a given problem, understanding and voicing the concerns of each party. This not only deconstructs the issue but also nurtures empathy.

High school (9–12) students can tackle advanced problem-solving strategies like the following.

- **Case studies:** Provide students with detailed case studies that require comprehensive problem deconstruction. These could range from historical events to current global challenges.
- **Debate and discussion:** Organize sessions where students debate different facets of a problem, defending or opposing certain stances. This sharpens their ability to see a problem from multiple angles.
- **Digital tools:** Introduce students to digital tools and software that can aid in deconstructing complex scenarios or data sets, further preparing them for real-world applications.

By tailoring how they teach problem deconstruction to students' developmental stages and comprehension levels, educators can ensure that the process is both engaging and effective. Over time, these strategies not only help students better understand the problems at hand but also equip them with the analytical prowess to approach any challenge with innovation and creativity.

In our increasingly interconnected world, innovative organizations—be it NASA or any other forward-thinking entity—benefit immensely from tapping into a diverse pool of minds, each bringing its unique viewpoint to the table. This diversity in thought and approach isn't just a by-product of varied personal experiences but can be significantly nurtured within educational environments. Instead of channeling students down a singular, predetermined path, an innovative learning paradigm encourages them to think expansively, question the status quo, and collaborate across boundaries. By instilling such a mindset from the very beginning, we cultivate a generation that's predisposed to look at problems from multiple angles, find solutions beyond the obvious, and readily collaborate with peers who have different perspectives.

It's essential to recognize that the core of innovation in learning lies in fostering a broad mindset that's curious, adaptable, and collaborative. Such a mindset will not only make students valuable contributors in diverse teams in the future but also prepare them for more specific frameworks and methodologies that they may encounter later in their learning journey, like the challenge-based approach. It also encourages effective use of available resources, facilitates the transfer of intellectual property, fosters a more innovative culture, and improves the ability to formulate problem statements or research requirements. Additionally, it offers savings in terms of money and time associated with innovative problem-solving techniques. By confronting students with practical problems that require them to use their knowledge and abilities to address the issue, this framework motivates them to think critically and creatively. By giving feedback on their responses, it also enables teachers to evaluate students' development in a more relevant way. A platform for cooperation between teachers, students, and other educational stakeholders may also be created using this architecture. In this renaissance, we can create innovative teaching techniques and plans that are adapted to the creativity and innovation potential of each student.

> **IBN AL-HAYTHAM THINKS CREATIVELY TO FIND INGENIOUS SOLUTIONS**
>
> Often hailed as the "father of modern optics," Ibn al-Haytham was a polymath who lived during the Islamic Golden Age. He was a physicist, mathematician, astronomer, and philosopher. His pioneering work in optics and the scientific method laid the foundation for future generations of scientists. Embodying the essence of creativity and innovative thought, Ibn al-Haytham was relentless in questioning, experimenting, and contributing to various fields of knowledge.
>
> One of Ibn al-Haytham's most significant achievements was challenging the then-prevailing theory of vision. While the popular belief was that rays came out of the eyes, making vision possible, Ibn al-Haytham proposed the opposite: that light rays entered the eyes. To prove his hypothesis, he conducted a series of experiments, including the use of the camera obscura—a dark room with a small hole allowing light to enter. Through rigorous testing and keen observation, he demonstrated how light behaved, revolutionizing our understanding of optics.
>
> Now imagine Lucas, a middle school student intrigued by the properties of sound. After learning about the basic principles in class, Lucas believes there could be innovative ways to manipulate sound waves for practical applications. He thinks of the noise pollution in his bustling neighborhood and wonders if there could be a way to reduce it. Drawing inspiration from Ibn al-Haytham's spirit of exploration, Lucas starts experimenting with different materials to create a makeshift sound barrier. Over time, with trials and errors, he crafts a simple yet effective prototype that diminishes outside noise when placed on windows, turning it into a school project and winning accolades.
>
> Both Ibn al-Haytham and Lucas embody the spirit of creativity, challenging existing beliefs or norms and pushing the boundaries of what's known. While al-Haytham tackled the intricacies of light, changing the course of scientific thought, Lucas took on a local issue with sound, demonstrating innovation's power at any age. Their stories underscore that creative thinking, when paired with curiosity and perseverance, can lead to groundbreaking solutions and discoveries—be it in medieval Cairo or a contemporary classroom.

Implement and Differentiate an Easy Activity to Nurture Creative Thinking and Innovative Action in K–12 Students

In an age where information is at our fingertips, what distinguishes truly educated individuals is not just what they know, but how they think and act on that knowledge. Just as muscles require regular exercise to grow stronger, the cognitive muscles of creativity and innovation need consistent practice. By infusing our classrooms with opportunities for students to engage in creative thinking followed by innovative action, we create a robust learning environment. Following are practical exercises differentiated for various grade levels that educators can employ to stimulate these critical faculties in their students.

Elementary School Students

At the elementary school level, students are at an ideal age to begin exercising their creative and innovative muscles. Their vivid imaginations are ripe for activities that challenge them to think beyond the conventional, and their cognitive skills have developed to a point where they can start to apply their ideas in more concrete ways. The activities of story cubes and creating an eco-friendly classroom harness these developmental strengths.

- **Story cubes:** To do this activity with your students, you will need dice with pictures on each side. These can be purchased or created with stickers on blank dice. Roll the dice and get several random pictures. Students must then create a story that links all these pictures together. This encourages creative narratives and unexpected combinations.

- **Eco-friendly classroom:** To do this activity, you will need recyclable materials (for example, cardboard, plastic bottles, and cans). Challenge the students to build something useful for the classroom using only the recyclable materials. This could be a pencil holder, a book stand, or anything else they can imagine. This practice enforces the idea of taking a concept and turning it into a tangible product or solution. Lead a discussion that includes the following.

  → *Set the context*—Begin by contextualizing the activity. Ask students to think about how every item they use in the classroom started as an idea or a concept. Encourage them to consider how these items are part of a story about solving problems or fulfilling needs.

  → *Use guided imagery*—Use guided imagery to help students visualize the transformation process. Ask them to close their eyes and imagine an inventor thinking of a new product, or a scientist considering how to solve a problem. Guide them to see the process of an idea materializing into something concrete.

  → *Facilitate connections*—Ask open-ended questions to help students draw parallels between storytelling and creating. For instance, ask, "How is developing a story like inventing something new?" or "Can you think of a character from a story who made something to solve a problem?"

  → *Encourage reflection*—Have students reflect on their own experiences of creating or building something. Ask, "Have you ever made something that started as just an idea? What was it, and how did you make it real?"

  → *Idea sharing*—Allow students to share their ideas openly without fear of judgment. This fosters an environment where creativity is valued and encourages them to brainstorm freely.

  → *Relate to personal experience*—Tie the activity to the students' lives by asking how they might use the object they plan to create. Discuss the practicality and potential impact of their creations on daily classroom activities.

→ *Discuss and debrief*—After the activity, lead a debriefing session. Ask students what they learned about turning ideas into reality, what challenges they encountered, and how they overcame them.

Middle School Students

For middle school students, who are transitioning from concrete operational thought to more formal operational thought processes, activities like maintaining an invention journal and building prototypes are highly beneficial. At this stage of cognitive development, they are beginning to think abstractly and critically, making it an opportune time to engage them in activities that nurture these skills.

- **Invention journal:** You will need a notebook or digital journal for each student. Encourage students to write down problems they encounter in their daily lives for a week. At the end of the week, students should pick one problem and brainstorm possible solutions. This activity allows students to practice recognizing problems in their daily lives, a skill that aligns with their developing ability to observe and analyze the world around them critically. As they jot down various problems, they engage in reflective thinking—a habit that is crucial in developing a critical mindset. When students choose a problem from their journal to brainstorm solutions, they are taking the first steps in the design thinking process. They learn to generate ideas without judgment, a skill that will become increasingly important as they progress through their education and into their careers.

- **Prototype building:** You will need basic crafting materials (paper, scissors, glue, cardboard) and a computer with design software (if available). Using their solutions from the invention journal, students will design and build a basic prototype of their solution. This can be a physical model or a digital representation. Building a prototype, whether physical or digital, allows students to transition from theoretical brainstorming to concrete application. This hands-on activity promotes problem solving and critical thinking, as students must consider the practicality of their designs and troubleshoot issues that arise during the creation process. It also provides an opportunity for them to learn basic principles of engineering and design, which can be particularly engaging at an age where many students are beginning to consider their future careers.

These activities are crucial at the middle school level, as they help students develop a sense of agency and capability in solving real-world problems, setting a strong foundation for high school, college, and beyond.

High School Students

High school students stand on the cusp of adulthood, where the educational focus shifts toward preparing them for real-world challenges. The exercises detailed here—societal debate and community project—are tailored to this age group because they require students to engage with complex issues critically and to apply theoretical knowledge practically. Both activities help shape students' identities as informed, capable, and proactive members of society, empowering them to become agents of change. Through these exercises, students can become not only academically competent but also socially responsible and innovative in their approach to the issues they care about.

- **Societal debate:** You will need articles or videos about a contemporary societal issue. Have students analyze and discuss the issue. Encourage them to think about potential solutions or improvements. They should consider the implications, benefits, and drawbacks of these solutions. Societal debate leverages high school students' developing ability to understand and discuss complex societal issues, such as environmental policies or social justice. They're encouraged to analyze various viewpoints, develop arguments, and propose informed solutions, practices that are essential for active citizenship.

- **Community project:** The community project activity takes the insights gained from the societal debate and challenges students to apply them. The materials needed for this project depend on students' proposed solution and could range from digital tools to raw materials such as wood, clay, or metal. Encourage students to take one of the solutions discussed in the societal debate and implement it at a small scale in their school or community. For instance, if the debate was about waste management, they could start a recycling initiative in school. This is about taking theoretical or conceptual solutions and implementing them in real-world scenarios. High schoolers are at an age where they can execute projects with a degree of independence and are ready to see the impact of their actions within their communities. Whether it's initiating a recycling program or developing a digital campaign for a cause, these projects enable students to transform conceptual discussions into tangible outcomes.

We've navigated a journey from the imaginative realms of elementary students to high school learners working toward positive social change. In each stage, the intertwined processes of creative thinking and innovative action provide a foundation for holistic learning. The true beauty of these exercises lies not just in the immediate results, but in the long-term impact on a student's mindset. As educators, our primary aim is to nurture not just repositories of knowledge, but proactive thinkers and doers, prepared to make meaningful contributions to the world around them.

Concluding Thoughts

Creativity and innovation, as explored in this chapter, aren't mere buzzwords but crucial elements in fostering an empowered learning experience. Drawing inspiration from history, notably Leonardo da Vinci's genius, we recognized that the confluence of imagination and rationality isn't a paradox but a potent blend that can lead to groundbreaking discoveries and change. This synthesis of fantasy and reality, a harmony of dreaming and doing, is vital for students in our contemporary age.

The structured environment of schools, with its standards and routines, can at times seem antithetical to these values. Yet, as the NASA example elucidated, even within confines, innovation can flourish provided there's a will to adapt and evolve. The key is to approach challenges from multiple angles, invite diverse perspectives, and break problems down to their core components—techniques that students can internalize and apply in various scenarios. By introducing them to the principles of deconstruction and analytical thinking, we're equipping them with tools to navigate an increasingly complex world.

This chapter and its practical applications serve to underline a broader theme of the book: teaching students not just to know, but to think and act meaningfully. The purpose of education, as highlighted throughout, isn't merely about acquiring knowledge but about internalizing a mindset—a way of approaching challenges, seeking solutions, and effecting positive change. And with the potent duo of creativity and innovation in our pedagogical arsenal, we're not just shaping learners but future leaders and visionaries.

You will never have a greater or lesser dominion than that over yourself.

—LEONARDO DA VINCI

Chapter 6

Habit 5: Self-Regulate

Students need to be able to evaluate their learning and make adjustments to the depth and breadth with which they pursue elements of that learning. They need to be able to decide with paths to take or not take in learning. They need to be able to persist, refrain, and change course when necessary. In other words, they need to be able to self-regulate. Self-regulation is the cornerstone of learner autonomy and a skill integral to effective education. It involves students' ability to initiate, maintain, control, and adapt their thoughts, emotions, and behaviors to achieve long-term educational goals. This self-directed practice is key to developing independent, motivated, and resilient learners who are equipped to meet the challenges of a rapidly changing world.

In revisiting the role of self-regulation in education, we see a movement from traditional models, which often emphasize rote learning and teacher-centric methods, to a learner-centered approach. By fostering self-regulation, students take ownership of their learning journey, employing strategies to monitor and self-correct their pathway to knowledge acquisition. This transformation aligns with a more personalized education system, one that values the unique abilities and learning styles of each student.

In this chapter, we delve into the multifaceted nature of self-regulation and its implications for teaching and learning. We explore the connection between self-regulation and the other eight habits, examining how the ability to self-regulate impacts a student's engagement with each of these habits. For example, self-regulation enhances collaborative learning by helping students contribute effectively in group settings, strengthens problem solving by aiding in the monitoring and adjustment of tactics, and bolsters critical thinking by encouraging students to reflect on their reasoning processes.

The scope of this chapter also covers practical strategies for educators to teach and support the development of self-regulation. We look at research that demonstrates the positive impact of self-regulatory practices on student outcomes, and I provide methods to create learning environments that cultivate these skills. Through a combination of theoretical insights and actionable techniques, you will gain a robust understanding of how to embed self-regulation in your teaching practices, thereby contributing to the broader renaissance in education.

Use Strategies to Promote the Development of Self-Regulation

Evidence from various studies highlights the efficacy of self-regulation in educational settings. For example, Barry J. Zimmerman's (2002) work on self-regulation has been influential, illustrating that students who are adept at self-regulating their learning are more likely to succeed academically. Additionally, Albert Bandura's (1982) research on self-efficacy complements this, showing that students' belief in their capabilities greatly influence their ability to self-regulate and achieve their goals. Moreover, the development of self-regulation has been linked to improved outcomes in various domains of student learning. Research by Angela Duckworth and Stephanie Carlson (2013) suggests that self-regulation, often operationalized as grit or perseverance, is a better predictor of student success than traditional measures such as IQ.

These studies provide the empirical foundation for the strategies and practices discussed in this chapter. They underscore the importance of teaching self-regulation and highlight the significant role educators play in fostering these skills in their students. Thus, as you delve deeper into this chapter, you will not only learn about the conceptual underpinnings of self-regulation but also how to practically apply research-backed strategies to nurture these skills in your students.

Self-regulated learning involves four distinct processes. Keep in mind, the processes do not always need to occur in the following order. Learners who are skilled at self-regulation engage in many of these processes simultaneously or modify the order as they grow more proficient at self-regulation.

1. **Planning and goal setting:** Students evaluate their own development relative to their goals as guideposts along the way. To set goals, students must first recall prior knowledge regarding the degree of difficulty of the activities involved in reaching goals as well as their own capabilities in the relevant subject area. Students should consider how much time they will need to complete an activity before developing a strategy for managing their time effectively. They might also think about certain learning that they will use to accomplish their goal or goals tactics (like quizzing themselves as they read, for example).

2. **Taking charge of the situation:** Students implement any learning tactics (such as rehearsal, elaboration, summarizing, or self-questioning) they chose during planning and goal setting to control the learning experience. Seeking assistance can also be considered a way of taking control, although this is only the case when the learner makes use of the assistance to further strengthen their own abilities or comprehension; seeking help is not a self-regulatory

behavior when it is used as a crutch to get an answer without putting in effort. Control also involves delaying enjoyable activities to make headway toward one's objectives, and it can take the form of employing attention-focusing strategies such as turning off all music, sitting alone, or going to the library. To put it another way, control can be defined as the general perseverance to cling to the techniques that work.

3. **Tracking progress and engagement:** Students are aware of their own levels of comprehension, motivation, feelings, and behavior in relation to achieving a goal. For instance, students have the ability to clarify for themselves what it is that they do and do not yet know by utilizing the metacognitive method they opted to apply in the goal-setting stage, which is to ask themselves questions. Keeping track of how much actual studying gets done with a study group is another method of self-monitoring, as is noticing which contexts and environments assist them to focus on their job.

4. **Engaging in metacognitive reflection:** Students use the knowledge they received during the earlier self-assessment activity. A student's perception of their own growth, or lack thereof, will be shaped by the degree to which they believe in their own skills. A student who has a solid belief that they are capable will, for instance, attribute a low grade on a mathematics test to the fact that they did not get enough sleep the night before or that they only spent a short amount of time studying, rather than attributing the low grade to a lack of intelligence. Responding to self-evaluation functions like a thermostat, allowing one to either crank up the dial in effort to increase progress toward one's goals or ease back in order to focus on other things. This adjustment may take the form of behaviors such as requesting help, being persistent, or switching up learning tactics.

To train students to self-regulate better through these four processes, you can provide support to bolster the students' sense of self-efficacy, encourage them to cultivate a growth mindset, and place an emphasis on learning rather than grades and marks. Teachers across grades K–12 might also try the following strategies to encourage students to develop and appropriately apply self-regulating tactics, working toward making the cycle of independent self-regulation a habit.

- **Align the mode of instruction:** Tailor teaching methods to match individual learning strategies, optimizing students' absorption of the material.

- **Incorporate positive feedback:** Use encouragement to reinforce students' successful behaviors and efforts, fostering a supportive learning environment.

- **Encourage concentration:** Implement strategies that help students focus their attention, which is crucial for maintaining engagement with tasks.

- **Help students track their own development:** Teach students to self-monitor and evaluate their progress, enhancing their ability to regulate their learning.

- **Evaluate like a detective:** Guide students in critical self-reflection, enabling them to assess and adjust their learning strategies effectively.

Align Modes of Instruction

Teachers align modes of instruction by assisting students in determining specific learning strategies that are appropriate for the goals they have set for themselves. Repetition, organization, or categorization of knowledge, mnemonic devices, or paraphrasing the material are some of the most effective ways to strengthen fundamental learning tasks such as storing information for memory recall.

When students are tasked with giving knowledge meaning, however, teachers must implement more complex instructional methods. Students have the option of creating a network of ideas by listing underlying causes or themes, outlining the structure of the process or paper, or diagramming spatial relationships as part of the process of building connections between new concepts and the learner's prior knowledge. Differentiating the mode of instruction helps students build stronger bridges between the two sets of information.

It is crucial for teachers to explicitly teach a variety of learning strategies to their students, as well as to enable and encourage their students as they select which learning strategy is most appropriate for the type of work they will be doing. For more in-depth information on aligning modes of instruction with content, consider reading *Classroom Instruction That Works: Research-Based Strategies for Increasing Student Achievement* (Marzano, Pickering, & Pollock, 2001).

Incorporate Positive Feedback

It requires practice to keep one's focus on a task. Educators can help students maintain their concentration by providing positive feedback on students' efforts. Students frequently internalize their teachers' evaluations of their work, which means that teachers have significant influence over whether students continue to engage in a task or give up on it. It is essential that educators recognize their significance in students' perceptions and cultivate a culture that recognizes and values errors as valuable learning opportunities. While positive feedback is crucial, it is also important to discuss problem areas in a genuine manner to pave the way for personal development. Constructive criticism, when delivered alongside positive feedback, helps students understand their mistakes and learn from them, reinforcing the idea that errors are part of the learning process.

To effectively incorporate positive feedback within the educational process, focus on strategies that reinforce the effort and the learning process rather than just the end result. This approach encourages students to persist in their tasks and view challenges as opportunities for growth. Here's how you can do this.

- **Provide specific praise:** Instead of general comments like "good job," offer specific feedback about what the student did well. For example, "Your use of evidence in this essay really strengthened your argument."
- **Encourage a growth mindset:** Praise efforts, strategies, and persistence over time. Highlight how students' actions lead to improvements and learning, reinforcing that they can develop their abilities with effort.
- **Use the feedback sandwich:** Start with something positive, discuss areas for improvement in the middle, and conclude with encouragement. This helps students receive constructive criticism within a supportive framework.
- **Give timely and regular feedback:** Provide feedback soon after tasks to help students immediately apply advice to their learning processes.
- **Cultivate an environment of trust:** Foster a classroom culture where students feel their contributions are valued, and mistakes are seen as a natural part of the learning journey.

- **Teach self-feedback:** Encourage students to self-assess and identify their own strengths and areas for growth, promoting independence and self-reflection.

By weaving these tactics into your teaching practice, you help students build resilience and take an active role in their learning journey, ultimately leading to a more engaged and motivated classroom.

Encourage Concentration

It is extremely beneficial to have a quiet space for individual work, and teachers can do much to make the learning atmosphere calm, quiet, and conducive to concentration. Beyond this, the most effective way for students to learn to control their own attention and impulses is through persistent and frequent practice, with the duration of sessions becoming progressively longer. Although working together and engaging in conversation are essential components of the educational process, maintaining self-control in a chaotic setting can be extremely difficult. This skill is of utmost significance in secondary school, since teenagers' higher-level critical thinking skills are significantly hampered by distractions. Teachers can provide students with complex, open-ended tasks that give students the opportunity to practice managing distractions and maintaining focus while tackling increasingly challenging academic work. This is a great way for teachers to further support the development of self-regulation in their students. Here's how teachers can do this.

- **Structure the learning space:** Arrange the classroom to minimize distractions. This might include seating arrangements that limit visual noise or a designated quiet zone for individual work.
- **Implement focus sessions:** Use techniques like the Pomodoro Technique, where students work for a set time on a task, followed by a short break. This helps to build concentration endurance gradually.
- **Mindfulness practices:** Begin classes with mindfulness exercises such as deep breathing or guided imagery to help students center their attention and reduce stress.
- **Academic challenges:** Provide tasks that require sustained attention and critical thinking, allowing students to practice maintaining focus through more complex, engaging work.
- **Tech-free zones:** Encourage periods where students put electronic devices away to reduce digital distractions.
- **Personalized goals:** Work with students to set personal focus goals and develop a plan to achieve them, fostering self-awareness and self-regulation skills.

By consistently applying these techniques, teachers support students in developing the concentration necessary for academic success and self-regulated learning.

Help Students Track Their Own Development

At the heart of monitoring and analyzing one's level of comprehension sit two questions: What do I know?, and How can I improve? Self-regulation involves students actively taking responsibility for their own learning by setting goals, monitoring their progress, and reflecting on their outcomes. Depending on the nature of the objective, students might challenge themselves to become more aware of the boundaries of their own knowledge by using techniques such as recall, practice, and extension. Following direct instruction with a brief summary of the lesson's most important takeaways is an example of one monitoring method. Students who are working to improve their reading comprehension can take a moment to stop and ask themselves questions about the text they are currently reading.

In addition to monitoring their own learning, students can also reflect on their development of other skills, such as managing their time. These students would do well to keep track of how they spend their time and then evaluate those data in relation to the objectives of the tasks they are working on. For instance, I might think that a good strategy for preparing for an assessment at the end of the semester is to spend two hours each week studying with a study group. This would be in addition to my own study time. Having said that, it is possible that I will discover that one of the two hours is typically spent engaging in social activities. Afterward, I will be able to adjust my behavior based on this new information moving ahead.

Helping students track their development is about fostering metacognitive skills and self-awareness. This involves the following.

- **Learning diaries:** Encourage students to keep a diary where they record what they've learned and their thoughts on the learning process. Review these diaries periodically with the students to discuss their reflections and identify patterns or areas for improvement.
- **Regular check-ins:** Schedule brief regular meetings with students to review their goals and progress, providing a structured opportunity for self-assessment.
- **Self-assessment tools:** Use rubrics or checklists that students can use to evaluate their own work. Guide them in setting criteria for what successful learning looks like and how to measure it.
- **Reflective questions:** Teach students to ask themselves reflective questions after completing tasks, such as, "What strategies worked for me?" and "What can I do differently next time?"
- **Visual progress tracking:** Have students create visual representations of their progress, like a chart or graph, to track achievements and identify areas needing attention.

These techniques give students a structured way to monitor their learning journey, making them active participants in their educational development.

Evaluate Like a Detective

When students reflect on their learning, they require a high level of resilience to investigate what worked and what didn't and to recover quickly from the inevitable highs and lows that come with the process of learning. Teachers can provide explicit instruction in metacognitive methods by chatting with students about how to evaluate themselves like a detective. Looking for concrete evidence of what they can improve helps students focus on changeable behaviors, such as effort and preparation, rather than fixed traits like personality or intelligence. For instance, a student with poor resilience who has just received feedback that she did poorly on a mathematics test might consider dropping mathematics altogether. On the other hand, if she were to exhibit emotional resilience, she might make the decision to reflect on the specific challenges that she struggled with to modify her approach to learning. After giving it some thought, she concludes that during the previous semester, she never went to the library by herself, recapped the information she had just learned to herself after each class, or approached the teacher for assistance. She thinks about whether these adjustments are worthwhile, plans how she will put them into effect, and then devises a strategy for how she will organize her time going forward.

Evaluating like a detective involves students taking an active role in critically analyzing their learning experiences and outcomes. Here's how to guide them.

- **Review feedback:** After receiving feedback, students should dissect it to understand what was effective and what wasn't. Ask them to identify the specific elements that contributed to their success or shortcomings.
- **Employ self-questioning:** Encourage students to ask themselves probing questions about their performance. For example, "What study strategies did I use, and how might different techniques improve my understanding?"
- **Analyze cause and effect:** Teach students to look for patterns in their performance. If they performed poorly on a test, have them analyze their study habits, emotional state, and understanding of the content prior to the test.
- **Develop a reflective practice:** Create regular opportunities for students to reflect on their learning, such as journaling or discussion groups, where they can analyze their strategies and think about how to adapt them for better outcomes.
- **Build resilience:** Discuss the importance of resilience and mindset. When faced with failure, rather than attributing it to a lack of ability, students should identify actionable steps to improve, such as seeking help or altering their study routine.
- **Create action plans:** Help students create specific action plans based on their analyses. These plans should detail what steps they will take to change their approach to learning and how they will implement these changes.

By fostering these investigative habits, you'll be equipping students with the skills to self-assess and pivot their learning strategies as needed, supporting their journey to becoming self-regulated learners.

Evaluate Students' Self-Regulation and Offer Them Opportunities to Practice

The dual objectives of periodically evaluating students' self-regulation abilities are (1) informing the teacher about their students' progress and (2) pushing students to practice self-awareness. Formal schoolwide exams of broader social-emotional topics, such as Panorama Education's (2024) robust and reliable Social-Emotional Learning Survey, are beneficial for collecting thorough data, but they are too extensive to effectively carry out more than once or twice each academic year. On a biweekly or monthly basis, teachers can measure students' levels of self-regulation in an informal setting. Figure 6.1 (page 96) and figure 6.2 (page 97) display self-regulation questionnaires for secondary and elementary students, respectively.

CIRCLE THE RESPONSE THAT BEST DESCRIBES YOU IN THIS MOMENT:

1. How willing are you to experiment with alternative methods if you reach a roadblock when acquiring new knowledge?
    a. Not at all likely
    b. Quite likely
    c. Likely
    d. Highly likely
2. How frequently, before beginning a tough project, do you think about the most effective ways to tackle the project?
    a. Very seldom
    b. Occasionally
    c. Fairly frequently
    d. Almost always
3. How frequently do you keep your attention fixed on the same objective for a period of several months at a time?
    a. Very seldom
    b. Occasionally
    c. Fairly frequently
    d. Almost always
4. How well are you able to maintain your focus when you are working on a project that is really important to you even if there are many other things going on around you?
    a. Not at all focused
    b. Somewhat focused
    c. Focused
    d. Very focused
5. How well are you able to continue working toward a significant goal even if you encounter a challenge along the way?
    a. Not very well
    b. Somewhat well
    c. Well
    d. Very well
6. How well do you pay attention and how well do you refrain from getting distracted?
    a. Not very well
    b. Somewhat well
    c. Well
    d. Very well
7. How frequently do you follow through and meet the goals you set for yourself?
    a. Very seldom
    b. Occasionally
    c. Fairly frequently
    d. Almost always

WRITE YOUR RESPONSE TO THE FOLLOWING OPEN-ENDED QUESTIONS.

8. How do you keep yourself motivated when a concept or lesson is not inherently interesting to you?

9. How do you refocus your attention once you become aware that you are distracted?

10. How did you react the last time you had a problem at school, and what did it teach you?

Figure 6.1: Student self-regulation check—secondary.

*Visit **go.SolutionTree.com/instruction** for a free reproducible version of this figure.*

CIRCLE YOUR ANSWERS.
1. How did you feel during today's lesson?
    a. 🙂 Happy
    b. 😐 OK
    c. 🙁 Confused
    d. ☹ Sad
2. What did you find hard?
    a. 🧩 Problem solving
    b. 📚 Reading
    c. ✏ Writing
    d. 🎨 Drawing
3. How did you solve the problem or challenge?
    a. 🧠 I thought hard about it.
    b. 📞 I asked a friend.
    c. ✋ I asked the teacher.
    d. 💡 I came up with an idea.
4. What can you do next time to help you understand better?
    a. 📖 Study more
    b. 📝 Practice more
    c. 🙋 Ask for help
    d. 💪 Try harder
5. Draw your solution.

Figure 6.2: Student self-regulation check—elementary.

*Visit **go.SolutionTree.com/instruction** for a free reproducible version of this figure.*

Teachers can leverage the self-evaluation questionnaires to create collaborative opportunities for students to actively engage in the process of self-regulation. These evaluations, while illuminating areas of strength and challenge, serve as a starting point for discussions between students and teachers on setting realistic, personally motivating goals that align with the student's aspirations and academic needs. They also play a pivotal role in developing coping skills by allowing students to identify stress points and work proactively to manage them.

The following strategies are all modes of helping students develop self-regulation skills.

- **Set personally motivating goals:** This involves helping students establish clear, relevant, and challenging yet attainable goals that are directly tied to their interests and learning paths.

- **Develop coping skills:** Teachers can guide students through strategies to manage stress and navigate academic and social pressures, fostering resilience and adaptability.

- **Use journaling:** Encouraging students to keep a journal offers them a private space to reflect on their learning, track progress, and articulate their thoughts and emotions, thus supporting the development of their self-regulation skills.

Set Personally Motivating Goals

The process of setting goals is an essential component of self-regulation. Dale Shunk and Barry Zimmerman's (2012) self-regulation theory, for instance, emphasizes the role of setting SMART goals as a foundation for self-regulated learning. Goal orientation significantly influences academic achievement through motivational components such as self-efficacy and effort regulation. These components mediate the relationship between goal setting and academic success, highlighting the importance of personal goals in fostering student engagement and perseverance (Frumos et al., 2024). It is important to acquire the skills necessary to set goals to avoid frustration, moderate anxiety, and set positive expectations. However, these goals will change quite a bit depending on the requirements of each individual student; for example, some students need to reduce their anxiety to succeed, while others might do better with a little bit more of it.

The individual knowledge that each learner possesses about what motivates them, whether it comes from within themselves or from outside sources, is an essential component of self-regulation. Learners need to be able to set personal goals that are attainable within a reasonable time frame in addition to cultivating positive beliefs that they can meet their goals and be successful in their endeavors.

A template for goal setting, like the one shown in figure 6.3, can support students in recognizing and implementing various methods of self-regulation. Learners select a goal they have for themselves, such as lowering the number of times they lash out in anger as a result of being frustrated. Learners then break down this objective into smaller, more manageable actions, such as setting a timer for five minutes whenever they feel upset and taking deep breaths during that time. In the last section of the template, students think of ways they might keep themselves motivated and on track to achieve their objective, such as promising themselves a treat after achieving a milestone along the way.

GOAL: _____

The following are the steps that I need to take to reach my goal.

1. _____
2. _____
3. _____
4. _____
5. _____
6. _____
7. _____
8. _____

The following are methods for maintaining my motivation and keeping myself on schedule.

1. _____
2. _____
3. _____
4. _____

Figure 6.3: Student goal-setting template.

*Visit **go.SolutionTree.com/instruction** for a free reproducible version of this figure.*

Develop Coping Skills

When successful learning requires that students cope with negative emotions and frustrations, and when there are no options for students who have difficulty doing so, learning can become inaccessible. This can be a problem for students who want to learn but are unable to do so. For most students, merely demonstrating self-regulation skills is not enough for them to develop these skills. They will require long-term apprenticeships that incorporate scaffolding, or the structured support you provide. Teachers can assist learners in selecting adaptive strategies for managing and directing their emotional responses to external events (such as strategies for coping with anxiety-producing social settings or for reducing task-irrelevant distractors) and internal events (such as strategies for coping with anxiety-producing social settings or for reducing task-irrelevant distractors) by using reminders, models, checklists, and similar tools (for example, strategies for decreasing rumination on depressive or anxiety-producing ideation). These scaffolds provide sufficient options for students to successfully and independently apply strategies regardless of individual differences.

You should offer differentiated models, stepping stones, and feedback for students in coping skills. Here are some examples.

- **Modeling:** Modeling is indeed a crucial teaching strategy, yet it's most effective when combined with other approaches. For instance, while modeling provides a visual and behavioral guide for students, it is the interplay between scaffolding and subsequent independent practice that fully ingrains coping skills. Consider modeling as the first step of a coping skill to show students how to approach a problem. But to develop true mastery, students also need to practice these strategies themselves, reflect on their effectiveness, and receive personalized feedback. This combination ensures that students not only see what to do but also learn how to adapt these strategies to their individual needs and contexts.

- **Checklists:** Offer students a checklist of coping methods that they can turn to whenever they feel worried or overwhelmed. The checklist can include methods as simple as taking a few calm breaths, counting to ten, writing down ideas and feelings, or talking to a trusted adult.

- **Role playing:** To assist students practice their coping abilities in real-life scenarios, teachers might employ role-playing exercises with their classes. For instance, a teacher may have students act out a scenario in which they are experiencing feelings of anxiety or being overwhelmed, and then have them practice utilizing a variety of coping skills to learn how to better control these feelings.

- **Reflection:** Urge your students to think back on the times when they faced difficult circumstances and how they used coping methods to deal with their emotions. They will have a better understanding of their own emotional responses as a result of this, as well as the ways they might utilize coping methods in the future.

Students need to learn a variety of strategies, such as reminders, models, checklists, and other similar tools, to develop effective self-regulation skills. These tools will assist students in determining the coping mechanisms for managing their emotions that are most effective for them individually.

Use Journaling

Keeping a journal is an effective method for introspection and growth on an individual level. Students gain several benefits from keeping a journal. In addition to helping students improve their writing skills, it can also assist them in better understanding their own thoughts and feelings. Additionally, it may assist them in thinking in a more ordered and reflective manner. Students can explore new ideas and express themselves freely in a protected environment when they keep a journal. They can also use journaling as a tool for self-expression and creativity. Finally, keeping a journal can be an effective method for relieving stress and assisting students in working through challenging feelings in a constructive manner.

Journaling is a teachable skill. Here are some teaching strategies.

- **Demonstrate the process:** Demonstrate journaling by writing in your own journal in front of the class or by reading aloud from your own journal. Students will gain a better understanding of the process, as well as a better sense of how they should approach writing in their journals, if they have an example to follow.

- **Give students prompts:** Give students questions or statements that motivate thinking on a variety of subjects or experiences. These prompts could be tied to current events or themes the class is covering, or they can be more open-ended questions that allow students to explore different ideas or feelings on their own terms. Either way, the purpose of these prompts is to get students thinking and talking.

- **Urge students to reflect:** Encourage students to reflect on what they have written in their journals by either asking them questions about what they have written or having them share extracts from their notebooks with the rest of the class (if they are comfortable doing so). Students will acquire insight into their own ideas and feelings as a result of this, and it will also help them become more reflective thinkers in general.
- **Provide assistance:** As a last step, provide students with support and direction when writing in their journals. This will allow students to feel safe expressing themselves without the fear of being judged or criticized by other people.

To effectively cultivate self-regulation in students, an interplay of personalized goal setting, resilience training, and reflective practices is key. Encouraging students to set personal goals fosters a sense of ownership and direction in their learning journey. When these goals are rooted in students' individual motivations and interests, students are more likely to engage deeply and persistently with their studies. Developing coping skills is equally vital; it equips students to handle academic and emotional challenges, thereby reinforcing their ability to stay the course despite setbacks. Finally, journaling serves as a reflective practice, allowing students to internalize their experiences, monitor their progress, and articulate challenges and triumphs. Together, these strategies form a cohesive framework for empowering students to take command of their learning processes, adapt to challenges, and emerge as self-sufficient learners capable of navigating the complex landscape of education and personal growth.

GEORGE WASHINGTON CARVER SELF-REGULATES

George Washington Carver, a renowned African American scientist and inventor, dedicated his life to agricultural research and education. His work revolutionized the agricultural economy of the United States. Carver's ability to overcome obstacles and his continuous pursuit of knowledge exemplify the essence of self-regulation and the drive for lifelong learning and personal development.

Carver faced numerous challenges, but his resilience and ability to self-regulate helped him to thrive. For instance, despite the lack of resources and formal education during his early years, Carver meticulously planned his studies, set personal goals, and sought out knowledge independently. He managed his time effectively, often studying late into the night, and remained focused on his objectives. This self-regulation enabled him to overcome significant obstacles and make groundbreaking discoveries in agriculture. He believed in the importance of setting achievable objectives, pursuing them with vigor, and adapting his approach as needed. This approach led him to discover hundreds of uses for crops like peanuts and sweet potatoes, thereby promoting sustainable agriculture.

Consider Marcus, a high school student interested in environmental science. Faced with academic setbacks, Marcus adopts Carver's self-regulative techniques, setting specific goals for his science fair project on sustainable farming. He mirrors Carver's disciplined approach by journaling his progress, setting daily and weekly milestones, and reflecting on feedback from teachers and peers. When he encounters difficulties, Marcus adapts his methods, experimenting with different farming techniques and learning from each trial. This persistent and reflective

> approach leads to a successful presentation at the science fair and a newfound confidence in navigating academic and personal challenges.
>
> George Washington Carver and Marcus demonstrate that self-regulation is a dynamic process involving goal setting, persistence, and adaptability. Their experiences highlight that disciplined self-regulation fosters innovation and personal growth, showing that disciplined perseverance, coupled with self-awareness, is key to overcoming challenges and achieving success.

Implement and Differentiate an Easy Activity to Nurture Self-Regulation in K–12 Students

Developing self-regulation in students is an essential component of education, allowing individuals to become active managers of their learning and behavior. This capacity is a strong predictor of academic success, more so than measures of intelligence. Instructing students in self-regulation involves equipping them with strategies to plan, monitor, and assess their learning and behavior. Teachers play a critical role in this process, offering scaffolded support to students as they learn to set and strive for personal goals, manage their emotions and behaviors, and reflect on their experiences.

In the classroom, self-regulation manifests in students' ability to set realistic goals, maintain focus amid distractions, and persist through challenges. As educators, our goal is to design activities that not only teach curriculum content but also integrate self-regulation skills development. Such skills are built gradually and require regular practice. The following sections offer a brief introduction and activity for each grade band. The activities provided here cater to the cognitive and emotional development appropriate to each educational level, encouraging students to become self-aware, goal-directed learners capable of adapting to various learning environments and demands.

Elementary School Students

Young learners benefit from concrete, engaging activities that connect to their immediate world. For example, you might introduce a "goal garden" where each student plants a seed for a personal goal they want to achieve, such as reading a book a week. They can then track their progress by adding petals to a flower on a classroom mural each time they move toward their goal, offering a visual and tangible representation of growth.

Middle School Students

At this stage, students can handle more abstract thinking and appreciate a degree of autonomy. Introduce a challenge wheel that they spin to land on a variety of self-regulation challenges, such as organizing their desk, planning their homework, or helping a classmate, which they must address within the week. This random selection adds an element of fun and unpredictability.

High School Students

High schoolers are preparing for the independence of adulthood and can manage more sophisticated self-assessment. Implement a personal progress conference where students prepare a presentation on their academic and personal growth over the semester, including goals set, progress made, and plans for improvement. This exercise helps them articulate their development and plan for the future.

By integrating these activities, you create opportunities for students to practice self-regulation across a spectrum of scenarios, fostering skills that they will use throughout their academic journey and beyond.

Concluding Thoughts

Self-regulation is a multifaceted skill crucial not only for academic success but also for personal growth and lifelong learning. It fosters a profound internalization of discipline and motivation, whereby learners set their benchmarks and strive to surpass them. The practice of self-regulation thus becomes a gateway to self-mastery, where students learn to harmonize their cognitive, emotional, and behavioral faculties. This alignment is imperative in navigating the diverse demands of educational pathways and life's challenges.

By focusing on self-regulation, educators pivot from a traditional, directive teaching model to one that is student centered, promoting autonomy and self-discovery. Students are encouraged to become introspective, analyze their performance, and refine their strategies for learning. They celebrate their successes and learn constructively from their failures, thus cultivating resilience. This empowerment allows students to take ownership of their learning, enhancing their ability to apply knowledge critically and creatively.

Emphasizing self-regulation in education has broader implications, producing individuals who not only have academic knowledge but also the competencies to thrive in an ever-evolving world. In fostering these skills, educators shape adaptable, innovative, and responsible citizens. This approach embodies a shift from rote learning to nurturing dynamic learners who are prepared to meet the complex demands of modern society with confidence and competence. In this renaissance in education, our responsibility as educators is to help prepare students for life.

Learning is the only thing the mind never exhausts, never fears, and never regrets.

—LEONARDO DA VINCI

Chapter 7

Habit 6: Transfer Learning

One of the biggest challenges in the traditional educational structure is the transfer of learning. Grant Wiggins and Jay McTighe (2005) define *transfer learning* as "the ability to adapt information and abilities learned in one environment to another" of (p. 4). They contend that students can cultivate transfer learning via instruction and practice, which they may acquire in a variety of contexts. Students learn to notice patterns and apply their knowledge and abilities in a variety of diverse settings, which contributes to the development of this habit of thinking.

Transfer learning is truly an area in which we need a renaissance. Educators understand that transfer learning is pivotal because it equips students to apply their knowledge and skills to new situations or problems, beyond the context in which they were originally learned. This adaptability is crucial in a world that is rapidly changing and where individuals often face complex and multifaceted problems. A renaissance in this area would mean revolutionizing how students learn, moving beyond rote memorization to a deeper understanding that enables them to connect concepts and apply them innovatively in different scenarios.

Transfer learning is not just about enhancing academic achievement but also about fostering lifelong learning and adaptability, skills that are increasingly valued in every sphere of life, from personal to professional. Students must be able to adapt the information and skills they have gained in one setting to another one through transfer learning, which is an essential habit of thinking.

Analytical thinking is a key component of transfer learning. It allows students to dissect complex concepts and tasks, identify their underlying principles, and then apply these principles to different contexts. Analytical skills enable learners to critically evaluate information, discern patterns, and make connections between seemingly disparate ideas, which are essential processes in the application of knowledge to new situations. By engaging in analytical thinking, students become adept at not only understanding content deeply but also recognizing its relevance in various settings, thus enhancing their ability to transfer learning effectively.

To grow as a critical and analytical thinker, deconstructing one's thoughts is an essential practice. Students can get a deeper understanding of and critical distance from ideas, debates, and views by learning to dissect and analyze their own and others' cognitive processes. Fruitful conversations and debates stemming from the deconstruction of ideas and arguments are integral to transfer learning as they provide a dynamic platform for students to apply and test their understanding in a collaborative context. Engaging in discourse allows learners to encounter diverse perspectives and challenges them to use their analytical skills to defend, refine, or rethink their positions. This process not only deepens their understanding of the original content but also requires them to adapt their knowledge to new and varied situations, which is the essence of transfer learning. By practicing the articulation of ideas and the defense or critique of arguments across different contexts, students enhance their ability to transfer what they have learned to novel scenarios outside the classroom.

In this chapter, we will examine the many methods through which students form the habit of transfer learning and become better at connecting their ideas to the big picture for direct application. We'll also look at why this practice is helpful for students and how you may include it in your lessons. The implementation section will provide practical strategies for you to integrate these methods into your teaching practice.

Embrace Failure

Transfer learning can be significantly hampered by the fear of failure. Since analytical thinking often occurs through trial and error, embracing failure becomes a critical component of this process, as it allows students to refine their understanding and apply their learning more adeptly in future contexts. Therefore, the acceptance of failure is not an impediment but rather a catalyst for the development of robust transfer learning. The fear of failure is a formidable barrier in applying acquired knowledge to new situations. For instance, a student who excels in mathematical principles in the classroom may hesitate to utilize those skills in a real-world budgeting scenario due to the fear of making mistakes in a less controlled environment. This apprehension can stifle the natural curiosity and confidence needed to experiment and apply learning in diverse contexts, thereby constraining the scope of the student's analytical thinking and the breadth of their transfer learning.

It's critical for students to understand that failure is a necessary component of learning and that they should not dread it but rather welcome it as a chance for improvement. There aren't many better ways to learn than to try something, fail, and then try it again in a different way. Most of us fail to reap the benefits of our unavoidable mistakes. Even when there are strong incentives, people still have a propensity to bury their heads in the sand and fail to learn from their mistakes, according to research by Lauren Eskreis-Winkler and Ayelet Fishbach (2019) of the University of Chicago's Booth School of

Business. Thankfully, these authors' work also provides advice on how to keep your ego and emotions from interfering with your ability to learn from mistakes. Their findings, which illustrate both what prevents people from making the most of their mistakes and how to get past these typical mental blockages, are also supported in research by Richard Davidson and Brianna Schuyler (2015). Here are some of the hurdles they identified that people often face in attempting to learn from mistakes.

- They fail to move beyond their subjective perceptions of themselves.
- They don't share with anyone.
- They stifle their emotions.
- They lose sight of why.
- They criticize themselves.

Teachers play a crucial role in guiding students to reframe obstacles as stepping stones toward growth. By explicitly addressing and transforming the hurdles students face into actionable, positive self-development steps, educators can effectively foster resilience and a growth mindset. In the upcoming sections, we'll delve into practical strategies you can utilize to help students overcome their self-imposed barriers. These will help you encourage your students to approach mistakes from an outside perspective, share their learning experiences, express their emotions productively, reconnect with their purpose, and replace self-criticism with constructive self-talk. Each of these reinforces the habit of transfer learning.

Approach Mistakes From an Outside Perspective

Learning is at the mercy of ego. Incorrect beliefs can be corrected, new information can be sought after, and horizons can be expanded. However, admitting you are incorrect undermines your perception of yourself as competent and intelligent. So how can students make sure their egos don't prevent them from improving? One method is to mentally remove oneself from the mistake they are attempting to learn from.

Adopting an objective observer's perspective of your own experiences can significantly alter your response to failure. Rather than asking "Why did I fail?" I might ask "Why did Nathan fail?" adopting a more detached viewpoint. This technique, which may initially seem counterintuitive, is supported by research indicating that self-distancing strategies mitigate the adverse effects of reflecting on negative experiences (Kross & Ayduk, 2011). Furthermore, studies have shown that such an approach can catalyze self-improvement, offering a productive means to process and learn from failures (Mischkowski et al., 2016). To guide students in using this technique, encourage them to write about their experiences from a third-person perspective, as if they are observing someone else, and discuss how this viewpoint changes their understanding and emotional response.

Share Mistakes With Others

Being transparent about mistakes can serve as a powerful motivator for both the person who made the mistake and others. Sharing the lessons learned from errors encourages a culture of openness and continuous improvement. It also helps to demystify the learning process, showing that progress often comes from understanding and working through our missteps. You can foster this culture of transparency by guiding students to view mistakes as opportunities for growth and by providing forums where they can comfortably share and discuss these learning experiences. This practice not only aids in normalizing the discussion of errors but also reinforces the habit of reflective practice, a cornerstone of transfer learning. Framing your failures in this way transforms blunders into practical life lessons, like how motivational speakers turn past mistakes into motivational gold. To create opportunities for students to share mistakes, consider implementing the following strategies.

- **Mistake of the week:** Dedicate a time each week for students to share a mistake they made and what they learned from it. This can be a part of a regular class meeting or an informal discussion session.
- **Reflection journals:** Encourage students to keep journals where they reflect on their mistakes and the lessons learned. Periodically, have them share their reflections with peers in small groups.
- **Peer review sessions:** Organize sessions where students can present their work, receive constructive feedback, and discuss any mistakes they made during the process.
- **Error analysis projects:** Assign projects where students analyze a past mistake in detail, exploring what went wrong, why it happened, and how they can avoid similar errors in the future.
- **Classroom discussions:** Create a safe space for open discussions about mistakes by modeling transparency yourself. Share your own mistakes and the lessons you've learned to set an example.

By integrating these practices into your teaching routine, you can help students develop a healthier relationship with mistakes, viewing them as essential steps in the learning journey.

Express Emotions Productively

In fostering a healthy learning environment, teachers can encourage students to express their emotions in constructive ways. Does failure make you feel good? No, it hurts terribly. Though unpleasant, it is a necessary evil. Nature uses pain to help us learn the proper way to behave. Therefore, suppressing pain suppresses learning. If you want your failures to ultimately make you smarter, you must allow yourself to feel them deeply. For example, social psychologist Joseph P. Forgas's (2017) research suggests that mild sadness can improve memory accuracy and judgmental strategies. Additionally, his studies elucidate how mood can impact cognition and motivation (Forgas, 1995).

Acknowledging the discomfort that comes with failure is important, but so is channeling these feelings into positive actions. Educators can work with students to articulate their emotions through reflective discussions, journaling, or art, providing them with the tools to express themselves safely and appropriately within the educational setting. By validating and guiding students' emotional expressions, teachers can help them process their feelings, learn from their experiences, and apply those lessons in future endeavors, enhancing their transfer learning skills.

Reconnect With Purpose

It's simple for students to fall into a cycle of self-criticism after making a mistake, questioning every move they made. Reflection and sadness are necessary parts of the process of coping with failure, but obsessing over the specifics of a mistake won't help someone recover and put what they've learned to use. So what exactly should students do? To help students reconnect with their purpose after a mistake, guide them through the following steps.

1. **Revisit their goals:** Encourage students to remind themselves of their long-term objectives, such as learning a new skill or pursuing a specific career. By focusing on these broader goals, they can see how short-term setbacks are just steps along their journey.
2. **Understand their "why":** Help students identify the underlying reasons for their pursuits. Understanding their motivation can strengthen their resilience and keep them grounded, even when faced with challenges.
3. **Shift focus to learning:** Encourage students to view mistakes as learning opportunities. Instead of fixating on what went wrong, prompt them to ask, "What can I learn from this experience?" This mindset shift can transform failures into valuable lessons.
4. **Celebrate small wins:** Remind students to acknowledge and celebrate their progress, no matter how small. Recognizing their achievements can boost their confidence and reinforce their commitment to their goals.
5. **Practice self-compassion:** Teach students to be kind to themselves in the face of failure. Self-compassion can mitigate the negative effects of self-criticism and help them maintain a positive outlook.

By following these steps, students can move beyond their mistakes, reconnect with their purpose, and continue their journey with renewed motivation and resilience.

Practice Self-Compassion

To reiterate, failure isn't supposed to feel good, but criticizing onself for errors demotivates and prevents learning important lessons from failure. Yes, students should consider what went wrong, but not waste time dwelling on their failings. Instead, they should practice self-compassion by speaking kindly to themselves, much like a friend would. To help students practice self-compassion, consider the following.

- **Encourage positive self-talk:** Teach students to speak to themselves with kindness and understanding, just as they would to a friend. Remind them to replace self-critical thoughts with supportive and encouraging ones.
- **Normalize mistakes:** Help students understand that making mistakes is a natural part of learning and growing. Share stories of successful people who have failed and emphasize that setbacks are common and not something to be ashamed of.
- **Reflect constructively:** Guide students to reflect on their experiences without judgment. Encourage them to identify what they learned from the mistake and how they can apply this knowledge in the future.
- **Employ self-compassion exercises:** Introduce exercises that promote self-compassion, such as writing a letter to themselves from the perspective of a supportive friend or practicing mindfulness and self-compassion meditations.

Additionally, keep in mind that mistakes are a part of being human and not something to be ashamed of. The question is not *if* you will fail, but rather *when*. What you can learn from the experience is the one and only real question you need to respond to. We should see failure as a learning opportunity rather than an embarrassing display of personal weakness and teach our students accordingly. With the straightforward methods and mindset shifts mentioned above, you can help students transform failure into a valuable experience. Remember, failure is a terrible thing to waste.

Use Analogical Thinking

Analogical reasoning is a fundamental aspect of how people think. It is the ability to see and use similarities between two situations or events. In fact, some researchers think that it is the most important way that humans think and sets us apart from other intelligent species (Gentner, 2003; Holyoak & Thagard, 1995). It is a key part of discovering new things, solving problems, categorizing things, and making decisions. Deep analogical thinking is the process of identifying conceptual connections between various scenarios or domains that may appear to have little in common at first glance. Analogical reasoning can be considered an extension of transfer learning. We may transfer the information we learn from one circumstance or event to another by identifying the similarities between two situations or occurrences. As a result, we can relate various ideas and use what we know in new situations. Analogical thinking enables us to apply what we already know in novel and imaginative ways, making it a potent tool for transfer learning.

Analogical reasoning makes the unfamiliar more comprehensible. It also enables us to comprehend things that we are completely unable to perceive. Students can understand the velocity of molecules by comparing it to the collision of billiard balls, and they can comprehend the workings of electricity by comparing it to the flow of water through a pipe. The neural networks of artificial intelligence were conceptualized as being similar to the neurons in the brain. Similarly, genetic algorithms are conceptually based on the principles of evolution by natural selection. In this analogy, the process of finding solutions to problems is compared to the evolutionary process. Just as in natural selection, where organisms with favorable traits are more likely to survive and reproduce, in genetic algorithms, solutions are tried and evaluated, and the more successful solutions pass on their properties to the next generation of solutions. This cycle continues, iteratively refining and improving the solutions over time.

The 17th century astronomer and mathematician Johannes Kepler, faced with the monumental task of explaining the celestial mechanics of planetary motion, ventured into uncharted territory. With no precedents to guide him, Kepler resorted to the use of analogies, drawing parallels between odors, heat, and light and the possible forces at play in the cosmos. This imaginative leap, positing the concept of "action at a distance" within the heavens, was a pioneering step in scientific thought. By comparing the movements of the planets to more tangible phenomena such as the way boats move or magnets attract, Kepler exemplified analogical thinking and transfer learning. He applied familiar principles to the unknown, thereby laying the groundwork for the laws of planetary motion and advancing our understanding of the universe (Martens, 2000; Voelkel, 1994).

Kepler had to deal with a challenge that was brand new to all of humanity, not just him. Since most issues are, of course, not brand new, we can draw on what Dedre Gentner (1983) refers to as "surface" comparisons from our own experiences. According to Gentner, if you are reminded of things that appear similar on the surface, many times they will also be similar in terms of their relationships. Remember, for instance, how you unclogged the bathtub drain in your previous apartment? When the kitchen sink in your new one becomes clogged, that will likely enter your mind.

But according to Gentner (1983), the notion that immediately applicable surface parallels apply to new situations is known as the "kind world" theory. A kind world is built on recurring patterns where problems can reliably be solved through prior knowledge. The modern world is not so benign; it calls for thinking that is independent of prior knowledge. We must be able to choose a strategy for issues we have never encountered, much like mathematics students. Gentner (1983) explains it like this: In the life we lead now, we need to be reminded of things that are relationally or abstractly connected. The more crucial this becomes, the more creative we must be.

Gentner aimed to understand whether Kepler's model of using distant analogies to solve problems could work in other circumstances. To explore this, she developed what she called the ambiguous sorting task. This task consists of twenty-five cards, each describing the workings of real-world phenomena. Each card fits into one of two main groups—one based on its subject matter (for example, economics, biology) and the other based on its underlying deep structure. Participants in the study group the cards based on these similarities (Gentner, 1983).

As an example of a deep structure, you could put together positive feedback loops like economic bubbles and the melting of the polar ice caps. When there is an economic bubble, people buy stocks or real estate with the hope that the price will go up. When people buy, the price does go up, which makes more people want to buy. When ice caps melt, they don't reflect as much sunlight back into space. This makes the Earth warmer, which makes more ice melt. Or, you could say that sweating and what the Federal Reserve does are both examples of negative feedback loops. Sweating cools the body so that it no longer needs to sweat as much. When the economy needs a boost, the Fed lowers interest rates. If the economy grows too quickly, the Fed raises rates to slow down the activity it started. The way that gas prices cause grocery prices to go up and the steps that a message takes to get from one neuron to another in your brain are both examples of causal chains. In these chains, one event leads to another, which leads to another, in a straight line.

Conversely, you could group changes in the Federal Reserve rate, economic bubbles, and gas prices together because they all have to do with economics. You could also put sweating and how nerve cells talk to each other under biology. Gentner gave the ambiguous sorting task to students from different majors at Northwestern University. Researchers found that all of the students figured out how to group things by subject matter. But fewer were able to group things based on deep structure. Students who had taken classes in many different fields, like those in the integrated science program, were especially good at finding common deep structures, though (Gentner, 1983).

By engaging in activities like the ambiguous sorting task, students practice discerning deep structures, which are often abstract and require higher-level thinking. This practice not only enhances their ability to categorize and link concepts within and across various disciplines but also primes them for innovative problem solving. Ultimately, the ability to identify and apply these foundational patterns empowers students to transfer their learning to new and diverse contexts, solidifying their grasp of the material and its applications in the real world.

Inform Transfer Learning Instruction With Constructivist Thinking

The goal of education is not to make information more readily available; rather, it is to show students how to take material that is readily available and turn it into knowledge they can apply—that is, transfer. Constructivist thinking, which posits that learners construct their own understanding and knowledge of the world through experiences and reflecting on those experiences, serves as a framework for transfer learning instruction. This approach emphasizes active learning, where students construct meaning based on their experiences and prior knowledge. Teachers facilitate this process by creating learning environments that encourage exploration, inquiry, and reflection.

Through constructivist methods, educators teach students not just to consume information but to critically evaluate it, make connections with what they already know, and apply it in various contexts—hence, informing the practice of transfer learning. This instructional focus ensures that students are prepared not only to understand new information but also to apply it in practical, often novel, situations.

Decades of research in the field of cognitive science have shown that the ability to transform accessible information into usable knowledge is not a passive process but rather an active one. John Sweller (1988), who developed cognitive load theory, illustrates the importance of managing mental resources to enhance learning. Additionally, in their book *How People Learn*, John Bransford, Ann Brown, and Rodney Cocking (2000) outline key findings on the active nature of learning and the construction of knowledge. A study by Paul Kirschner, John Sweller, and Richard Clark (2006) reinforces the importance of guided instruction in learning. They argue that minimally guided instruction is less effective and efficient than instructional approaches that place a strong emphasis on guidance of the student learning process. Additionally, a study by John Hattie and Gregory Donoghue (2016) in their meta-analysis on the impact of learning strategies highlights the significant role of teaching methods that engage students actively in the learning process. Moreover, work by Deans for Impact (2015) has underscored the cognitive principles that align with active learning and knowledge transfer, emphasizing that learners must actively participate in the learning process for deeper understanding and application of knowledge. This body of work collectively informs and supports the constructivist approach to teaching and transfer learning.

Constructing usable knowledge, applicable to future decision making, requires more than just the ability to perceive information. It also demands active information processing skills such as selective attention, integrating new information with prior knowledge, strategic categorization, and active memorization. Individuals vary widely in their ability to process information and in their access to prior knowledge, which affects their capacity to assimilate new information. Educators play a crucial role in this process. By carefully planning and presenting information, they can provide the necessary scaffolding to ensure that all students can access and learn the material. This scaffolding helps bridge the gaps in students' prior knowledge and enhances their ability to process and integrate new information effectively. The following actions help streamline that planning and presentation of information to support transfer learning as a habit.

- **Use selective attending:** Teach students to focus on the most pertinent information, filtering out less relevant data, which aids in the efficient allocation of cognitive resources for deeper processing.
- **Integrate new information with prior knowledge:** Encourage students to connect new concepts to existing cognitive frameworks, facilitating a more robust and meaningful understanding of the material.
- **Use strategic categorization:** Instruct students in organizing information into meaningful categories, which can help them recognize patterns and relationships, making the recall and application of knowledge more efficient.
- **Engage in active memorization:** Move beyond simple repetition by using techniques that embed information into long-term memory through understanding and association, ensuring that knowledge is accessible for future application.

Use Selective Attending

Selective attending is the cognitive process of focusing on relevant stimuli while ignoring distractions, and it is integral to the practice of transfer learning. Learners cultivate this skill through targeted activities. By honing selective attention, students learn to discern which information is essential and relevant to the task at hand, a fundamental step in applying knowledge to new situations.

First, educators can implement activities that require students to identify key concepts within a complex narrative or problem. This could involve analyzing case studies or real-world scenarios where students must sift through details to determine the crux of an issue. Teaching students to ask questions like "What is the primary goal?" and "Which information is necessary to achieve this goal?" can foster selective attention.

Second, educators might use collaborative projects to reinforce selective attending. In group work, students encounter a multitude of ideas and must learn to negotiate and prioritize information collaboratively. By guiding students to establish clear objectives and criteria for relevance, educators help them practice filtering information as a team.

Third, technology can be a double-edged sword, offering myriad distractions but also tools for practicing selective attention. Educators can utilize apps that help students practice concentration, such as those that offer timed reading or listening tasks with a focus on main ideas and details. By gradually increasing the complexity and the presence of distractors, students can build resilience against common disruptions.

Fourth, teachers can incorporate mindfulness practices into the classroom to enhance students' ability to concentrate. Mindfulness exercises that encourage students to focus on their breath or a single thought can train their minds to return to the relevant task when distractions arise, which is a valuable skill when they need to apply learning in a new context.

Finally, educators can model selective attending by thinking aloud as they work through a problem, explicitly noting irrelevant information and explaining why certain details are being set aside. This modeling provides a clear example for students to emulate when they are tasked with applying their knowledge in various scenarios.

By building the skill of selective attending, educators equip students with the ability to focus on applicable knowledge and skills in any learning situation, thereby enhancing their transfer learning capabilities.

Integrate New Information With Prior Knowledge

When you integrate new information with what you already know, you forge connections that transform discrete facts into applicable knowledge. Begin this process in your classroom by encouraging your students to engage in think-pair-share exercises. This will prompt them to actively consider how new concepts relate to their existing knowledge. Next, guide them in creating concept maps, which visually link new ideas to established ones, clarifying their interrelations.

Further integrate new and prior information by introducing case-based learning, which gives students opportunities to apply familiar knowledge to new scenarios, reinforcing their adaptability and problem-solving skills. Encourage them to conduct comparative analyses, actively juxtaposing new material against what they know, which enhances discernment and deepens understanding.

Finally, institute a practice of reflection. Have your students journal or participate in discussions that tie new lessons back to prior learning. This not only solidifies their knowledge but also fosters an intuitive sense of how to apply this integrated knowledge to diverse situations. Through these strategies, you enable your students to master the art of transfer learning, equipping them with the skills to apply knowledge in a multitude of contexts.

Use Strategic Categorization

Strategic categorization is a vital cognitive strategy that supports transfer learning by helping students organize information in ways that enhance recall and application. As you teach, introduce classification tasks that challenge students to group concepts based on underlying principles or characteristics. This method aids them in distinguishing between different sets of information and understanding when and how to apply these categories in various contexts.

Incorporate sorting exercises into your lessons, where students categorize items or concepts into predefined or self-generated groups. Such activities encourage them to analyze attributes and identify patterns, fostering a deeper grasp of content that is critical for transfer learning. As they become adept at categorization, they will be better equipped to apply these skills to unfamiliar situations.

Additionally, you should have your students engage in discussions that require them to categorize different viewpoints or approaches within a particular discipline. This not only promotes critical thinking but also helps them understand that they can approach certain problems in multiple ways, depending on the categorization framework they apply.

You can also use case studies in your teaching that require analysis and categorization of information to solve complex problems. This teaches students to identify relevant categories of information in real-world situations, a skill that is transferable to various academic and professional fields.

Finally, it is beneficial to regularly assess and refine the categorization strategies students use. By providing feedback and discussing the effectiveness of different categorization approaches, you can guide students in developing more sophisticated methods of organizing information, which is a crucial aspect of transfer learning. Through these strategies, students learn to sort and classify knowledge effectively, enabling them to apply their learning in new and diverse situations.

Engage in Active Memorization

Active memorization transcends mere rote learning; it involves engaging with the material in a way that embeds it into long-term memory, fostering the ability to recall and apply the information in various contexts. This is key to transfer learning.

As you teach, prompt your students to employ elaborative rehearsal by making connections between new information and what they already know. *Elaborative rehearsal* is a memory technique that involves thinking about the meaning of the term to be remembered, as opposed to simply repeating the word to oneself. It involves forming associations between new information and existing knowledge to facilitate deeper understanding and long-term retention. This can involve explaining new concepts in their own words, creating analogies, or teaching the material to a peer. These activities ensure that memorization is not only active but also meaningful, laying the groundwork for students to transfer knowledge to different scenarios.

Implement *spaced repetition,* a technique where students review information at increasing intervals, in your instruction. Spaced repetition leverages the psychological spacing effect, where recall is improved over time, allowing students to gradually build a durable memory trace of the learned material.

Introduce mnemonic devices in your teaching. These tools, like acronyms, rhymes, or the method of loci, can be particularly useful in memorizing complex information. The *method of loci* is a mnemonic device that involves associating items to be remembered with specific physical locations, using visualizations of familiar places to organize and recall information. Mnemonics serve not only as memory aids but also as ways to re-engage with content, making the retrieval process active and thus strengthening the potential for transfer.

Employ active application tasks such as problem-solving exercises that require students to use memorized information in new ways. For instance, you might ask students to solve novel mathematics problems using a formula they have memorized, which can aid in transferring their knowledge to various types of problems.

Finally, encourage your students to reflect on their memorization processes. Through reflection, they can identify which strategies are most effective for them, thereby understanding how to memorize new topics in the future. This metacognitive aspect of active memorization is a powerful ally in transfer learning, as it empowers students with self-directed tools for learning.

Implement Effective Transfer Learning Strategies

The following sections provide practical strategies to help you facilitate transfer learning in your classrooms. By focusing on background knowledge, patterns and big ideas, processing and visualization, information retrieval and transfer learning, and mental models, you can create a robust learning environment that enhances students' ability to apply knowledge across various contexts. Each section offers actionable steps and examples to guide you in implementing these strategies effectively.

Background Knowledge

When information is presented in a manner that primes, activates, or provides any prerequisite knowledge, it makes the information more accessible to learners and increases the likelihood that those learners will assimilate the information. When some students lack the background knowledge that is essential to assimilating or using new information, barriers and inequities are created in the learning environment. However, there are also barriers for students who have the necessary background knowledge but may not realize that what they know is relevant to the course they are taking.

These obstacles can be simplified if there are a variety of options to choose from that either supply or activate the pertinent prior knowledge, or link to the prerequisite information in another location. The following list presents suggested options.

- Anchor instruction by linking to and activating relevant prior knowledge. For example, before starting a new mathematics unit, review key concepts from previous units that the new unit will build on.
- Employ graphic organizers like Venn diagrams or mind maps to help students visually connect new information with what they already know.
- Present important prerequisite ideas in advance through demonstration or models. Show a science experiment or model a mathematics problem to give students a concrete understanding before they explore the concept further.
- Bridge conceptual gaps with appropriate analogies and metaphors. Compare the structure of an atom to a solar system to help students grasp the concept more easily.
- Establish unmistakable links between different subject areas. Integrate a history lesson with literature by reading historical fiction that reflects the time period being studied, providing context and enhancing comprehension.

Patterns and Big Ideas

One of the primary distinctions between novices and experts in any given field is the ability to differentiate what is essential from what is unimportant or irrelevant. Since experts can quickly identify the most important information, they are able to effectively allocate their time by quickly locating the appropriate "hooks" for incorporating the most valuable new information into their existing body of knowledge.

As a direct consequence of this, one of the most effective ways to make information more accessible is to provide explicit cues or prompts that assist individuals in attending to those characteristics that matter the most while avoiding those that matter the least.

- In text, graphics, diagrams, and formulas, highlight or emphasize the most important elements.
- To put an emphasis on important ideas and connections, make use of outlines, graphic organizers, unit organizer routines, concept organizer routines, and concept mastery routines.

- Make use of a variety of examples, as well as nonexamples, to highlight important characteristics.
- Make use of visual cues and auditory prompts to direct attention to important aspects.
- Recall already-learned skills to solve unfamiliar problems.

Providing students with explicit cues or prompts that assist them in attending what matters the most while avoiding what matters the least is one of the most effective ways to make information more accessible.

Processing and Visualization

Processing and visualizing information frequently requires mental strategies and skills to transform information into useable knowledge. These mental strategies can be either cognitive and metacognitive. Cognitive strategies involve selecting and manipulating information so learners can summarize, categorize, prioritize, and contextualize it for better understanding and retention. Visualization techniques or graphic organizers can help in this process by making abstract concepts more concrete.

Metacognitive strategies are higher-order processes where learners monitor and regulate their cognitive strategies, reflecting on how they learn and adapting their methods for maximum efficacy. As an educator, you should instruct your students in both types of strategies: employing cognitive strategies for immediate learning tasks and metacognitive strategies to evaluate and refine their learning processes over time.

Learners have very diverse abilities, and well-designed materials can provide customized and embedded models, scaffolds, and feedback to help learners make effective use of those strategies. The following practices will help you do so.

- Provide clear instructions for each stage of a sequential process. Break down complex tasks into manageable steps and offer detailed guidance for each step.
- Give students a choice of different organizational methods and strategies. Offer various tools such as tables, algorithms, or flowcharts to help them organize and process information.
- Provide interactive models that guide exploration as well as new understandings. Use simulations or interactive diagrams to help students visualize and manipulate information dynamically.
- Establish stepped scaffolds that will support various information processing strategies. Create layered supports that gradually remove assistance as students become more proficient.
- Make different points of entry to a lesson available, as well as alternative routes through the material. Offer diverse methods of engagement, such as exploring big ideas through dramatic works, arts and literature, film, and media.
- Break down the information into more manageable chunks. Segment information into smaller, more digestible parts to facilitate understanding and retention.
- Make information available in stages. Present content incrementally, using techniques like sequential highlighting to focus attention.

- Take away any distracting elements that aren't absolutely necessary to accomplishing the learning objective. Simplify visual aids and materials to focus on essential content, removing extraneous details.

Learners with more experience draw on their previous information and experiences to help them more easily process new information when they encounter it. However, a significant number of students lack both the experience and the skills to direct them as they pursue their education. These students benefit from direct instruction and practicing the strategies for selecting and manipulating information to better summarize, categorize, prioritize, visualize, and contextualize what they are learning.

Research studies by Nelson Cowan (2012) on cognitive chunking and Mark Haystead (2009) on graphic organizers suggest that teaching students to break down information into smaller components and employing strategies like explicit prompts, graphic organizers, concept maps, and strategic instruction can significantly enhance student achievement. Furthermore, educational expert Daniel Willingham (2009) provides practical insights on strategy instruction that are deeply rooted in classroom application. These sources underscore the efficacy of these methods in facilitating students' information processing and contributing to their academic success.

Information Retrieval and Transfer Learning

The amount of memory and transfer scaffolding that individual students require to improve their capacity to access their previous learning varies from student to student. Because learning is not about acquiring individual facts in isolation, and students require multiple representations for this to happen, it is only natural that all students could gain something from assistance in transfering the information that they already possess to other contexts. They might learn this information without support and without the use of multiple representations, but that information would be inaccessible to new circumstances. Techniques that heighten the memorability of the information and prompt and guide learners to employ explicit strategies support memory, generalization, and transfer. Educational psychologists and cognitive scientists refer to these techniques as "memory boosters," which include the following techniques.

1. **Suggest to students that they make use of mnemonic devices and techniques.**
    a. Easy-to-see examples, such as imagining what knowledge you want to keep in your head
    b. Methods of paraphrasing, such as restating the material in your own words after you have summarized it
    c. The method of loci, which links new information with a well-known location or path
    d. Opportunities for reviewing material and practicing, such as quizzes and practice assessments
2. **Establish connections between the new information and previously learned material with note-taking aids.**
    a. Concept maps, such as mind maps or spider diagrams

b. Graphic organizers, such as Venn diagrams, flow charts, Cornell notes, or two-column notes

c. Word webs, which illustrate the interconnections between similar words by linking them with lines and arrows

d. Half-full concept maps, in which two distinct ideas are each represented by one half of a circle, and the halves of the circle are connected to one another by arrows to demonstrate how the ideas relate to one another

3. **Incorporate cutting-edge ideas into tested paradigms and environments.**

    a. Literary devices such as analogy and metaphor, as well as the performing arts, musical composition, and cinema, to simplify information and make it simpler to comprehend.

    b. Real-world scenarios that give students opportunities to put what they've learned into practice in a variety of settings while providing them with support

        i. Construct a playground according to the principles of physics, such as by applying Newton's laws of motion to the design of a swing set

        ii. Present a variety of problems that can be solved by linear equations, such as determining the slope of a line when given two points on the line

4. **Review significant ideas and their interrelation at frequent intervals.** Schedule frequent reviews of important ideas and their interconnections by allocating time once a week specifically for review.

Mental Models

In the fast-paced world, lifelong learning is essential, but determining how to learn effectively can be challenging. The key to effective learning is not simply increasing the material or time spent learning but improving the learning process itself. In his book *Ultralearning*, Scott Young (2019) suggests using mental models to accelerate learning across various subject areas. *Mental models* are frameworks that help individuals understand and navigate complex concepts by relating new information to existing knowledge. Young (2019) compiled a list of the most fundamental mental models, which include the following. As educators, you can help students use these models to enhance their learning.

- **Memory strengthens by retrieval:** Encourage students to test themselves regularly rather than passively reviewing notes. Retrieval practice helps reinforce memory more effectively than simply rereading information. Suggest students space out their self-testing sessions to enhance memory retention through delayed retrieval.

- **Knowledge grows exponentially:** Emphasize the importance of mastering basic concepts before moving on to more complex topics. This foundational knowledge allows students to build and expand their understanding more effectively. Use Bloom's taxonomy to guide students in starting with a broad overview before diving into details.

- **Creativity is mostly copying:** Teach students that creativity often involves combining existing ideas in new ways. Encourage them to explore different subjects and hobbies to draw from a wide range of experiences and memories, fostering innovative thinking.
- **Success is the best teacher:** Help students find a balance between challenging themselves and experiencing success. While struggle is part of learning, consistent failure can be demotivating. Provide opportunities for students to achieve success and build confidence in their abilities.
- **Knowledge becomes invisible with experience:** Explain to students that skills become automatic with practice, reducing the mental effort required to perform them. However, this can make it difficult to teach these skills to others. Encourage students to reflect on their learning process and break down complex tasks into teachable steps.

ADA LOVELACE CONNECTS DOTS ACROSS DOMAINS

Ada Lovelace, often recognized as the world's first computer programmer, stands as an icon of interdisciplinary thinking. The daughter of the renowned poet Lord Byron, Lovelace combined her artistic heritage with her passion for mathematics, demonstrating a unique ability for transfer learning. She foresaw the creative potential of Charles Babbage's Analytical Engine beyond its immediate mathematical applications.

While collaborating with Babbage, Lovelace was introduced to the concept of the Analytical Engine, a mechanical general-purpose computer design. She was entranced by its capabilities. But unlike most, she imagined the engine's potential to venture into fields like music and art, illustrating its capacity to create complex patterns akin to composing elaborate symphonies or crafting intricate artwork. Her extensive notes on the engine include what is recognized as the first algorithm intended for implementation on a computer, marking her role in history.

Jasmine, a modern-day high school student, mirrors Lovelace's multidisciplinary mindset. Passionate about biology and digital design, she created an app that visualizes the intricate processes of human cells in an engaging and interactive manner. By doing so, she helps students understand complex biological systems through a more visual and interactive medium, fostering a deeper comprehension of the subject.

Ada Lovelace's ability to perceive the Analytical Engine's potential across varied fields is akin to Jasmine's blending of biology with digital design. Both figures showcase the power of interdisciplinary thinking and its role in innovation. They exemplify the essence of transfer learning, illustrating how knowledge in one domain can deeply enrich and inform another. In a world increasingly defined by its interconnectedness, such an ability to weave together diverse disciplines is more valuable than ever.

Implement and Differentiate an Easy Activity to Nurture Transfer Learning in K–12 Students

To effectively foster transfer learning in K–12 education, create activities tailored to the developmental capacities of your students. At each educational stage, you must construct experiences that enable students to apply and adapt what they learn to different contexts, not merely memorize facts. Your goal is to develop students' ability to recognize patterns, conceptualize principles, and apply their understanding to solve problems in unfamiliar situations.

Elementary School Students

When working with elementary school students, it's imperative to capitalize on their innate curiosity and desire to engage with the world around them. To this end, structure activities that blend play and education, making learning both enjoyable and impactful. A practical example is initiating a classroom garden project. This not only grounds their understanding of plant biology in tangible experience but also nurtures a sense of responsibility and stewardship over the natural world.

Begin by discussing the life cycle of plants, from seed germination to pollination. Then, guide your students as they select seeds, prepare soil, and plant their own garden. This hands-on approach not only solidifies their scientific knowledge but also teaches patience and care. As the plants grow, encourage your students to observe the effects of sunlight and water, thereby drawing direct connections to the environmental science curriculum.

Extend this learning by having students apply these insights to real-life scenarios, such as determining suitable plants for a home garden based on the local climate and soil conditions. Enrich this activity by integrating other subjects, such as mathematics for measuring growth and art for journaling plant progress. Through this multifaceted approach, students begin to see the relevance of their classroom learning in everyday life, setting a strong foundation for the development of transfer learning skills.

Middle School Students

As middle school educators, you are positioned to harness the burgeoning abstract thinking abilities of your students. This is an opportune time to introduce interdisciplinary projects that require them to synthesize knowledge from various academic domains. An example of a rich, integrative project is the construction of a model ancient civilization.

Invite your students to investigate and recreate an ancient society, like Egypt or the Mayan civilization. Begin with history lessons, exploring the timeline, key events, and societal structures. Then, delve into the literature of the era, examining myths, stories, and written records to gain insight into the culture and values of the people. In science, analyze the natural resources and geography that shaped the civilization's development. Incorporate mathematics by having students calculate architectural dimensions of pyramids or temples based on historical data, using scale to create accurate models. Encourage them to consider the mathematical systems the civilization might have used, including their approach to astronomy and agriculture.

By coordinating these subject areas into a unified project, you not only engage your students in active learning but also demonstrate the interconnectedness of human knowledge. This not only reinforces their cognitive skills in each discipline but also teaches them how these disciplines interact, laying the groundwork for transfer learning as they begin to understand that solutions to complex problems often require a multifaceted approach.

High School Students

High school students stand on the cusp of adulthood, where critical thinking and independence become crucial. At this stage, you should challenge them to engage with complex issues that demand a mature understanding and an integrated approach to problem solving. A capstone project presents an ideal opportunity for students to consolidate and apply their learning in a meaningful way.

Guide students to select a pressing global issue—climate change, inequality, or public health, for example—and explore it in depth. This project should be expansive, encouraging students to conduct independent research, analyze data, and explore theoretical frameworks across subjects like economics, political science, environmental studies, and ethics.

Encourage students to approach their chosen issue from multiple angles. For instance, if they are exploring clean water access, they should understand the scientific principles of water purification, the geographical distribution of water resources, the political challenges in infrastructure development, and the economic impact of water scarcity. In doing so, they will need to employ advanced research methods, engage in critical discussions with peers and experts, and develop strong reasoning to defend their viewpoints. Their final task is to devise innovative, sustainable solutions that reflect a sophisticated synthesis of the knowledge they've gained throughout their education.

By navigating such a project, students not only demonstrate their subject mastery but also their ability to transfer and adapt that mastery to address real-world challenges. This is the essence of transfer learning at the high school level: preparing students not just for tests, but for thoughtful, informed citizenship.

Concluding Thoughts

We have journeyed through the essential skills of fostering transfer learning and explored how these skills can prepare students to apply their knowledge in various contexts. This process, anchored in constructivist thinking and active learning, empowers students to construct meaning from their experiences and to integrate new information effectively. By encouraging students to recognize patterns and differentiate essential information from the irrelevant, we enhance their cognitive and metacognitive abilities.

Throughout this chapter, we have emphasized the importance of processing and visualization techniques, equipping students with strategies for better understanding and retention. Additionally, we have implemented techniques for information retrieval and transfer learning, guiding students to apply their knowledge in new and diverse scenarios. Mental models provide frameworks that accelerate and deepen learning across various subjects. By integrating these approaches into your teaching practice, you are not merely disseminating information but facilitating a transformative process that prepares young minds to meet the unknown with confidence and agility. The habit of transfer learning, as highlighted, transcends the classroom and becomes a cornerstone of students' educational and professional futures.

As we conclude this chapter, let us reaffirm our commitment to nurturing inquisitive and adaptable minds capable of rigorous evaluation and open to continuous learning. Through this dedication, we create a learning environment that values the exchange of ideas and the application of knowledge in meaningful ways. Our goal is to inspire a new generation of learners—learners who can think critically, act wisely, and contribute positively to the ever-evolving dialogue of our society. In embracing these methodologies, we equip our students not only to excel academically but also to navigate the myriad challenges of the modern world with resilience and innovation. The journey of fostering transfer learning is ongoing, and as educators, our role is pivotal in guiding students to harness their full potential and achieve lasting success.

Obstacles cannot crush me. Every obstacle yields to stern resolve. He who is fixed to a star does not change his mind.

—LEONARDO DA VINCI

Chapter 8

Habit 7: Ask Questions

In the realm of education, the art of questioning is not merely about seeking answers but about fostering an environment where critical thinking and inquiry are the cornerstones of learning. The value of this kind of questioning—a rigorous, evidence-based approach—is profound. It equips students with the ability to not just accept information at face value but to scrutinize it, to see beyond the obvious, and to engage with the material in a way that cultivates deep understanding. This habit of questioning is essential, as it encourages learners to develop a sound, skeptical stance toward knowledge, which is instrumental in an ever-evolving world.

Bertrand Russell, the esteemed 20th century philosopher, eloquently championed this form of inquiry. He argued for the necessity of free thought, emphasizing that educational systems should promote the impartial pursuit of knowledge and remain vigilant against the acceptance of unverified beliefs. Russell posited that many of the world's quandaries could be ameliorated if judgments were consistently based on evidence and held with a level of confidence proportional to that evidence. This perspective is not just historical musing but is incredibly relevant in contemporary education, where true questioning can often be overshadowed by a rush toward standardized answers.

When Russell stated, "The world needs open hearts and minds, which can't come from rigorous systems, old or new," he underscored a profound educational philosophy (quoted in Monk, 1996). This is why asking questions is such an important habit of thinking. The world's need for "open minds and hearts" is crucial. Cultivating this in young students is not just about equipping them with knowledge, but also about nurturing the kind of critical thinking, empathy, and ethical understanding that future leaders require. An open mind allows for the questioning and exploration of new ideas, fostering innovation and problem solving. An open heart is equally important, as it encourages compassion and cooperation—skills that are vital for addressing the complex social and humanitarian issues that will define students' generation. By fostering these qualities, educators help prepare students to contribute positively to an interconnected and rapidly changing world.

The potency of higher-level questioning in education lies in its ability to drive transformation and stimulate growth. When students engage in such inquiry, they challenge existing norms and push the boundaries of conventional thought. Posing "What if...?" questions is not merely an exercise in curiosity but a powerful tool that has historically catalyzed change and innovation. This form of questioning underpins the scientific method and has sparked countless advances, as every notable innovation or technological breakthrough began with someone questioning what was possible. These questions invite us to imagine different futures and to explore the pathways to those realities, thereby holding intrinsic value in their capacity to expand our understanding and shape our world.

As teachers, we frequently pose questions to the class. Are all queries, however, created equal? Inquiry-based learning is more than just asking questions: it's about engaging students in activities that foster critical thinking and exploration. Inquiry should be the foundation of our education system because it is through questioning and exploring that we not only discover new knowledge but also learn to apply it critically.

This chapter embodies the investigative stance central to scientific inquiry, urging educators and students alike to adopt a mindset that favors curiosity and rigorous examination over rote memorization. This approach to teaching and learning is vital for cultivating the habits of mind necessary for a renaissance in education that champions critical thinking and innovation. By integrating these strategies into your teaching, you contribute to a shift in educational paradigms, where inquiry becomes the heartbeat of the classroom, pumping vitality into every lesson and empowering students to become thinkers and problem solvers prepared to face the challenges of the future.

Activities that effectively promote inquiry will be the focal strategies of this chapter and include class discussions, debates, and organized controversy, which create a dynamic environment for students to delve into topics deeply. In the pages that follow, you will be introduced to strategies that foster an inquisitive approach in the classroom. From adjusting your mindset to let inquiry lead; to asking profound, open-ended questions; to crafting activities that require students to investigate what is true and what is not, this chapter provides actionable insights. You'll learn how to create a classroom environment where inquiry is not just encouraged but is the driving force behind all learning activities.

Let Inquiry Pave the Way

Every learner should have the chance to enjoy the thrill of inquiry. The goal of teaching is to create an environment and orchestrate an inquiry that paves the way for students to progress to more complex levels of thought. However, due to the vast difference between traditional instruction and inquiry-based learning, teachers often have questions and hesitations. Here, we address several common worries about inquiry in the classroom.

First, teachers often ask, "How can we expect students to ask questions without first providing them with content knowledge?" Lessons that involve inquiry do not preclude the transmission of knowledge. The teacher provides this support whenever students need additional conceptual or procedural knowledge to advance in an inquiry. Inquiry gives students the freedom to choose how they will use the knowledge they learn in a meaningful context. Additionally, students are more likely to listen and participate actively in what the teacher or another student has to say if they ask for an explanation (Chi & Wylie, 2014). Being receptive to the many ways in which students think is the foundation for personalized learning. It means being aware of how to develop each student's thinking , and being open to changing your whole-group and small-group plans based on real-time data. I contend that all of curricula could be taught through inquiry, but that this may not be practicable due to school, district, and state structures.

Another common question is, What if students don't ask questions? We can address this in two ways. The first answer begins by piquing students' natural curiosity by setting the prompt just above their level of comprehension. Next, provide students with structured question stems and observation prompts to guide their inquiry. This approach ensures that even if students are hesitant to ask questions independently, they have a framework to help them engage with the material. Next, model the questioning process by demonstrating how to ask effective questions and think critically about the content. This modeling can inspire students to adopt similar strategies in their own learning. Finally, praise all contributions and return to those contributions as they emerge during the inquiry. If you don't get any questions, ask students if they understood the prompt before moving on to a teacher-led, structured inquiry. Inquiries may appear slowly; the development of shared knowledge results in a deeper comprehension of the procedure. It may take time and adjustment to the learning plan for students to formulate inquiries, but once they do, students frequently push themselves to achieve goals at a higher level than expected to answer their own questions.

The second answer to the question of students not asking questions is that it's important to directly teach students how to ask questions. I recommend starting slowly with classes that are new to inquiry and progressing to open inquiry over months rather than in a matter of weeks. Before using a preplanned structure for the remainder of the inquiry, you may allow students to ask questions and make observations regarding the prompt at the beginning of the class. Before allowing students to produce and develop their own ideas in later inquiry, you may offer them a variety of paths to choose. The investigative thinking processes are likely to initially present difficulties for students (and teachers!) who are used to repetition. In your initial efforts, take an organized strategy.

In addition to worrying about how to respond if students don't answer questions, elementary teachers particularly may wonder, "Are you sure I can use inquiry with my young students?" There are two approaches to improve the accessibility of inquiry. First off, you can assume greater responsibility for the inquiry's structure by, for instance, creating a road map for students to follow in the first class and then organizing subsequent lessons in response to their queries and observations. Second, inquiry prompts can be both recognizable and unusual. For example, if teaching a science lesson on ecosystems, you might use a common example like a forest ecosystem (recognizable) alongside a less familiar one like a deep-sea hydrothermal vent ecosystem (unusual). The familiar forest ecosystem gives students a foundation of prior knowledge to build on, while the unusual hydrothermal vent ecosystem piques their curiosity and inspires them to learn more. This combination encourages students to analyze and compare the two ecosystems, fostering deeper engagement and understanding.

Figure 8.1 (page 128) shows examples of using inquiry in various contexts.

SUBJECT AREA	PROMPT	QUESTIONS	PRAISE
Mathematics	What is the connection between a circle's area and circumference?	What are some facts about circles? What is the formula for calculating a circle's area? What is the formula for calculating a circle's circumference? How can we compare the area and diameter of a circle using these formulas?	You did a great job considering circles and their characteristics! Let's find out what else we can discover.
Science	How does light impact plant growth?	What do plants need to grow? How does light differ from other environmental conditions in the way it affects plants? What tests might we run to determine how light impacts plant growth?	Wonderful suggestions on how to test this question! Let's find out what else we can discover.
Social Studies	What impact did industrialization have on the development of European cities in the 19th century?	What did European cities look like before industrialization? How did industrialization affect European cities during this time? What were some of industrialization's beneficial and detrimental consequences on European cities at the time?	You did a great job considering how industrialization affected European cities! Let's find out what else we can discover.
English Language Arts	How does a writer's word choice affect the tone and style of their writing?	What are some instances of terms that, depending on usage or context, have a distinct connotation or meaning? How do writers employ particular phrases to establish a particular tone or mood in their writing? How does a writer's word choice affect the overall tone and style of their writing?	Wonderful suggestions about how writers might convey meaning through language! Let's find out what else we can discover.
STEM	How might a designer apply engineering concepts to create a bridge that can withstand heavy winds?	What substances are most suitable for making bridges? What principles of engineering should be taken into account while designing a bridge? How can a designer test the bridge's durability to make sure it can resist heavy winds?	Well done considering how to create a safe and secure bridge! Let's find out what else we can discover.
Music	How do rhythm and tempo impact a piece of music's overall sound?	How are rhythm and tempo different from one another? How do different tempos and rhythms produce various tones in a piece of music? How might musicians use rhythm and tempo to achieve a certain effect?	Fantastic suggestions for using tempo and rhythm to produce captivating musical effects! Let's find out what else we can discover.
Art	How can we utilize color to convey feeling in a painting?	Which hues represent which feelings? How can we employ color combinations in a painting to get the desired effect? How does a painting's emotional resonance differ depending on how we use light and shadow?	Well done considering how to utilize color to evoke feeling in a painting! Let's find out what else we can discover.

Figure 8.1: Inquiry lesson starters.

*Visit **go.SolutionTree.com/ instruction** for a free reproducible version of this figure.*

It's clear that the path to true understanding and innovation in the classroom is paved with questions. By embracing and structuring inquiry-based learning, you cultivate a learning environment that values curiosity and critical thinking. This environment not only inspires students but also prepares them to navigate an ever-changing world. Through the art of inquiry, educators can transform passive learning into an active exploration that equips students with the tools they need for lifelong learning. Let this be the guiding principle as you continue to shape the minds and futures of your students.

Supplement Procedural Questions

When trying out inquiry in the classroom, many educators (myself included) fall into the trap of asking procedural questions. Procedural questions focus on the steps or methods needed to reach an answer and don't connect to a broader idea. Typically, they do not require students to understand underlying concepts but rather to follow a specific set of instructions or a defined process. While these questions are crucial for developing technical skills and accuracy, they often fall short in promoting deeper conceptual understanding or encouraging students to make connections beyond the procedure itself. Teachers also need to ask students higher-order thinking questions like why the formula works or help them try to figure out if an algorithm works on different problems or in different contexts.

What teachers do after they prompt students with higher-order thinking questions is also important. Rather than letting students grapple with confusion, teachers often respond to their solicitations with hints that morph an inquiry problem into a procedural one. An *inquiry problem* is a question or challenge designed to stimulate curiosity and require students to use higher-order thinking skills to explore, investigate, and derive answers. When students are playing multiple choice with the teacher, they are seeking rules and trying to turn a conceptual problem they don't understand into a procedural one they can just execute. Humans are quite skilled at completing tasks with the least amount of effort necessary. Soliciting hints toward a solution is both clever and expedient. But when it comes to learning concepts that can be broadly wielded, expedience can backfire. By the time the students are done soliciting hints from the teacher and solving the problems, the inquiry process has turned back to a rote transmission of information.

It's hard for educators to not fall into this trap; it's uncomfortable to see students struggle and to not feel in control of the classroom when we can't anticipate where the exploration of a topic will go. To avoid this, provide scaffolding that guides students without giving away the answers. Encourage them to discuss their ideas in small groups, offer open-ended questions that lead them to think deeper about the problem, and provide periodic check-ins to ensure they are on the right track while still maintaining the inquiry-based nature of the lesson. This way, students obtain information through guided discovery rather than direct transmission, maintaining the integrity of the inquiry process.

Here are some strategies for avoiding the traps of over-reliance on procedural questions in your class.

- **Create one problem with many parts:** An entire class period could involve going over just one problem with many parts, requiring many questions to address.
- **Give students a way to share their ideas:** When a student offers an idea for how to approach a problem, rather than engaging in multiple choice (having students select from predetermined options) or asking for "better" ideas or

answers, have the student come to the board and put a magnet with their name on it next to the idea. Or, if you're in an online collaborative space, put a digital sticky note next to the ideas.

- **Create a captain's log of the class's collective intellectual voyage:** Using a Japanese strategy called *bansho*, make conceptual connections over the course of collective problem solving to visually map out and reinforce understanding. The bansho method involves displaying students' ideas, solutions, and strategies on a large board, creating a visual record of the class's thought processes. By continuously adding to this log, students can see the evolution of their learning, identify connections between different concepts, and reflect on their progress.

The following sections detail each of these strategies.

Create One Problem With Many Parts

Creating a single problem with many parts for your students to work on throughout a class period is a transformative strategy that promotes critical thinking and problem-solving skills. Begin with a central issue that has breadth and depth that students can dissect and approach from multiple angles. For instance, in a social studies class, you could pose a situation such as the impact of a historical event on various aspects of society. Students would need to analyze the political, economic, social, and cultural ramifications, understanding how these elements intertwine. In a science class, you might present a real-world problem like climate change, asking students to explore its causes, effects, and potential solutions. They could examine scientific data, debate policy responses, and propose innovative technologies to mitigate its impact. In a mathematics class, you could introduce a complex scenario such as planning a community garden, where students must use geometry to design the layout, algebra to budget costs, and statistics to predict yield and resource needs. These multifaceted problems encourage students to apply knowledge from various disciplines, fostering a deeper and more integrated understanding of the subject matter.

Encourage collaborative work, where students can debate and discuss the facets of the problem and guide each other through the layers of complexity. This approach not only enhances their interpersonal skills but also fosters a community of learners who can collectively build a comprehensive understanding of the issue at hand. As they navigate the problem, prompt them to consider implications, alternatives, and possible solutions. This teaches them to appreciate the nuance and complexity of real-world issues, a skill that is invaluable both in academic settings and in life.

By dedicating a class period to a multilayered problem, you create an immersive learning environment where students are actively engaged in discovery and exploration. They begin to see the relevance of their learning as they apply academic concepts to the scenario, gaining a deeper and more nuanced understanding of the subject matter. This method not only encourages students to move beyond seeking the right answer but also to develop a curiosity about the interconnectedness of ideas and concepts, echoing this chapter's advocacy for a more inquiry-based approach to learning.

Give Students a Way to Share Their Ideas

To nurture a culture of sharing and collaboration in your classroom, establish varied channels for students to express their ideas and thinking processes. Encourage them to articulate their perspectives on complex problems or concepts, allowing them to move away from simply reciting standard answers and toward developing their viewpoints. In a literature class, for example, instead of asking students which character they most identify with, prompt them to create a character web on a collaborative board, physically or digitally. Here, they can post insights into the motivations and relationships of different characters, inviting peers to connect and expand on these ideas.

This visual and interactive method can lead to richer, more engaging discussions that reveal the depth of each student's understanding and creativity. It can break down barriers to participation, as even those who are typically more reserved may feel more comfortable contributing in a less formal, more dynamic setting. As students learn to respect and build on one another's thoughts, they develop a shared body of knowledge and become more invested in the learning process.

Providing students with the opportunity to showcase their thinking empowers them to take risks and think more deeply. In a mathematics setting, for instance, after solving a problem, students could post different methods and strategies they used to reach a solution. This strategy highlights that there are multiple ways to approach and solve problems, emphasizing that the process and the reasoning behind it can be just as important as the correct answer. As they interact with the diverse approaches of their classmates, students enhance their ability to think flexibly and critically—key skills in fostering an inquisitive mindset and promoting the in-depth exploration central to this chapter.

Create a Captain's Log of the Class's Collective Intellectual Voyage

Creating a captain's log for your classroom's collective intellectual journey is a powerful way to visualize and document the progression of learning throughout a course. This log becomes a living record of the class's explorations and discoveries. Begin by designating a prominent space in the classroom to display the log. Start with a central theme or question that will guide your class's journey. As students contribute their insights, solutions, and reflections, add these to the log in a structured and interconnected manner. Use visual elements such as diagrams, flowcharts, and mind maps to illustrate the relationships between different concepts and ideas. Encourage students to add their own contributions, making the log a collaborative and dynamic tool that grows with the class's understanding. For example, if your class is studying ecosystems, start with a central question like "How do different organisms interact within an ecosystem?" As students explore this question through various activities and discussions, document their findings on the log. Include diagrams of food webs, notes on symbiotic relationships, and reflections on human impact. This ongoing record not only helps students see the bigger picture but also fosters a sense of ownership and engagement in their learning process.

As you and your students embark on various academic endeavors, from unraveling complex scientific theories to dissecting the motifs in a piece of literature, document every new piece of knowledge and each question raised in this log. It's not merely about recording right answers; it's about capturing the richness of classroom discussions, the variety of perspectives considered, and the evolution of your students' thinking. As students contribute to the captain's log, they see how their individual contributions fit into a larger, collaborative understanding of the subject matter.

Display the captain's log prominently in the classroom or virtually in an online learning environment. Regularly revisit and update it, encouraging students to reflect on their learning journey. This ongoing process not only reinforces the material covered but also promotes a sense of accomplishment as students visually observe how much ground they've covered. Over time, this log will not only illustrate the detailed network of knowledge your students have built but also highlight the learning processes that were most effective, guiding future instructional strategies. The sample log entries in figure 8.2 serve as a template for how this might look across different subjects.

SUBJECT AREA	EXAMPLE CAPTAIN'S LOG ENTRY
Mathematics	Today, we collaborated to solve a challenging algebraic equation. We spoke about several approaches we might take to the problem and ultimately came up with a solution that worked for everyone. To illustrate our process and the connections between many ideas, including substitution, elimination, and graphing, we constructed a learning landscape in our online collaborative document.
Science	Today, the class collaborated to find a solution to a climate change problem. We spoke about the many theories and hypotheses we might use to solve the issue before coming up with a solution that was backed up by data from trials and research. To illustrate our process and how we linked many concepts, like greenhouse gases, global warming, and increasing sea levels, to arrive at our conclusion, we built an anchor chart.
Social Studies	Today's class collaborated to find a solution to the challenge of misinformation in American society. We spoke about the several angles we might take on the issue before coming up with a solution that was backed up by data from a variety of sources, including news stories, interviews with experts, and historical records. To illustrate our journey and how we integrated many facts and concepts—such as technology evolution and policies—to arrive at our conclusion, we constructed a learning landscape.
English Language Arts	The class today collaborated to find a solution to an issue involving symbolism in literature. We spoke about the several literary techniques we could employ to solve the issue before coming up with a solution that was backed up by evidence from numerous texts, including poems, short stories, novels, and other works. To illustrate our journey and how we related several literary devices, including imagery, metaphor, and allegory, to come to our conclusion, we built an anchor chart.

Figure 8.2: Captain's log example.

*Visit **go.SolutionTree.com/instruction** for a free reproducible version of this figure.*

The captain's log is more than a mere chronicle; it is a testament to the journey of learning. It encapsulates the twists and turns of inquiry, the collaborative efforts of your class, and the growth that each student has contributed to the collective voyage. Let it stand as a reminder of where you've been and as an inspiration for where you will go, continuing to light the way for future explorations in your educational odyssey.

HYPATIA OF ALEXANDRIA ASKS QUESTIONS

Hypatia of Alexandria stands as an emblem of wisdom, resilience, and the pursuit of knowledge in a predominantly male-dominated society. As a female mathematician, astronomer, and philosopher during the final century of the Roman Empire, Hypatia was not only recognized for her profound knowledge but also for her ability to question and challenge the status quo, epitomizing the vital habit of asking questions.

> Hypatia's tenure as the head of the Platonist school at Alexandria saw her impart knowledge on a vast array of topics from mathematics to the philosophies of Plotinus and Aristotle. However, her legend extends beyond her roles as a teacher and scholar. Hypatia was known to openly critique established theories, pushing the boundaries of understanding in her time. An example of this is her work on the *Almagest*, a seminal text on astronomy, where she offered clear and innovative solutions to mathematical problems. By revisiting and questioning existing works, she shed light on areas of ambiguity, further enriching the academic discourse of her era.
>
> Leo, a junior high student, is inspired by Hypatia's indomitable spirit of inquiry. In his history class, while studying ancient civilizations, he doesn't just passively absorb information. Instead, he wonders about the why and how behind historical events and decisions. This inquisitiveness leads Leo to launch a project where he attempts to connect the philosophical beliefs of ancient societies with their political and social decisions, looking for patterns and motivations. His project not only garners admiration from his peers and teachers but also sparks vibrant class discussions.
>
> Both Hypatia and Leo showcase a profound commitment to asking questions, refusing to simply accept surface-level explanations. Hypatia's interrogation of ancient texts and Leo's pursuit of underlying patterns in history underscore the significance of a questioning mindset. Such an approach not only deepens understanding but can also catalyze innovations and fresh perspectives, regardless of the field of study.

Implement and Differentiate an Easy Activity to Nurture Genuine Inquiry in K–12 Students

To foster genuine inquiry among K–12 students, you can implement activities that encourage skeptical thinking and critical analysis. One such approach is inspired by Carl Sagan's (1996) concept of a "baloney detection kit," a set of principles and strategies for evaluating the validity of information and arguments. This kit provides a framework for students to develop critical thinking skills by learning how to question and analyze information they encounter. It includes the following nine concepts as tools for thinking (Sagan, 1996).

1. Verification of the facts
2. Debate of substance
3. Precedence of expertise over authority
4. Multiple hypotheses
5. Removal of self from concept
6. Measurable hypotheses
7. Proper function of *every* link in the chain
8. Occam's razor (the simplest solution is most likely the best one)
9. Possibility of disproving your hypothesis

These tools can be integrated into classroom activities to nurture inquiry and promote a healthy skepticism toward unsupported claims. For instance, in science projects, students can be guided to verify facts by cross-checking multiple sources and debating the substance of their findings. By emphasizing the precedence of expertise over mere authority, students learn to value well-supported arguments. Encouraging them to formulate multiple hypotheses and test them with measurable outcomes ensures a comprehensive understanding of scientific inquiry.

A classroom exercise could involve presenting students with a controversial claim and guiding them through the process of dissecting it using the baloney detection kit. Students would verify facts, debate the substance of the claim, and propose multiple hypotheses. They would then test these hypotheses and apply Occam's razor to determine the simplest explanation. Throughout this process, they would learn the importance of being able to formulate and grasp a reasoned argument, as well as the critical skill of detecting flawed or false arguments.

By integrating these intellectual exercises into their curriculum, educators can nurture a culture of genuine inquiry and critical thinking among students, equipping them with the tools to navigate and assess the vast amount of information they encounter daily.

From the formative years in elementary school to the pivotal high school periods, we'll explore how to implement and differentiate inquiry-based activities to suit each developmental stage. The aim is not just to teach students to think but to think well—equipping them with the tools of skeptical thinking and the know-how to apply these tools critically and creatively. Through this guided approach, students will become adept at assessing claims, engaging substantively with complex ideas, and evolving into informed individuals ready to face the challenges of our dynamic world.

Elementary School Students

Develop an activity called "Detective Club," where students become fact finders. Introduce them to the basics of verifying information by using simple, observable experiments in the classroom. Encourage them to ask questions about what they see and guide them in understanding why asking for evidence is important. For instance, when discussing weather, have them collect data on temperature, wind, and precipitation, promoting hands-on verification. Here are specific strategies to incorporate the Detective Club into your classroom.

1. **Verification of the facts:** Create a fact-finder game where students must decide whether a statement about nature (for example, "The sky is blue because of the ocean") is true or false, encouraging them to find evidence in books or credible websites.

2. **Debate of substance:** Host classroom debates on which animals make the best pets, focusing on using facts rather than opinions to support students' arguments.

3. **Precedence of expertise over authority:** Discuss what makes someone an expert (for example, a doctor or a scientist) versus an authority figure (for example, a celebrity endorsing a product) through role-playing activities.

4. **Multiple hypotheses:** Introduce a simple scientific question and brainstorm various possible explanations, teaching the concept of forming multiple hypotheses.

5. **Removal of self from concept:** Teach the importance of being open-minded by having students draw or write about an idea, then exchange with a classmate to consider different perspectives.

6. **Measurable hypotheses:** Conduct simple experiments where students can make predictions and then measure results, such as plant growth with varying amounts of sunlight.
7. **Proper function of every link in the chain:** Demonstrate a simple chain reaction with dominoes and discuss what happens if one domino doesn't fall.
8. **Occam's razor:** Present a problem with two potential solutions, one simple and one complex, and discuss why the simpler one might be better.
9. **Possibility of disproving your hypotheses:** Encourage a Myth Busters activity where common myths are tested and potentially disproved.

Middle School Students

Create a debate forum called "the Challengers," encouraging students to discuss and defend different viewpoints on a given topic, such as the impact of historical events. This will instill a habit of engaging with substance over rhetoric. Incorporate activities that require them to research and present multiple hypotheses for scientific phenomena, fostering an appreciation for diverse perspectives and critical analysis. Here are specific strategies to incorporate the Challengers into your classroom.

1. **Verification of the facts:** Have students conduct a simple research project on a historical figure, verifying different "facts" they find in various sources, and then presenting which are true and which are myths.
2. **Debate of substance:** Organize debates on more complex topics like renewable energy, encouraging the use of data and research to support students' points.
3. **Precedence of expertise over authority:** Analyze case studies where expert opinions were disregarded in favor of authority figures and discuss the outcomes.
4. **Multiple hypotheses:** For a given scientific phenomenon, like climate change, have students come up with and test different hypotheses.
5. **Removal of self from concept:** Discuss cognitive biases and have students write an argument, then rewrite it from an opposing viewpoint.
6. **Measurable hypotheses:** Engage in more sophisticated experiments that require precise measurement and data analysis, such as chemical reactions with different variables.
7. **Proper function of every link in the chain:** Study the food chain of an ecosystem and analyze the impact if one species is removed.
8. **Occam's razor:** Apply Occam's razor in scientific scenarios, such as choosing between competing theories based on simplicity.
9. **Possibility of disproving your hypothesis:** Host a science fair where students present projects designed to test and potentially disprove their own scientific hypotheses.

High School Students

Initiate a project-based module titled "Inquiry Incubator," where students take on complex issues like climate change, applying all aspects of the baloney detection kit. They will learn to separate their personal beliefs from evidence-based conclusions, design measurable experiments, test their hypotheses, and practice applying Occam's razor to find the simplest, most logical solutions.

1. **Verification of the facts:** Challenge students to verify news articles by cross-referencing multiple sources, identifying biases, and presenting their findings to the class.
2. **Debate of substance:** Hold formal debates on social issues, requiring students to use substantial evidence and clear logical arguments to defend their positions.
3. **Precedence of expertise over authority:** Evaluate historical or current events where expert advice was critical and create presentations on the importance of expert opinion over authority.
4. **Multiple hypotheses:** Assign a complex problem, like a health issue, and require students to propose multiple hypotheses and investigate their validity through research.
5. **Removal of self from concept:** Have students critically analyze of their own research papers, identifying areas where personal bias may have influenced their conclusions.
6. **Measurable hypotheses:** Design comprehensive experiments or social science surveys with quantifiable hypotheses and statistical analysis.
7. **Proper function of every link in the chain:** Evaluate complex systems, like an economic model, to identify and explain the importance of each component's functionality.
8. **Occam's razor:** Critically examine case studies in various disciplines, applying Occam's razor to form conclusions.
9. **Possibility of disproving your hypothesis:** Conduct advanced research projects where disconfirmation is a key part, encouraging rigorous testing and peer review.

Figure 8.3 gives a high school–level example using the concept of climate change.

EXAMINING HOW CLIMATE CHANGE AFFECTS THE ENVIRONMENT

Step 1: *Verify the facts*—In the first step, students will gather information about climate change and its impacts on the environment. To ensure accuracy, they will rely on trustworthy resources including scientific publications, official reports, and other credible sources.

Step 2: *Have a substantive debate*—Students present their results. They will provide their proof and discuss why they think it is reliable. Along with listening to opposing viewpoints, they will take those viewpoints into account in their own arguments.

Step 3: *Ensure experts take precedence over authority*—Students will seek out authorities on climate change and its consequences on the environment. They will pay attention to what these professionals have to say about the subject and use that knowledge to guide their own judgments.

Step 4: *Form multiple hypotheses*—Students will develop a number of hypotheses on how climate change is harming the ecosystem. They will next use accurate data analysis to obtain information from dependable sources and evaluate each idea.

Step 5: *Remove yourself from your concept*—Students take a step back from their preconceived notions about climate change and its consequences on the environment. They will approach the situation objectively, without prejudice or preconceived ideas, to make a judgment that is based on information rather than opinion.

Step 6: *Make your hypothesis measurable*—Students will set measurable objectives for each hypothesis they have developed on the impact of climate change on the environment. This can entail tracking over time variations in temperature, sea level, or other environmental conditions.

> **Step 7:** *Analyze every link in the chain to see that it is functional*—Before drawing any conclusions about how climate change will affect the ecosystem, students must make sure that every link in their chain of evidence is operational. This entails making sure that it is completely true and that all sources are trustworthy before taking any inferences from the data.
>
> **Step 8:** *Apply Occam's razor*—When analyzing their ideas regarding how climate change affects the environment, students must take Occam's razor into account. This indicates that before examining more complex answers, students should seek out simple ones first since they are more likely to be accurate than intricate ones with lots of variables. The simplest explanation for the observed increases in global temperatures is that human activities are increasing greenhouse gas emissions, which are trapping more heat in the atmosphere and warming the planet.
>
> **Step 9:** *Disprove your hypothesis*—Students must now make an effort to disprove each hypothesis they have developed on the impact of climate change by assembling data that either support or refute it. This aids students in better understanding how climate change is affecting our world, allowing them to go forward with educated judgments.

Source: Sagan, 1996.
Figure 8.3: Using the baloney detection framework in learning.

Each of these activities not only supplements procedural questions with open-ended inquiry but also aligns with the overarching goal of cultivating critical thinking and skepticism—skills that are crucial for navigating the information-rich 21st century. Such a framework not only introduces students to critical thinking but also iteratively develops their skills as they progress through their education, fostering lifelong habits of inquiry and reflection.

Concluding Thoughts

I'll close this chapter by returning to Bertrand Russell. The importance that Russell placed on unrestricted and uninhibited inquiry is still important today. The spirit of asking questions should serve as the bedrock of our educational system since it is essential to our progress. To pique students' interests and encourage them to pursue their inquiries, we need to spark their curiosity through activities such as classroom discussions, debates, organized controversy, baloney detection, debriefings of difficult cases, simulations, and role plays. We should also encourage students to discuss their points of view in a convincing and comprehensive manner. When we do this, we can make sure that students have the tools they need to defend their viewpoints and that they have a solid understanding of the interrelated ideas that comprise a subject. That leads us to our next habit of thinking, evaluating evidence.

There is no result in nature without a cause; understand the cause and you will have no need of the experiment.

—LEONARDO DA VINCI

Chapter 9

Habit 8: Evaluate Evidence

A revitalized education paradigm that values a multiplicity of viewpoints encourages students to actively ask questions and seek information from diverse sources. This inquisitive approach is fundamental to developing their ability to critically analyze data, recognize logical inconsistencies, and assess the validity of evidence. Engaging in this rigorous questioning process not only sharpens their understanding but also equips them with the analytical tools necessary for thoughtful inquiry and reasoned decision making. By teaching the habit of evaluating evidence, we support students in becoming more educated citizens who are better able to make sound choices based on the facts rather than relying solely on their feelings or opinions. Inquiry and the ability to formulate pertinent questions (see chapter 8 page 125) are crucial skills that can assist students in effectively evaluating available facts and data, and teaching students to think critically about the evidence they come across is an important component of inquiry. Students can acquire the skills essential to make judgments based on sufficient information if they are taught in the classroom to engage in inquisitive behavior by formulating inquiries and conducting investigations.

The questioning mind probes deeper and does not accept information at face value. When students learn to ask the right questions, they begin to peel back the layers of data and statements presented to them, seeking the core of reliable evidence. This methodical skepticism is not a sign of distrust, but a hallmark of a critical thinker—a necessary approach in a world saturated with information of varying credibility. As educators, our mission is to instill in students the ability to not just gather evidence, but to also interrogate it to understand its origin, context, and meaning. This critical evaluation begins with inquiry. By asking pointed, purposeful questions, students can discern between what is substantiated and what is mere conjecture. The strength of their future arguments and the solidity of their conclusions hinge on this foundational skill. Hence, inquiry does not just lead to the evaluation of evidence; it is the very bedrock on which the evaluation is built.

In this chapter, you will embark on a journey through the intricate relationship between inquiry and the evaluation of evidence. We explore how to cultivate a culture of questioning in the classroom, how to guide students in formulating powerful questions, and how to critically assess the information they uncover. You will learn practical strategies for teaching students to think like detectives, sifting through the noise to find the signal. By integrating the principles laid out in this chapter, you prepare your students to construct well-informed perspectives rooted in solid evidence and clear reasoning, thus connecting to the main point of cultivating informed, reflective, and engaged citizens.

Teach Students the Meaning of Evidence

The first step in instructing students how to analyze evidence is to assist them in comprehending what the term *evidence* means. Explain to them that evidence consists of any piece of information they may use to back up a claim or provide a response to a query. Show them some examples of the many kinds of evidence that are available, such as statistics, quotations from experts, or testimonies from eyewitnesses. When it comes to making judgments or developing views, explain why it's critical to take into account all available sorts of evidence. To begin a conversation about evidence with your students, consider the following middle school class discussion.

> **Teacher:** The proof that we have of the sun and the stars comes not just from direct observation but also from deductions and inferences that draw from those observations. When we see the flickering of the stars and compare it to the constant brightness of our own sun, we may determine that the stars are other suns that are very far away. By seeing how the Earth's shadow appears on the moon during a lunar eclipse, we may draw the conclusion that the Earth is spherical in shape. Observing how the constellations appear to move across the night sky over time enables us to draw the conclusion that the Earth rotates around the sun. The fossil record allows us to extrapolate that there have been shifts in the way life has evolved on earth over time. When we examine the geological record, we may infer that the climate of the Earth has undergone shifts throughout the course of time. When we examine the chemical makeup of rocks and minerals, we may determine the distinct conditions in which they originally formed. All these inferences and deductions present us with evidence that contributes to our advancement in comprehending the world around us.
>
> The word "evidence" is the response to both of these inquiries. There are times when having proof implies being able to truly see or hear, feel, or smell that something is true. Astronauts have reached a distance far enough from earth to confirm visually that the planet is spherical. There are times when our eyes require assistance. With the naked eye, the evening star seems to be a bright twinkling light in the sky, but, when viewed through a telescope, this evening star reveals itself to be a magnificent ball that is really the planet Venus. An observation is the name given to something that one acquires knowledge of by direct seeing or hearing, or feeling....
>
> Scientists, engineers, and scholars utilize evidence to learn about the world. Instinctive reactions have their place in science as well, but they should only be used to generate

> hypotheses, which should then be verified by seeking evidence. A scientist may have a hunch about a concept. This is not a particularly compelling argument in favor of believing something. However, it may be a compelling argument for conducting an experiment or searching for evidence. When looking for new ideas, scientists frequently rely on their intuitive impulses. However, these impulses do not hold any weight unless they are backed by evidence.
>
> What actions may we take in response to all of this?
>
> **Student 1:** We can start by making observations and noting down everything we see, just like scientists do when they begin their experiments.
>
> **Student 2:** We should always look for evidence to support our ideas and not just rely on what we think might be true. This means doing experiments or finding reliable sources of information.
>
> **Student 3:** It's important to ask questions and be curious. If we have a hunch about something, we should try to test it out and see if there's any evidence that supports it.
>
> **Student 4:** We should learn to differentiate between what we know for sure from evidence and what we think might be true based on our instincts. This helps us stay objective.
>
> **Student 5:** When we come up with new ideas, we should discuss them with others to see if they can find any evidence that either supports or disproves our thoughts.

These responses highlight the importance of evidence-based thinking and encourage students to practice scientific inquiry by relying on both intuition and evidence in a structured manner.

Another discussion form considering evidence could take might consider popular beliefs, such as in the following.

> **Teacher:** The next time someone tells you something that seems significant, you should ask yourself, "Is this the type of thing that people know because of evidence? Or is it the type of thing that people only believe because it has been passed down through the generations or a friend told them something at lunch?" And the next time someone tells you that something is true, ask them, "What kind of evidence is there for that?" And if they are unable to provide you with a satisfactory response, I hope that you would give great consideration to anything they say before you accept it as truth.
>
> What are things you've heard today that you could ask, "What evidence is there for that?"
>
> **Student 1:** I heard that eating chocolate every day is good for your health. What evidence is there for that?
>
> **Student 2:** Someone said that the moon landing was faked. What kind of evidence do they have for that?
>
> **Student 3:** A friend mentioned that drinking lots of water helps you concentrate better. Is there any scientific evidence for that?
>
> **Student 4:** I read somewhere that listening to classical music makes you smarter. What studies support that claim?
>
> **Student 5:** I was told that staying up late can make you more creative. What kind of research has been done on that?

These responses illustrate the importance of questioning the basis of information and highlight the value of seeking evidence to support claims. This practice helps students develop critical thinking skills and encourages a culture of inquiry in the classroom. The class could record the results of this discussion and revisit it throughout the year as they conduct their own investigations and seek out evidence.

Employ the Scientific Method in Evaluating Evidence

After establishing a foundational understanding of what constitutes evidence, the instructional focus must shift to the methods of assessing its validity. At the heart of this inquiry is the scientific method, an unparalleled tool in the arsenal of evidence evaluation. It is a method with a built-in error-correcting mechanism, which is vital in overcoming the biases and emotional influences that can distort objective analysis. To ensure a comprehensive understanding, let's delve into the commonly known steps of the scientific method and illustrate their application across various subject areas.

1. **Observation:** Identify a phenomenon or problem that needs explanation. For instance, in a history class, students might observe patterns in historical events, such as the causes of revolutions.

2. **Question:** Formulate specific questions about the observation. For example, students might ask, "What were the common factors that led to different revolutions?"

3. **Hypothesis:** Develop a testable hypothesis or prediction. In this case, students could hypothesize that economic hardship is a primary cause of revolutions.

4. **Experiment:** Design and conduct experiments to test the hypothesis. In studying revolutions, this might involve gathering data from historical documents, literature, or social studies, and looking for patterns that support or refute the hypothesis.

5. **Data collection:** Gather and record data systematically. Students could compile data on various revolutions, noting economic conditions, social unrest, political factors, and so on.

6. **Analysis:** Analyze the collected data to determine whether they support or refute the hypothesis. Students would look for correlations and trends in their data to see if economic hardship consistently precedes revolutions.

7. **Conclusion:** Draw conclusions based on the analysis. If the data support the hypothesis, students conclude that economic hardship is a significant factor. If not, they revise their hypothesis.

8. **Report:** Share the results for review and replication. Students could present their findings in essays, presentations, or class discussions, allowing peers and teachers to review and critique their work.

9. **Replication:** Encourage other students to replicate the study to verify the results. This step reinforces the importance of validation and peer review in establishing credible knowledge.

Understanding and applying these steps allows students to systematically evaluate evidence, ensuring their conclusions are based on reliable and reproducible data. This process fosters critical thinking and nurtures a scientific mindset, equipping students with the skills necessary to navigate a world filled with information and misinformation. As the previous example of studying historical revolutions proves, this method is not limited to the sciences; it is a universal framework that can be adapted to any field requiring critical analysis and evidence-based conclusions. In literature, as another example, students can use the scientific method to analyze themes and character development.

In addition to applying the scientific method, it is crucial to teach students to critically examine the sources of their evidence. Encourage them to do the following.

- **Question the accuracy of data:** Ensure that the data are gathered using reliable and valid methods.

- **Assess the credibility of expert opinions:** Consider the qualifications and potential biases of the experts.

- **Discern underlying biases or conflicts of interest:** Identify any potential motivations that might influence the data or conclusions.

In the context of evidence evaluation, the scientific method is not just another supporting tool; it is the backbone of a robust inquiry. It requires the evaluator to place truth-seeking above personal bias or comfort. It is less about identifying the source of biases and more about comprehending their influence on the body of knowledge. Ensuring the reliability of evidence is paramount, and this means subjecting it to independent verification, as advocated by Sagan (1996).

This focus on the scientific method, combined with a critical examination of evidence and sources, will enable students to distinguish between what is substantiated and what is conjecture. By integrating these approaches into your teaching practice, you can help students develop the habit of transfer learning, enabling them to apply their knowledge and skills in diverse and meaningful ways throughout their lives.

Delve Into Data Sets and Arguments

It is essential for students to learn how to evaluate the reliability of evidence by searching for patterns or trends within data sets and examining arguments for logical fallacies. Help them hone these abilities by assigning a variety of sources and discussing their results with either you or their peers. Developing students' capacity to assess the reliability of evidence is a multifaceted process that involves engaging them with practical, hands-on activities. Students can achieve this by delving into various data sets to search for patterns and assess arguments for logical consistency. Here are detailed methods and examples of how to guide students in this endeavor.

- **Data analysis projects:** Have students collect data on a current event or scientific phenomenon, then analyze these data for trends and anomalies. For instance, students might gather data on local weather patterns over a month and then discuss how these patterns compare with long-term climate data. This encourages familiarity with data collection methods and statistical analysis.

- **Case study reviews:** Provide students with case studies from diverse sources, such as academic journals, news outlets, or historical events. Have them identify the thesis, supporting evidence, and potential biases or logical fallacies within the arguments presented. For example, a case study could involve reviewing the evidence supporting the health benefits of a new diet. Students would evaluate the quality of the evidence, identify any misleading statistics, and discuss the findings.
- **Debate sessions:** Organize debates where students are assigned positions that they may or may not personally agree with. This requires them to research evidence supporting their side while also anticipating counterarguments. For example, a debate might center on the impact of technology on mental health, with students using evidence to support their stance.
- **Peer review exercises:** Have students swap research papers or essays with a classmate and perform a peer review. They should focus on assessing the strength of the evidence supporting the thesis and the validity of the arguments. This exercise teaches students to critique constructively and consider different perspectives.
- **Role-playing simulations:** Create a simulation in which students must adopt the role of a professional within a field—such as a scientist, journalist, or policymaker—and make decisions based on the evidence presented to them. This could involve a scenario where they act as city council members deciding on a new public policy, requiring them to sift through various data and reports to make an informed decision.

In addition, students can evaluate evidence anytime they're reading, engaging with a lesson, working on a project, researching for a paper, and so on. Figure 9.1 provides a checklist you can use with students.

- ☐ **Identify what constitutes evidence:** Any item of information that supports a claim or answers a question is evidence. Examples include numerical data, expert quotes, or firsthand accounts.
- ☐ **Evaluate the evidence:** Apply the principles of the scientific method and consider any potential biases when evaluating the evidence.
- ☐ **Pose inquiries:** Ask intelligent questions that promote critical analysis of the available evidence.
- ☐ **Analyze data:** Investigate data sets for patterns or trends and look for logical flaws in arguments.
- ☐ **Assess the sources:** Determine where the information came from, how reliable it is, and whether the author has any biases or conflicts of interest that could affect the perspective conveyed in an article.
- ☐ **Affirm the questions or problems that were posed:** Acknowledge the importance of the questions raised and reflect on whether they demonstrated critical thinking.
- ☐ **Put suggestions into action:** Collaborate to come up with possible solutions. Encourage students to try out one of the new ideas mentioned in discussions with classmates or teachers.

Figure 9.1: Evidence evaluation checklist.

Visit go.SolutionTree.com/instruction for a free reproducible version of this figure.

By integrating these activities into your curriculum, you help students develop a systematic approach to evaluating evidence. They learn not only to recognize robust evidence but also to question and verify information before accepting it as true. These skills are vital for their academic growth and for navigating the increasingly complex information landscape they will encounter outside the classroom.

Encourage Insightful Questions

We can help students become more informed decision makers and better equipped to make sound judgments based on facts rather than emotion or opinion if we teach them how to evaluate evidence through inquiry and ask good questions. It takes practice and skill to be able to ask insightful questions. Helping your students get better at asking questions is one of the most important things you can do for them as a teacher. However, the first thing that we can demonstrate to students is that they should never stop questioning things. The one who asks the most questions and reflects on those questions is the person who is learning the most. You are presenting students with examples of how to ask appropriate questions that stretch their thinking and require greater levels of reflection when you model collaborative dialogue.

You can use the following strategies during classroom discussions and encourage students to do the same.

- **Request responses and reflection:** When students articulate their thoughts and back them with evidence, they practice the critical assessment of that evidence. They learn to not just form opinions but to substantiate them, an essential skill in evidence evaluation. For example, after a student presents an idea, ask them to explain what evidence supports their conclusion and how they arrived at their reasoning.

- **Encourage follow-up questions:** By not accepting the first response as definitive, students learn to dig deeper. This practice is vital for evaluating evidence thoroughly, prompting them to look beyond surface-level information and assess the robustness of the evidence presented. For example, if a student answers a question, prompt them with, "Can you explain further or provide more details on why you think this is the case?"

- **Listen before answering:** Attentively listening to others' contributions before responding teaches students to consider multiple perspectives, an approach crucial for critical evaluation of evidence. For example, have students summarize their peer's argument before adding their own points to ensure they fully understand their peer's perspective.

- **Respond to agreements or disagreements:** When students express their agreement or disagreement with evidence presented by others, they practice evidence evaluation. They learn to discern the quality and relevance of evidence in supporting arguments. For example, encourage students to state why they agree or disagree with a point made and what evidence supports their stance.

- **Bring up related thoughts:** This emphasizes the importance of connecting ideas, which is fundamental to evaluating evidence. By introducing related thoughts and continuing the dialogue, students engage in comparative evaluation, enhancing their ability to discern the strength of different pieces of evidence. For example, ask students to relate the current discussion to previous lessons or concepts, exploring connections and contrasts.

The exchange of ideas through questioning and dialogue is essential in developing critical thinking and evidence-evaluation skills. Two-way dialogues that invite a multitude of ideas and perspectives enrich students' understanding and prompt them to apply evidence-based reasoning in a more engaged and rigorous manner. These strategies serve as practical tools to embed the principles of evidence evaluation within classroom discussions, enhancing students' analytical skills and preparing them for complex problem-solving tasks.

We should constantly reevaluate our convictions as critical thinkers as our fields advance and the environment we live in changes. By discussing these numerous points of view and the many values they represent as a class, students learn how to accept a range of contradicting ideas seriously. Through assignments, class discussions, and research projects that demand putting aside preferred viewpoints to seek out and consider a variety of legitimate evidence and claims about an idea to see it in all of its complexities and produce more integrated and relevant thinking, students need explicit practice in trying on these multiple stances.

MARIE CURIE EVALUATES EVIDENCE

Marie Curie, a pioneering scientist, left an indelible mark on the world with her groundbreaking research on radioactivity. A two-time Nobel Prize winner in both physics and chemistry, Curie's meticulous approach to scientific investigation underscores the essential habit of evaluating evidence. Her journey from struggling student in Poland to revered scientist in France exemplifies the importance of rigorous data analysis and the pursuit of truth.

Marie Curie's pioneering research on radioactivity—a term she coined—involved painstakingly processing tons of pitchblende to isolate mere grams of the new elements polonium and radium. Her rigorous scientific process demanded precise measurements, exhaustive observations, and continuous verification of data. It was this unwavering commitment to evaluating evidence and reevaluating her methodologies that led to her groundbreaking discoveries. Her detailed notebooks, some of which remain radioactive and are stored in lead-lined boxes, stand as a testament to her meticulous approach and serve as a chronicle of her dedication to understanding the mysteries of the atomic world.

Naomi, a tenth-grade student inspired by Curie's legacy, decides to embark on a project exploring the effect of different light conditions on plant growth. Emulating Curie's thoroughness, Naomi meticulously records her observations, regularly photographs her samples, and seeks peer reviews of her methodologies. As she compiles her data, she identifies anomalies and decides to rerun portions of her experiment to ensure accuracy. Her detailed final report doesn't just present findings; it also offers an introspection into the experimental process, challenges

> faced, and their resolutions, underscoring the importance of evaluating evidence in scientific inquiry.
>
> Both Marie Curie and Naomi emphasize the importance of critically evaluating evidence in their pursuits. Curie's relentless scrutiny of her experimental results and Naomi's dedication to ensuring the accuracy of her findings highlight the pivotal role of evaluation in drawing meaningful conclusions. Through their stories, we're reminded that the rigor of the process is as crucial as the discoveries themselves, urging learners to consistently question, validate, and refine their understanding based on the evidence at hand.

Implement and Differentiate an Easy Activity to Nurture Evaluating Evidence in K–12 Students

Developing the skill to critically evaluate evidence is a fundamental part of a student's educational journey, serving as the cornerstone for informed decision making and rational thought. In an age where information is as varied in quality as it is abundant, the ability to discern the credible from the questionable is more important than ever. As educators, our role is to introduce, develop, and refine this skill across all grade levels, ensuring students can approach evidence with a discerning eye. By carefully crafting age-appropriate activities, we create opportunities for students to practice and master this essential skill in a way that resonates with their stage of cognitive development. What follows is an adaptable activity framework, designed with the understanding that as students progress through their education, their ability to engage with and evaluate evidence should similarly advance.

Elementary School Students

Introduce the concept of evidence evaluation through a "mystery box." Place an object in a box so students cannot see it. Provide a series of clues, some true and some false, about the object. Ask students to determine which clues are reliable and make guesses about what's inside.

- Prepare a set of clues about the object, ensuring a mix of accurate and inaccurate statements.
- Present the clues one by one and discuss with the class which could be true or false, encouraging them to explain their reasoning.
- After presenting all the clues, have a class vote on what students think is in the box before revealing the object.
- Reflect on the activity by discussing which clues were misleading and which helped in evaluating the mystery object accurately.

Middle School Students

Develop critical analysis skills with a "detective case files" activity. Create a fictional crime scene with a variety of evidence for students to analyze. Students must use their reasoning to piece together the evidence and solve the case.

- Create a scenario with a set of evidence, witness statements, and red herrings.
- Have students work in groups to evaluate the reliability of each piece of evidence.
- Ask each group to present their hypothesis based on the evidence they have deemed credible.
- Conclude by discussing which pieces of evidence were most helpful and why some could be discounted.

High School Students

For high school students, organize a research-based debate. Students will research a given topic, gather evidence, and present their findings to support their stance, while also critically evaluating the opposition's evidence.

- Assign a controversial topic and divide students into pro and con groups.
- Task each group to research and gather evidence, then present their arguments in a structured debate format.
- During the debate, encourage students to question the evidence presented by the opposing side critically.
- After the debate, have students reflect on the strengths and weaknesses of the evidence presented by both sides.

By progressively building on these activities, students from kindergarten to twelfth grade can develop and refine their ability to evaluate evidence, which is essential for critical thinking and informed decision making.

Concluding Thoughts

We have navigated through the foundational skills of asking critical questions and moved toward understanding how such inquiry can lead to a deeper evaluation of evidence. This process, rooted in a healthy skepticism and an open mind, allows learners and evaluators alike to grow through comparison and contrast of different viewpoints and data. The practice of critical thinking, as emphasized throughout this chapter, requires us to temporarily suspend our biases and entertain a variety of perspectives. By fostering an environment where multiple viewpoints are not just tolerated but are genuinely considered, we catalyze the growth of our students as evaluators who can dissect arguments, discern the quality of evidence, and construct well-reasoned conclusions. In this way, we equip them with the necessary tools to not only thrive in academic settings but to become informed and thoughtful citizens.

Remember, critical thinking is not innate—it is learned and honed. It flourishes in settings that encourage questioning and where students can explore diverse viewpoints without apprehension. In bringing various perspectives into harmony within the classroom, we encourage students to embrace complexity and engage in thoughtful discourse.

The skills they develop will not only serve them in their academic pursuits but will also enable them to navigate the myriad challenges of the modern world.

Thus, as we conclude, let us recommit to the cause of nurturing inquisitive minds that are capable of rigorous evaluation and open to the insights that such evaluations reveal. In doing so, we affirm our dedication to creating a learning space that values the exchange of ideas and the rigorous analysis of evidence. Through this commitment, we aspire to inspire a new generation of learners—learners who can think critically, act wisely, and participate fully in the ongoing dialogue that shapes our society.

The noblest pleasure is the joy of understanding.

—LEONARDO DA VINCI

Chapter 10

Habit 9: Embrace Lifelong Learning and Perseverance

As we embark on the exploration of habit 9, embracing lifelong learning and perseverance, it's fitting to pause and reflect on the cohesive tapestry we've woven with the previous eight habits. Each habit, unique in its essence, threads together to fortify the fabric of learning, equipping students with a multidimensional skill set that enhances their ability to absorb, process, and apply knowledge effectively.

From the outset with habit 1, cultivate diverse curiosity, we've laid the groundwork for an expansive and exploratory approach to knowledge, allowing students to cast wide intellectual nets and reel in a wealth of understanding from various disciplines. This set the stage for habit 2, take risks, which encourages students to step beyond the comfort of the familiar, propelling them into realms of learning where true innovation and discovery lie. With habit 3, use humor, we infuse learning with the joy and engagement that comes from wit, easing the way into more profound insights. Following this, with habit 4, create and innovate, students are not just receivers of information but become creators, actively constructing knowledge and solutions, applying their ingenuity to real-world situations.

As students journey through learning, habit 5, self-regulate, ensures they are equipped to navigate the emotional and cognitive challenges they encounter, fostering resilience and introspection. Habit 6, transfer learning, emphasizes the interconnectedness of knowledge, encouraging students to weave together insights from various contexts to create a richer tapestry of understanding. The threads of inquiry and skepticism are then brought forth in habit 7, ask questions, and habit 8, evaluate evidence. These habits underscore the importance of curiosity and critical thinking, challenging students to delve deeper and substantiate their knowledge with well-founded evidence.

Now, arriving at habit 9, we recognize that the true essence of education lies not just in the acquisition of facts but in fostering an enduring spirit of learning and the grit to persevere through challenges. It is the resilience developed through perseverance and the adaptability fostered by a commitment to lifelong learning that truly equip students to succeed—not only within the walls of a classroom but also as they navigate the broader world.

This chapter invites educators and students alike to see learning as a journey without end, where perseverance is as crucial as the knowledge we carry with us. It's an empowering reminder that education is a dynamic and lifelong endeavor, with each habit playing a pivotal role in shaping competent, curious, and resilient individuals. Students of all ages would benefit from developing the vital life skill of perseverance. It is the capacity to carry on despite encountering obstacles and experiencing failure. Students can develop resilience, self-confidence, and a sense of success by learning how to persevere, which can be taught to students in the classroom. Additionally, it may assist them in becoming more successful in school as well as in life. In this chapter, we will review the different ways in which educators might instill a sense of perseverance in their students, including fostering a growth mindset, implementing goal-setting strategies, encouraging reflective practice, and using constructive feedback. The following strategies help develop these aims, and in using them, educators can better equip their students to embrace lifelong learning and the inevitable challenges that come with it.

Establish Objectives

The first thing that educators must do to teach students perseverance is to support them in developing goals that are both attainable and worthwhile. The goals that students set should be SMART.

- **Specific:** Goals should be clear and specific to provide students with direction. Instead of setting a goal like "get better at math," help students define exactly what they want to achieve. For example, "Improve my grade in algebra from a B to an A by the end of the semester."

- **Measurable:** A goal must have criteria for measuring progress. If students can't measure it, they can't manage it. For instance, if a student's goal is to read more, a measurable goal would be "Read one book every month." This allows them to track their progress clearly.

- **Attainable:** Goals need to be realistic and attainable. While it's good to encourage students to dream big, their goals should be within reach. For example, if a student is struggling with basic algebra, a goal like "Complete all algebra homework assignments on time and attend after-school tutoring once a week" is attainable and sets a clear path to improvement.

- **Relevant:** The goals should matter to the student and align with other relevant goals. We need to ensure that the goal taps into the student's interests and aspirations. For example, if a student is passionate about the environment, a relevant goal could be "Start a recycling program at school by the end of the year."

- **Time bound:** Every goal needs a target date so that there is a deadline to focus on. This part of the SMART goal criteria helps to prevent everyday tasks from taking priority over longer-term goals. An example could be "Learn to type forty words per minute by the end of the quarter."

When setting goals, it is beneficial for students to do the following.

- Write down their goals to make them tangible.
- Break down larger goals into smaller, actionable steps.
- Review their goals regularly, with teacher guidance, and adjust as necessary.
- Celebrate, with teacher support, small successes along the way to maintain motivation.

When working with students to develop goals, it is essential to stress that those objectives should center on something they are enthusiastic about and that they are prepared to put in a lot of effort to achieve. They will be more motivated to keep going even when things get challenging because of this. The process of accomplishing a goal requires help and encouragement from teachers, which you should provide throughout. This may involve providing feedback on progress or offering words of support when things become challenging. Furthermore, it is essential for educators to demonstrate tenacity by demonstrating their own dedication to accomplishing their objectives. Students will gain a better understanding of how they can attain success via consistent effort and dedication as a result.

Let's take the example of a student, Alex, who wishes to improve his writing skills. A SMART goal for Alex might be, "By the end of the semester, I will write three well-structured essays that receive a grade of at least B+, attending two writing workshops per month and meeting with my teacher biweekly for feedback." This goal is specific (well-structured essays, grade of B+), measurable (three essays, two workshops per month, biweekly meetings), attainable (with dedicated effort and support), relevant (improves writing skills), and time bound (by the end of the semester).

By incorporating these elements of SMART goal setting into your teaching practices, you can support students in creating meaningful and attainable goals that encourage persistence and the pursuit of excellence. This process not only aids in achieving specific objectives but also fosters a mindset geared toward growth and continuous improvement.

Cultivate an Environment for Effort

To teach perseverance effectively, a supportive and constructive learning environment is paramount. Within this space, students must feel comfortable experimenting, taking calculated risks, and sometimes failing, knowing that their efforts are valued. The role of the educator is to model respect and foster a culture that not just tolerates, but encourages asking questions, challenging norms, and exploring uncharted territories of thought. For example, when students work collaboratively on a science experiment, the focus should be on the collaborative process and scientific inquiry, not just the correctness of the result.

Regular opportunities to engage in problem solving teach students the tenacity needed to tackle complex issues. These can range from mathematical puzzles that require iterative attempts to thematic group discussions that challenge students to find consensus or create solutions to social issues. For example, students complete a history project where they research and propose solutions to a historical conflict, considering the perspectives of all parties involved. By structurally embedding such activities into the curriculum, students naturally develop resilience as they navigate various challenges.

Recognizing effort over outcomes is crucial in teaching perseverance. Students should understand that while achieving goals is important, the dedication and hard work they put in are equally valuable. This approach reinforces the intrinsic value of learning and the importance of persistent effort. Teachers can implement this by creating a wall of effort (as opposed to a wall of fame) that publicly acknowledges students' efforts, or by providing personalized feedback that highlights the diligence and strategies the student employs, rather than just the grade achieved. Such recognition should not be limited to academic achievements but extended to include the effort put into all aspects of school life. For instance, recognizing a student who has shown improvement in participation or helped peers sends a powerful message that all efforts toward personal and communal growth are noticed and valued.

These strategies collectively create an educational ecosystem that not only values the end product but also cherishes the learning journey. By linking respect, problem solving, effort recognition, and a supportive environment, educators can instill in students the grit needed to persevere and the curiosity that fuels lifelong learning. This holistic approach ensures that students are not just prepared for the exams they will face in school but are also equipped with the resilience and love for learning that they will need throughout life.

In cultivating an environment that champions effort, it is indeed fitting to incorporate strategies or facets that directly contribute to this goal. Two such pivotal facets are teaching self-reflection and supporting students in overcoming anxiety of public speaking. These are not peripheral elements but central to fostering a culture that recognizes and values effort. Here's how you can introduce and integrate these facets into the environment for effort.

Teach Self-Reflection

Self-reflection is an integral skill in the pursuit of lifelong learning and the cultivation of perseverance. To establish this connection, it's important to highlight how self-reflection aids students in recognizing their learning patterns, assessing their challenges, and developing strategies to overcome obstacles. Emphasize that self-reflection is not a passive activity; rather, it is a dynamic process that prompts learners to engage actively with their educational journey.

When you teach self-reflection, you empower students to take charge of their learning. This self-empowerment is a cornerstone of perseverance. Students who reflect are better equipped to identify the strategies that work for them, understand the reasons behind their setbacks, and devise plans to move forward. Such metacognitive skills are vital for lifelong learning, as they lay the foundation for continuous improvement and adaptation.

Moreover, the ability to self-regulate through self-reflection directly feeds into a student's capacity to persevere. By understanding their emotions and reactions to various academic challenges, students can manage their motivation and maintain their focus on long-term goals, despite short-term difficulties. They learn that setbacks are part of the learning process, and by analyzing their own experiences, they can develop resilience, adapt their methods, and persist in their educational endeavors.

Therefore, as part of your curriculum, integrate activities that encourage students to reflect on their learning experiences regularly. For instance, after completing a task or project, have students write a brief reflection on what they learned, challenges they faced, and how they overcame them. Offer various templates and frameworks to guide their self-assessment, allowing them to understand and articulate their learning process. This approach not only helps them to see the value of persistence but also ingrains a habit of lifelong learning, as they continuously seek to understand and improve themselves.

Additionally, provide students with tools for collecting and charting their own behavior data to monitor changes in those behaviors. Utilize various tools (for example, charts, templates, feedback displays) that depict progress in a manner that is both understandable and timely. Students can use checklists to monitor their own progress in meeting goals related to their behaviors. The checklists should include items that are specific to the student's goals and behaviors. To effectively monitor and encourage the development of desired behaviors in students, a behavior tracking chart can be a simple grid that allows students to add a sticker or a check mark each day they meet a specific behavioral goal, such as "raised hand to speak" or "completed homework on time." Progress trackers are another tool, often in the form of a bar graph or line chart, where students can visually map their progress over time toward a particular goal, like increasing the number of books read or improving test scores in a subject area.

Digital apps can also provide a platform for behavior monitoring, offering interactive and engaging ways for students to track their habits. These apps might include features for setting goals, receiving reminders, and viewing progress reports, which can be particularly motivating for tech-savvy students.

Additionally, reflective journals can be a valuable aid, providing a space for students to write daily or weekly reflections on their behaviors, note strategies that were effective, and plan how to overcome any challenges faced. This encourages metacognitive skills of self-evaluation and planning.

Incorporating these tools into classroom routines not only helps students track their behaviors and progress but also teaches them valuable organizational and self-assessment skills that are essential for lifelong learning and perseverance.

Support Students in Overcoming Public Speaking Anxiety

Public speaking is a skill that, when developed, can significantly enhance a student's perseverance in learning. The act of speaking in front of others requires one to confront and overcome internal barriers, such as anxiety and fear, which builds resilience. As students practice public speaking, they learn to persist through initial discomfort, developing confidence not only in their oratory abilities but also in their capacity to tackle other challenging learning scenarios. This resilience transfers to various aspects of their education, encouraging them to face academic challenges with the same tenacity. Moreover, public speaking necessitates preparation and the acquisition of knowledge, which aligns with the principles of lifelong learning. Each speaking opportunity becomes a microcosm of the larger learning process, where research, organization, practice, and reflection are key components. Supporting students in overcoming their fear of public speaking, therefore, does more than just prepare them for presentations; it instills in them the qualities necessary to persist in their learning journey. This section will explore strategies and techniques to help students build this crucial skill, ultimately contributing to their development of perseverance in learning.

The brain controls your body, but your body can also influence the brain. Simple physical actions can "hack" your brain and help you regain control over your nerves. However, understanding how stress manifests in the body is crucial. Fear and excitement are distinct emotions, but our bodies perceive them similarly, activating the autonomic nervous system (ANS). The ANS regulates functions like heart rate, digestion, and respiratory rate and is divided into the sympathetic nervous system, responsible for the fight-or-flight response, and the parasympathetic nervous system, responsible for the rest-and-digest response.

When faced with a public speaking scenario, the sympathetic nervous system activates, increasing heart rate and releasing adrenaline to prepare your body to respond. Understanding the role of the ANS can help students manage stress by using techniques to stimulate the parasympathetic nervous system and induce calm.

Although merely being aware of this fact can help control stress, neuroscientists suggest taking it a step further. People can decrease the physical responses caused by stress by consciously controlling their body and breath. In a learning environment, managing anxiety involves reducing stress and equipping students with strategies to perform under pressure. The ability to control physiological responses to anxiety is a powerful skill that can enhance students' academic performance and well-being. We are all familiar with taking a long, slow breath to ease our nerves. Conscious breathing is a simple yet effective technique to manage stress and anxiety, which can significantly impact students' stress levels and their ability to focus and perform under pressure. This chapter has highlighted the importance of creating a supportive learning environment that fosters resilience and perseverance. Integrating conscious breathing into your teaching practice aligns perfectly with these goals.

Encourage students to practice conscious breathing by focusing on taking deep, deliberate breaths to maximize oxygen intake and release tension. Here's a simple method to guide them.

1. **Inhale deeply:** Breathe in slowly and deeply through your nose, filling your lungs completely.
2. **Pause briefly:** Hold your breath for a moment to allow oxygen to fully saturate your lungs.
3. **Exhale slowly:** Breathe out slowly and completely through your mouth, releasing all the air from your lungs.

Practicing this method can quickly activate the body's relaxation response, counteracting the rapid heart rate and shallow breathing associated with anxiety. By teaching students this simple yet powerful breathing exercise, you can provide them with a tool to self-regulate their stress response in various academic settings, from presenting in front of the class to taking an exam.

Integrating such techniques into the classroom not only addresses immediate anxiety but also promotes lifelong skills in managing stress and cultivating perseverance in learning. This approach supports the broader objective of helping students develop the habit of transfer learning, as it equips them with strategies to remain calm and focused, enabling them to apply their knowledge and skills more effectively in diverse and challenging situations.

By making conscious breathing a regular part of your classroom routine, you create an environment where students can practice and refine their stress management techniques. This not only enhances their current academic performance but also prepares them for future challenges, reinforcing the idea that learning is a dynamic and lifelong journey. Through this practice, you help students build resilience and self-confidence, essential components of a successful and fulfilling educational experience.

Nurture Collaboration and Community

Learning to think interdependently is a skill students should cultivate as lifelong learners. Enhanced cooperation and understanding can lead to solutions that are advantageous to all humans. I also believe strongly that interdependent thinking cultivates constructive connections and provides a more harmonious educational setting. By adopting an interdependent mindset, students may better understand the needs and viewpoints of others and collaborate with them to reach a common objective. It entails realizing that our choices and actions affect other people and that we frequently function as part of a wider system or network of interactions. Students who think interdependently see their classmates' value and can cooperate with others to attain common goals. They can empathize with others and adjust their behavior accordingly. The ability to think collaboratively is useful in professional, academic, and interpersonal settings. The capacity to work well with others and coordinate actions toward a shared objective is crucial for success in many team-based settings. It can also be significant when numerous persons or groups have a vested interest in a decision or outcome, since this increases the likelihood that everyone's voice will be heard and their concerns will be addressed. All students need to be able to communicate and work together productively within a learning community if they are to be successful in the 21st century. Although some learners will find this task simpler than others, accomplishing it should still be a priority for all students.

It is possible to significantly expand the number of opportunities for support by distributing mentoring through a carefully structured network of peers. This support includes both learning how to collaborate effectively and mastering academic content. A flexible rather than a fixed grouping structure enables better differentiation and multiple roles, in addition to offering opportunities to learn how to collaborate with others in the most efficient manner. Learners should have access to a variety of options for how to acquire and apply these essential skills. Establish collaborative learning groups that have well-defined aims, functions, and responsibilities, as follows.

- **Develop schoolwide programs that encourage and support positive behavior, making sure to differentiate the programs' goals and services:** Examples of such programs include the following.
  - → Positive behavioral interventions and supports (PBIS) improve school climate, reduces disciplinary incidents, and increases academic performance through regular training for teachers, consistent behavior expectations across the school, a system for tracking behavior data, and recognition programs for positive behavior.
  - → Social and emotional learning (SEL) programs enhance students' emotional well-being, improve academic outcomes, and reduce behavioral issues through curriculum integration, classroom activities that promote social-emotional skills, teacher training, and parent engagement initiatives.
  - → Mentorship programs build positive relationships, improve academic performance, and increase student engagement through regular mentor-mentee meetings, goal-setting activities, academic support sessions, and social events to foster relationships.
  - → Restorative practices reduce conflicts and behavioral issues, improve relationships among students and staff, and create a supportive school environment through restorative circles, conflict resolution training, peer mediation programs, and regular community-building activities.
  - → Schoolwide recognition programs motivate students to excel, create a positive school culture, and reinforce desired behaviors through monthly or quarterly awards ceremonies, recognition boards, certificates of achievement, and special privileges or rewards for recognized students.

- **Guide learners through the process of when and how to ask their peers or teachers for assistance:** Here is sample language for student instructions.
    - → Before beginning the work as a group, have a conversation with the other people in the group about the kinds of support you might require and how you might provide the most effective support for one another.
    - → If you find yourself unable to go on with the group work or in need of assistance, your first step should be to discuss potential solutions with the other members of your group.
    - → If you are still unable to devise a solution, ask your fellow students for assistance to understand the issue and the many options available for addressing it.
    - → If your group members are unable to give support, you should seek help from your teacher. Describe the issue and outline your previous efforts to find a solution.
    - → Once you have gotten assistance from either your classmates or the teacher, think about what you have learned and how you can use it in the next collaborative endeavors.
- **Construct communities of students who share interests or activities and encourage them to interact with one another:** For example, you can create a coding club where students interested in programming can collaborate on projects, share knowledge, and participate in coding challenges. This not only fosters a sense of community but also enhances their skills through peer learning and collaboration.
- **Set expectations for the work that all groups will do (for example, rubrics, norms, and so on):** Some students, but not all of them, find that working on prolonged projects and activities with other classmates helps maintain their interest in participating in those endeavors. This collaborative approach not only sustains their engagement but also instills essential skills of lifelong learning and perseverance.

By working together on long-term projects, students learn the value of persistence, the importance of teamwork, and the ability to overcome challenges—qualities that will serve them well throughout their educational journey and beyond.

CHARLES IGNATIUS SANCHO PERSEVERES

Charles Ignatius Sancho's life story is a testament to resilience, versatility, and the pursuit of enlightenment. Born on a slave-trader ship crossing the Atlantic, Sancho later became a free man in England and wore multiple hats: composer, writer, actor, and businessman. He stands out as one of the first Black Britons known to have voted in an election and is celebrated for his eloquent letters that shed light on 18th century Black British life, while simultaneously advocating against slavery and for the rights of Black individuals.

> Despite the societal challenges he faced as a Black individual in 18th century England, Sancho refused to be bound by the limitations placed on him. He educated himself and opened a grocery shop in Westminster, where he became a respected member of his community. His collection of letters not only showcases his literary talent but also offers valuable insights into the sociopolitical atmosphere of his time, demonstrating his active role in shaping public opinion against the abhorrent trade in human beings.
>
> Consider Sarai, a high school student of immigrant parents. She often faces cultural barriers and stereotyping at school. However, inspired by figures like Sancho, she uses her unique position to foster understanding. Sarai starts a project to document the oral histories of other immigrants in her community, highlighting their experiences, dreams, and contributions. By weaving these into a digital archive and creating a series of podcasts, Sarai brings to the fore unheard voices, thus challenging preconceived notions and building bridges.
>
> Charles Ignatius Sancho and Sarai both represent the strength of character and the drive to not only transcend societal boundaries but to also make a lasting positive impact. While Sancho leveraged his writing to challenge the establishment and uplift Black voices, Sarai utilizes modern technology to share immigrant stories, promoting inclusivity. Their tales are stark reminders that, regardless of one's background or the era in which one lives, perseverance paired with creativity can foster understanding and ignite meaningful change.

Implement and Differentiate an Easy Activity to Nurture Perseverance and Lifelong Learning in K–12 Students

To foster perseverance and lifelong learning across all grade levels, educators can implement a goal-setting activity called "My Learning Journey." This activity helps students set personal learning goals, reflect on their progress, and understand the value of resilience and adaptability in their educational growth. My Learning Journey is a structured activity tailored to guide students through the process of identifying, planning, and achieving their academic and personal growth goals. In this activity, students will articulate clear and actionable goals that are meaningful to them, breaking down these objectives into manageable steps. This strategy encourages them to become agents of their own learning, enhancing their self-awareness and ability to self-reflect.

As they engage with My Learning Journey, students are encouraged to maintain a growth mindset, recognizing that intelligence and ability can develop with effort, good strategies, and support from others. They will document their progress, reflect on successes, and identify areas for improvement, which promotes metacognitive skills. This reflection is critical as it helps students understand *how* they learn, not just *what* they learn.

This activity also serves as a platform for students to practice perseverance. By setting long-term goals and identifying short-term objectives, students can experience the process of persisting through challenges and setbacks. They learn to see mistakes not as failures, but as opportunities for learning and growth—essential components of lifelong learning.

Educators support students by providing regular check-ins and facilitating discussions about strategies that can help overcome obstacles. These conversations can lead to a deeper understanding of resilience, helping students internalize that perseverance is about continuing to move forward, even when progress seems slow.

Throughout My Learning Journey, students also celebrate their milestones, no matter how small. This positive reinforcement helps build confidence and motivation, reinforcing the value of their efforts and the personal satisfaction that comes from striving to meet their goals.

By participating in My Learning Journey, students from all grade levels develop a tool kit of strategies for effective learning that they can carry with them beyond the classroom. This activity not only aligns with academic curriculum goals but also supports the broader objective of preparing students to be adaptable, resilient, and lifelong learners.

Elementary School Students

For elementary students, My Learning Journey is an engaging, hands-on project that makes the abstract concept of goal setting tangible. Young learners start by choosing a goal that excites them, such as mastering a new reading level or learning a science concept. They then draw a winding road on a large poster board, which represents their journey toward this goal. Along this road, they mark significant milestones. These are minigoals, such as recognizing a certain number of sight words or completing a science assignment, that lead step by step to the end objective.

Students can decorate their roads with drawings and stickers that reflect the subject they're exploring, making the journey visually appealing and personally significant. Each time they reach a milestone, they can celebrate by adding a vibrant sticker or a bright star to that spot on the road, which serves as a visual reminder of their progress and the importance of consistent effort. The physical act of adding these markers reinforces the satisfaction of achieving each step, nurturing an early appreciation for perseverance. Teachers can incorporate these milestones into the classroom routine, allowing students to share their progress, thus creating a culture of encouragement and mutual support.

Middle School Students

Middle school students, who are developing greater independence and critical thinking skills, will benefit from a My Learning Journey booklet as it prompts deeper self-reflection. This personal booklet contains pages for different goals, each detailing a specific plan of action. For instance, a student aiming to improve their writing might set goals for submitting essays to writing contests or starting a blog. They note actionable steps, anticipated challenges, and potential solutions for each goal.

Students also set deadlines, creating a sense of urgency and accountability. This booklet becomes a living document that they can refer to, ensuring they stay on track with their objectives. Sharing these booklets with classmates allows for peer-to-peer learning and feedback, fostering a community where students learn from each other's journeys and strategies. Teachers can facilitate sessions where students discuss their experiences with goal setting, challenges they've faced, and how they've adapted their strategies, encouraging a collaborative learning environment.

High School Students

High school students, preparing for the independence of adulthood, can leverage technology to manage My Learning Journey. They use online tools to create a digital log of their goals, which could range from academic achievements to personal development targets like leadership skills. This digital format allows for flexibility and creativity; students can blog about their experiences, post video updates, or even create podcasts discussing their learning process.

The digital journey encourages students to be proactive and adaptable, traits essential for success in both higher education and the workplace. They also have the opportunity to explore digital literacy as they engage with various platforms and media, a key competence in the digital age. The process of regularly updating their digital journey encourages students to self-assess and adapt their approaches to learning, emphasizing the ongoing nature of personal and academic growth. Students can share their progress in regular class discussions or online forums, with students providing insights and support to one another, fostering an environment where perseverance is recognized and valued.

In all grade bands, My Learning Journey is a progressive activity that evolves with the students' age and abilities. It encourages regular reflection, reassessment, and the understanding that learning is a continuous journey with ups and downs. It also reinforces that the ability to persist leads to success.

Concluding Thoughts

We have come full circle, appreciating how the final habit of embracing lifelong learning and perseverance interlocks with the previous eight to form a robust framework for educational success. This chapter has emphasized that the journey of learning is perpetual and woven into the fabric of life itself, extending far beyond academic pursuits. From igniting diverse curiosities to cultivating the steadfastness required for taking risks, from the levity of humor to the boldness of creation and innovation, each habit progressively builds on the last. The critical skills of practicing self-regulation, transferring learning, asking questions, and evaluating evidence are not mere techniques but are the bedrock of a learner's mindset.

Now, with habit 9, we recognize that the true spirit of education is in nurturing an unwavering drive to learn and the resilience to persist through life's challenges. It is about equipping students with not just knowledge but the tenacity to apply it, adapt it, and advance it through all stages of life. We have explored practical strategies within this chapter to foster these traits. Each approach reinforces the idea that learning is a dynamic process that rewards persistence and adaptability.

As educators, parents, and mentors, the charge is clear: inculcate these habits within our students and ourselves, recognizing that each student's journey is unique yet universally requires encouragement, support, and the space to grow. This chapter has provided the tools and understanding necessary to cultivate a generation of learners who are not only well educated but well prepared for the undulating road of life's learning journey. Thus, we conclude this exploration of habits with the affirmation that learning is an endless adventure that demands continuous engagement, critical reflection, and the courage to persist. It is our collective responsibility to ensure that learners are not just passing through a phase of education but are embarking on a lifelong expedition of intellectual discovery and personal growth.

Part II

In part II, you will dive into the challenge-based framework, building on the nine habits of thinking that were the focus of part I. You will see how these habits are integral to structuring learning experiences that are authentic, interactive, and deeply connected to real-world contexts. This section guides you, step by step, in applying the challenge-based framework to create dynamic educational settings where students actively engage with their learning process.

You will learn how to articulate clear student goals, formulate essential questions that challenge and extend understanding, and integrate academic standards to ensure rigor and relevance. Furthermore, you will explore the *engineering design process* to foster a problem-solving mindset, underpin the importance of teacher and student practices, and understand the role of assessment in the challenge-based framework.

With each chapter, you'll gain deeper insights into implementing the challenge-based framework at various educational levels, learning to adjust and apply its components to suit the developmental stages of your students. This part of the book equips you with the knowledge to transform theoretical concepts into practical applications that will prepare your students to thrive in an interconnected and ever-changing world.

Chapter 11

Integrate the Challenge-Based Framework and the Habits of Thinking

Woven within the fabric of the challenge-based framework is an age-old allure of interconnected thinking, reminiscent of polymaths of the past, who saw no boundaries between art and science. Under the umbrella of the challenge-based framework, students are not merely passive recipients of fragmented knowledge but active explorers, seeking threads that tie together disparate fields of study. For instance, they might bridge the logical precision of mathematics with the creativity of computer coding or find an intersection between engineering principles and artistic creation. They could even leverage cutting-edge technology to decipher the mysteries of scientific data.

Using the challenge-based framework is not merely about igniting a polymath spirit; it is your structured pathway to weave the habits of thinking into the very fabric of learning. Within this framework, you'll guide students to apply their interdisciplinary skills in a cohesive, real-world context. To guide you through the essence of the challenge-based framework, this chapter unfolds a comprehensive exploration of the framework's structure and its transformative power in the learning environment. You will discover how the framework provides a scaffold for integrating habits of thinking into the curriculum, promoting a culture of inquiry and innovation. You'll learn the key components of the framework and witness its application through vivid classroom examples. We will explore the framework's flexibility, considering numerous examples of the framework set to a variety of different challenges, including challenges differentiated by grade band. Finally, the Concluding Thoughts section provides an opportunity to reflect on how the framework and habits can work together to deepen student learning.

The Anatomy of the Challenge-Based Framework

Every masterpiece is composed of individual brushstrokes, and the challenge-based framework is no exception. The following components are essential parts of the framework. Together they work to equip students with the skills, knowledge, and mindset to navigate and shape the world as compassionate, informed, and proactive citizens. The framework's components include the following.

- **Student goal:** The goal is the core of the framework. As teachers, it is our primary focus because it articulates precisely what we want students to achieve and understand.

- **Essential question:** The goal is followed by the indispensable essential question, which propels us headlong into the heart of the challenge. It presents a complex problem or situation for students to engage with, requiring investigation, critical thinking, and problem solving to navigate. This dilemma, whether posed by the instructor or discovered through inquiry by the students themselves, becomes the focal point of their exploration and drives their pursuit of knowledge and innovative solutions.

- **Standards integration:** This component aligns learning outcomes with broader educational objectives. It ensures that the challenge-based framework is not an insular approach but rather integrates seamlessly with established academic standards and the essential 21st century skills. This fusion ensures that while students are engaged in meeting real-world challenges, they are also achieving key curriculum milestones and building competencies such as critical thinking, collaboration, communication, and creativity that are crucial for success in today's dynamic world.

- **Engineering design process:** The engineering design process charts the course for student engagement with a project or challenge, delineating the sequence of actions for students to take. It is a deliberate method where students apply habits of thinking at each step. By incorporating these habits, students move from identifying problems to creating and refining solutions, transforming theoretical understanding into practical application. This iterative process not only fosters a deeper grasp of content but also hones the very skills necessary for innovation and problem solving in complex, real-world contexts.

The following sections cover the framework's components in detail.

Student Goal

The student goal articulates the desired outcome of the learning experience. It serves as a clear statement of intent, providing a target for students to aim for and a benchmark against which they can measure progress. In practice, this goal must be SMART to ensure it is meaningful for students. For instance, in a primary classroom, the goal might be as straightforward as "Design a simple machine using recycled materials," whereas for high school students, it could be more complex, like "Develop a sustainable business model for a local community business."

Arriving at the student goal can vary depending on the context and the specific needs of the students. As the following list notes, the process can be teacher driven, student driven, or a collaborative effort.

- **Teacher-driven goals:** In some cases, especially with younger students or when introducing a new concept, the teacher may set the goal to provide clear direction and structure. For example, the teacher might choose a goal like "Create a model of the solar system" for an elementary science class.
- **Student-driven goals:** As students develop more autonomy, they might set their own goals based on their interests and strengths. For instance, a high school student interested in environmental science might set a goal like "Investigate the impact of plastic waste in our local river and propose solutions."
- **Collaborative goals:** Often, the most effective goals are developed collaboratively. This approach ensures that the goal is both challenging and attainable, leveraging the strengths and interests of all group members. For example, in a group project on renewable energy, students might collectively decide to "Design and build a functional solar-powered device."

The process of choosing a goal, and who chooses it, may be even more finely parsed depending on the circumstances, such as outlined in the following list.

- **Teacher-guided situations:** The teacher might present several potential goals, connected to learning topics, for example, and facilitate a discussion to help students choose the most relevant and engaging one.
- **Student-led situations:** Students might brainstorm individually or in groups, then present their ideas to the class for feedback and refinement.
- **Collaborative situations:** A combination of teacher guidance and student input can be used to refine the goal, ensuring it is both meaningful and achievable.

The following list offers how-to pointers to apply when choosing goals.

- **Facilitate discussions:** Start with a brainstorming session where students can freely share their ideas. Use guiding questions to help focus their thinking.
- **Use the SMART criteria:** Teach students about the criteria for SMART goals and have students apply them to their proposed goals.
- **Encourage reflection:** Ask students to reflect on their interests, strengths, and areas they want to improve. This can help in setting a goal that is both motivating and challenging.
- **Provide examples:** Share examples of well-defined goals from previous projects to give students a clear idea of what they should aim for.
- **Iterate and refine:** Allow time for students to revise their goals based on feedback from peers and the teacher. This iterative process helps in honing a goal that is precise and attainable.
- **Document the goal:** Have students write down their goals and keep them visible throughout the project. Regularly revisit the goal to check on progress and make adjustments as needed.

By involving students in the goal-setting process, educators not only foster a sense of ownership and motivation but also teach important skills in planning, reflection, and self-assessment.

Essential Question

The essential question prompts deep thought, sparks curiosity, and drives the inquiry process. It is open ended, thought provoking, and aligned with the student goal, challenging students to think critically about significant issues.

In the template, the student goal comes first because it ties directly to the content standards students must address. The student goal articulates the desired outcome of the learning experience, providing a clear target and ensuring that educational standards are met. Once the student goal is established, the essential question is then derived from it to guide the inquiry process and provide context for the learning journey.

For instance, if the student goal is "Develop a sustainable business model to reduce plastic waste in our community," the essential question might be, "How can local businesses implement sustainable practices to reduce plastic waste?" This alignment ensures that the essential question is purposeful and directly supports students achieving their goal.

See figure 11.1 for an example of how to arrive at the essential question from a student goal that encompasses addressing learning standards.

- **Student Goal:** Develop a sustainable business model to reduce plastic waste in our community.
- **Content standards and learning outcomes:**
    - **Science standard:** Understand the impact of human activities on the environment and developing solutions to minimize negative effects (ESS3.C; NGSS Lead States, 2013).
    - **English language arts standard:** Conduct research to answer a question, drawing on several sources, and generating additional related, focused questions for further research and investigation (CCSS.ELA-LITERACY.W.11-12.7; National Governors Association Center for Best Practices & Council of Chief State School Officers, 2010a).
    - **Social studies standard:** Analyze economic principles and the role of businesses in addressing societal issues (National Council for the Social Studies, n.d.).
- **Essential Question:** How can local businesses implement sustainable practices to reduce plastic waste?

Once you and your students have arrived at an essential question, refining the question is often necessary. The following list offers how-to pointers for designing and refining essential questions.

- **Start with the student goal:** Begin by clearly defining the student goal, which is based on the content standards. This goal provides the foundation for the essential question.
    - **Example goal:** "Develop a sustainable business model to reduce plastic waste in our local community."
- **Identify key concepts:** Look at the key concepts and skills embedded in the student goal. These will help shape the essential question.
    - **Example concepts:** Sustainability, business practices, environmental impact
- **Make questioning open ended:** Ensure that questions cannot be answered with a simple "yes" or "no." Open-ended questions invite exploration and discussion.
    - **Example question:** Instead of asking, "Is plastic waste a problem?" ask, "What are some ways in which plastic waste can be a problem?"
- **Encourage critical thinking:** Craft questions that require students to analyze, synthesize, and evaluate information. A good essential question will challenge students to think deeply and consider multiple perspectives.
    - **Example question:** "What are the most effective strategies for local businesses to minimize their plastic waste footprint?"
- **Connect to real-world issues:** Align the question with real-world problems and applications. This connection makes the inquiry more meaningful and engaging for students.
    - **Example question:** "How can our community benefit from businesses reducing plastic waste?"
- **Align with learning goals:** Ensure that the essential question aligns with the overall learning goals and standards. The question should drive students toward achieving specific educational outcomes.
    - **Example alignments:** The essential question should help students explore the science of environmental impact, the economics of business practices, and the skills of conducting research and presenting findings.

- **Refine through collaboration:** Involve students in the process of refining the question. Encourage them to suggest modifications or additional questions that deepen the inquiry. This collaborative process helps to ensure that the question is relevant and engaging for all students.
  - → **Example refinement:** Have students brainstorm additional questions like, "What role can technology play in reducing plastic waste?" or "How can consumer behavior influence business practices?"
- **Use clear and precise language:** Avoid jargon or overly complex language. The question should be clear and understandable, prompting immediate engagement from students. For instance, consider the difference between these two versions of an essential question:
  - → **Jargony essential question:** "How does the application of algebraic principles facilitate the solving of univariate linear equations within various mathematical contexts?"
  - → **Straightforward essential question:** "How can we solve equations with one variable?"

    The straightforward question uses simple language that students can easily understand, allowing them to immediately grasp the concept and engage with the material. In contrast, the jargony question uses technical terms and complex sentence structures that may confuse students and hinder their understanding. By prioritizing clarity and simplicity in your language, you can make learning more effective and inclusive.
- **Be flexible:** Allow the question to evolve as the inquiry progresses. Sometimes, initial questions lead to new and deeper questions. Be open to refining the question to better suit the direction of the inquiry.
  - → **Example progression:** If students find new aspects of the issue during their research, adjust the essential question to incorporate these insights. A preliminary essential question might be, "How do plants grow?" After students learn more about their topic, they might ask, "How do different environmental factors affect plant growth?" And later still, they might ask, "How does this urban environment around our school, characterized by numerous buildings, asphalt surfaces with heat-holding properties, and various forms of human-dominated traffic influence plant growth?"

By following these pointers, teachers can design and refine essential questions that drive meaningful inquiry and align closely with student goals and learning objectives, ensuring a cohesive and purposeful learning experience.

Figure 11.1: Example of moving from a student goal to an essential question.

Standards Integration

Standards integration ensures that the learning experience aligns with educational benchmarks and that students are developing the necessary skills to meet academic requirements. This involves mapping the challenge-based activities to relevant content standards such as Common Core, Next Generation Science Standards, or other curricular guidelines.

The following five-step process of mapping standards can be undertaken individually or collaboratively with colleagues.

1. **Identify relevant standards:** Begin by identifying the content standards that are most relevant to the challenge. For example, if the challenge involves designing an efficient community space, identify mathematics standards related to geometric concepts and measurements.

2. **Align activities with standards:** Match each activity within the challenge-based project to specific standards. Ensure that the activities provide opportunities for students to practice and demonstrate the skills and knowledge outlined in the standards.

3. **Create a standards map:** Develop a visual or written map that clearly shows how each activity aligns with the standards. This map can serve as a guide for planning, instruction, and assessment.

4. **Collaborate with colleagues:** While some educators might choose to map standards individually, collaborating with colleagues can enhance the process. Working in teams allows for the sharing of expertise, resources, and ideas.

Collaborative planning sessions can ensure a comprehensive and coherent approach to standards integration.

5. **Review and adjust:** Continuously review and adjust the mapping as needed. Based on student feedback and assessment data, make modifications to ensure that all standards are being adequately addressed.

Following are two examples of standards integration mapping in challenge-based projects.

- **Challenge:** Apply geometric concepts to design a community space that efficiently supports multiple activities, including research, collaborative learning sessions, and community presentations.
    - **Mathematics standards:**
        i. **CCSS.MATH.CONTENT.HSG.CO.D.12:** Make geometric constructions (National Governors Association Center for Best Practices & Council of Chief State School Officers, 2010b)
        ii. **CCSS.MATH.CONTENT.HSG.MG.A.3:** Apply geometric methods to solve design problems (National Governors Association Center for Best Practices & Council of Chief State School Officers, 2010b)
    - **Activities:**
        i. Students use geometric tools to create design blueprints.
        ii. Students calculate areas and perimeters to optimize space usage.
        iii. Students present their designs and explain the geometric principles used.

- **Challenge:** Analyze the impact of a historical event on modern-day society, in this case, the impact of the building of the Union Pacific railroad on Indigenous economies in the Great Plains.
    - **Social studies standards:**
        i. **NCSS.D2.His.1.6-8:** Analyze connections between events and developments in broader historical contexts (National Governors Association Center for Best Practices & Council of Chief State School Officers, 2010a)
        ii. **NCSS.D2.His.3.6-8:** Use questions generated about individuals and groups to analyze why they, and the developments they shaped, are seen as historically significant (National Governors Association Center for Best Practices & Council of Chief State School Officers, 2010a)
    - **Activities:**
        i. Students research historical events and their long-term impacts.
        ii. Students create presentations or reports connecting historical events to current societal issues.
        iii. Students participate in debates or discussions on how history has shaped modern society.

Standards integration helps to maintain academic rigor within the framework, ensuring that students are engaged in meaningful and standards-aligned learning experiences. By collaborating with colleagues and continuously refining the mapping process, you can create well-rounded and effective challenge-based learning projects.

Engineering Design Process

The engineering design process is a series of steps that students follow to systematically solve a problem or meet a challenge. It echoes the processes used by engineers and designers, fostering a mindset of iteration, testing, and continuous improvement. It includes stages such as the following.

- **Ask:** Students identify the problem.
- **Imagine:** Students brainstorm possible solutions.
- **Plan:** Students develop a blueprint for their ideas.
- **Create:** Students construct or implement their solution.
- **Improve:** Students evaluate and refine their solutions.

At each stage, teacher practice supports student actions, facilitating a cycle of experiential learning and practical application. The relevance of this process in education is profound—it not only mimics the real-world problem-solving methods but also instills in students the skills of resilience, adaptability, and critical thinking, which are vital in any discipline or profession they choose to pursue. The steps of the engineering design process (annotated with pointers and tips for each step and overall) are as follows.

1. **Ask:** This is the initial stage in the process of designing a solution to a challenge. In this part of the lesson, students will determine an issue or a difficulty that they wish to overcome. They need to think critically about the issue at hand by posing questions about it and coming up with viable answers. This is the stage where you'd ask students an essential question or where students would create their own shared or individual essential question.

    a. *Pointer*—Encourage students to identify the problem clearly and gather information.

    b. *Helpful tip*—Use guiding questions like, "What problem are we trying to solve?" and "What do we need to know to solve this problem?

    c. *Activity example*—Research the impact of plastic waste in the community.

2. **Imagine:** The second phase in the process requires students to put their imaginations to work to come up with potential answers to the problem that they discovered in the first step. They need to evaluate a variety of approaches to the issue and think about how their proposed solution may really operate in the real world. If you need to teach specific content standards or skills, this is the stage you'll do that in. You can do this in whole-group or small-group settings; for instance, you can teach the content one small group at a time while other students are working in collaborative groups on their challenge. The intent is for the learning to transfer to the next phases of the process.

    a. *Pointer*—Brainstorm possible solutions and think creatively.

    b. *Helpful tip*—Create a safe space for brainstorming where all ideas are welcome. Encourage wild and creative ideas without immediate judgment.

    c. *Activity example*—Generate ideas on how to reduce plastic waste in local businesses.

3. **Plan:** Once students have determined a possible solution to the problem, they may move on to planning how to implement the answer. This involves conducting research on the essential materials and tools, developing a schedule for the challenge's completion, and detailing any actions necessary for the effective execution of their solution.

    a. *Pointer*—Develop a detailed plan for the chosen solution.

    b. *Helpful tip*—Use tools like flowcharts, diagrams, and checklists to organize thoughts and outline steps.

    c. *Activity example*—Outline the steps to implement a recycling program in local businesses.

4. **Create:** This is the step when students really put their idea into action by constructing their answer (in the form of a design, product, presentation, and so on) with the help of the resources and tools they discovered in the planning stage. They should document their progress in case they need to refer back to it later on in the process.

    a. *Pointer*—Implement the plan and build the solution.

    b. *Helpful tip*—Provide resources and materials needed for creation. Allow students to experiment and make adjustments as they work.

    c. *Activity example*—Design and distribute recycling bins and educational materials to local businesses.

5. **Improve:** Once the students have completed their solution, they should analyze it and make any adjustments or improvements depending on what they discovered when testing or implementing their project. Before putting the finishing touches on the project and showing it to others for their comments or ratings, improvement is an essential step since it resolves any problems.

    a. *Pointer*—Test the solution and make improvements based on feedback.

    b. *Helpful tip*—Encourage peer reviews and iterative testing. Ask questions like, "What worked well?" and "What can we do better?"

    c. *Activity example*—Collect feedback from businesses and community members, then refine the recycling program based on their input.

As part of the challenge-based framework, the engineering design process is not just a sequence of actions; it's a mindset that students adopt to approach problems systematically, mirroring the iterative nature of professional practices in fields spanning from engineering to social innovation. This process teaches students to be not just problem solvers but problem finders, creators, and refiners. It's an educational spiral where each step builds on the previous, and knowledge is deepened through application and reflection.

As educators, you will guide students through this spiral, reinforcing the idea that learning is not linear but cyclical. Each iteration through the engineering design process empowers students to refine their understanding, improve their creations, and think more deeply about the implications of their work. By embedding these practices in the classroom, you are preparing your students to navigate a world where challenges are complex, solutions are not immediately apparent, and perseverance is key to innovation. This dynamic, fluid approach to learning encapsulates the heart of the challenge-based framework, fostering not only academic growth but the development of essential life skills. Through the engineering design process, the challenge-based framework develops learners who are ready to tackle the multifaceted challenges of tomorrow with confidence, competence, and creativity.

> **ADDITIONAL TIPS FOR EDUCATORS USING THE ENGINEERING DESIGN PROCESS**
>
> ☐ **Start small:** Begin with a simple challenge to familiarize students with the engineering design process. Gradually introduce more complex problems as their confidence and skills grow.
>
> ☐ **Facilitate collaboration:** Encourage students to work in teams. Collaboration fosters diverse perspectives and helps students develop communication and teamwork skills.
>
> ☐ **Integrate reflection:** After each iteration of the engineering design process, have students reflect on what they learned. Reflection helps deepen understanding and reinforces the cyclical nature of learning.
>
> ☐ **Use real-world problems:** Connect classroom activities to real-world issues. This makes learning relevant and engaging for students.
>
> ☐ **Provide continuous support:** Offer guidance and support at each stage of the engineering design process. Be available to answer questions and provide resources.
>
> ☐ **Celebrate successes and failures:** Celebrate both successes and failures as part of the learning process. Encourage a growth mindset by showing that mistakes are opportunities for learning.

Challenge-Based Instruction and Habits Integration

The interplay between habits of thinking and the challenge-based framework is fundamental since these habits animate the framework and give it life in practice. As educators, you weave these habits into each element of the framework, ensuring they are not simply things you teach but are lived and experienced by students. Weaving the habits means integrating them into daily activities and interactions, creating a learning environment where these habits are consistently practiced and reinforced.

Examples of weaving the nine habits of thinking into the framework include the following (figure 11.2).

---

1. **Cultivating diverse curiosity:**
    a. **In practice:** During the Ask phase of the engineering design process, encourage students to explore multiple sources of information and perspectives. Use activities like research projects and interviews with experts to broaden their understanding.
    b. **Activity example:** Have students interview community members or professionals related to their project to gain diverse insights and spark curiosity.

Figure 11.2: The nine habits of thinking in the challenge-based framework.

continued →

2. **Taking risks:**
    a. **In practice:** In the Imagine phase, create a safe space for brainstorming where all ideas are welcome. Encourage students to propose bold and innovative solutions without fear of failure.
    b. **Activity example:** Conduct a brainstorming session where students generate as many ideas as possible, emphasizing that no idea is too far-fetched.
3. **Using humor:**
    a. **In practice:** Integrate humor into classroom discussions and activities to create a positive and engaging learning environment. Use humor to make complex concepts more relatable.
    b. **Activity example:** Use humorous videos or skits to introduce a challenging topic, making it more accessible and enjoyable for students.
4. **Creating and innovating:**
    a. **In practice:** During the Create phase, encourage students to think outside the box and experiment with different materials and methods. Provide opportunities for artistic expression and creative problem solving.
    b. **Activity example:** Organize a maker space where students can use various materials to make prototypes of their ideas.
5. **Self-regulating:**
    a. **In practice:** Teach students to set goals and monitor their progress. Use reflection journals and self-assessment tools to help them develop self-regulation skills.
    b. **Activity example:** Have students keep a reflection journal where they regularly record their progress, challenges, and strategies for improvement.
6. **Transferring learning:**
    a. **In practice:** Help students apply what they have learned in one context to new and different situations. Use cross-curricular projects to reinforce this habit.
    b. **Activity example:** Design a project that combines science and art, such as creating a scientific illustration, to help students transfer skills between subjects.
7. **Asking questions:**
    a. **In practice:** Foster a culture of inquiry ecouraging students to ask deep, meaningful questions throughout the learning process. Use questioning techniques to guide exploration and discovery.
    b. **Activity example:** Implement a "question of the day" routine where students come up with a thought-provoking question related to their current project.
8. **Evaluating evidence:**
    a. **In practice:** Teach students to critically evaluate the sources and validity of the information they gather. Use activities that require analysis and evidence-based reasoning.
    b. **Activity example:** Conduct a source-evaluation workshop where students assess the reliability and relevance of different information sources.
9. **Embracing lifelong learning and perseverance:**
    a. **In practice:** Encourage a growth mindset and resilience. Highlight the importance of perseverance through challenges and continuous learning.
    b. **Activity example:** Share stories of famous innovators who overcame failures and persisted, and have students reflect on how they can apply similar perseverance in their projects.

By integrating these habits into every phase of the challenge-based framework, you create a dynamic learning environment where students not only learn academic content but also develop essential life skills. This approach ensures that these habits are not just abstract concepts but are actively practiced and embodied in the students' daily learning experiences.

For each component of the framework—student goal, essential question, standards integration, and engineering design process—the habits of thinking provide a metacognitive layer guiding teacher actions and supporting student behaviors. Examples of how this might work include the following.

- **Student goal:** By cultivating diverse curiosity (habit 1), teachers encourage students to set goals that are broad in scope and rich in possibility, while students themselves take risks (habit 2) by setting ambitious targets that stretch their capabilities and understanding.
- **Essential question:** The practice of asking questions (habit 7) becomes central as teachers model how to formulate questions that probe deeply and meaningfully, and students evaluate evidence (habit 8) to refine their questions and ensure they are significant and relevant.
- **Standards integration:** Teachers employ transfer learning (habit 6) to connect academic standards to real-world challenges, while students use self-regulation (habit 5) to manage their learning processes and ensure alignment with these standards.
- **Engineering design process:** This is where the synergy of habits and framework becomes most visible. As students ask, imagine, plan, create, and improve, they are continuously drawing on habits such as using humor to maintain engagement (habit 3), leveraging creativity and innovation in the design (habit 4), and embracing lifelong learning and perseverance as they refine their solutions (habit 9).

Each of these habits supports the framework's goal to cultivate learners who are ready to meet the complexities of the world with confidence and skill. Educators would consciously plan and document which habits a project will include through the framework. This deliberate planning ensures that these habits are explicitly taught, practiced, and reinforced throughout the project. By integrating the habits into the project plan, educators can create specific activities, reflections, and assessments that focus on developing these essential skills. The following are five practical steps for planning and documenting habits.

1. **Identify key habits:** At the start of the project, identify which habits of thinking are most relevant to the project goals and essential questions. For example, if the project involves a lot of research and data analysis, habits like evaluating evidence and asking questions might be prioritized.
2. **Incorporate habits into learning objectives:** Explicitly include the selected habits in the learning objectives and outcomes of the project. This ensures that both educators and students are aware of the focus on these habits.
3. **Design activities to practice habits:** Plan specific activities for students to practice the selected habits. For instance, if creativity and innovation are a focus, design brainstorming sessions and creative problem-solving tasks.
4. **Reflect and assess:** Include reflections and assessments that specifically address the habits of thinking. Have students reflect on how they applied the habits and assess their growth in these areas.
5. **Document the process:** Keep a record of how the habits are integrated into the project. This documentation can include lesson plans, activity descriptions, student reflections, and assessment results. This not only helps in planning but also in sharing best practices with colleagues.

By consciously planning and documenting the use of habits within the challenge-based framework, educators can ensure these critical skills are not just abstract background concepts but that students actively and intentionally develop them. This approach leads to a more structured and impactful learning experience, preparing students to navigate the complexities of the modern world with greater confidence and competence.

In terms of assessment, the challenge-based framework leverages a holistic approach, viewing the output—whether a product, design, or presentation—as a representation of the student's learning journey. The template in figure 11.3 (also found as a reproducible at the end of the chapter and online at **go.SolutionTree.com/instruction**) acts as a map, charting both the expected educational outcomes and the process by which these outcomes are realized. It is through this dual lens of product and process that the effectiveness of the challenge-based framework can be gauged, with the embedded habits of thinking providing the qualitative texture that gives depth to quantitative achievements.

STUDENT GOAL:

ESSENTIAL QUESTION:

STANDARDS INTEGRATION:

ENGINEERING DESIGN PROCESS:

Teacher Actions and Support	Student Actions and Behavior
Ask:	*Ask:*
Imagine:	*Imagine:*

Plan:	Plan:
Create:	Create:
Improve:	Improve:

HABITS OF THINKING:

Teacher Actions and Support	Student Actions and Behavior
Habit 1: Cultivate diverse curiosity	**Habit 1:** Cultivate diverse curiosity
Habit 2: Take risks	**Habit 2:** Take risks
Habit 3: Use humor	**Habit 3:** Use humor
Habit 4: Create and innovate	**Habit 4:** Create and innovate

Figure 11.3: Challenge-based framework template.

continued →

Habit 5: Self-regulate	Habit 5: Self-regulate
Habit 6: Transfer learning	Habit 6: Transfer learning
Habit 7: Ask questions	Habit 7: Ask questions
Habit 8: Evaluate evidence	Habit 8: Evaluate evidence
Habit 9: Embrace lifelong learning and perseverance	Habit 9: Embrace lifelong learning and perseverence

ASSESSMENTS:

TEACHER REFLECTION: WHAT DID I DO SUCCESSFULLY? WHAT WILL I DO DIFFERENTLY NEXT TIME?

*Visit **go.SolutionTree.com/instruction** for a free reproducible version of this figure.*

Therefore, as you assess, look beyond the finished product of the student project to the habits that underpinned its creation. This is where true growth and learning are visible, and the template enables this comprehensive assessment. It is not only about what students create but also about how they think and develop as learners and individuals throughout the challenge-based framework.

Moving from the foundational aspects of the challenge-based framework and the integral habits of thinking, we now transition to practical, real-world applications of these concepts through the following examples of challenges suited to each educational stage. Each challenge exemplifies how the framework and habits interweave to create an enriching learning environment tailored to the developmental needs of different age groups.

Challenge-Based Framework Examples for Different Grade Bands

The examples of challenges for elementary and secondary grade bands in figures 11.4 and 11.5 (page 182) respectively illuminate how the challenge-based framework, paired with the deliberate cultivation of habits of thinking, can be applied to real-life learning scenarios. These are not just activities; they are experiences crafted to meet students where they are, push their boundaries, and expand their horizons.

STUDENT GOAL:
Develop a comprehensive recycling program for the school that reduces waste and educates the community about sustainable practices.

ESSENTIAL QUESTION:
How can we design and implement an effective recycling program in our school that maximizes waste reduction and promotes environmental awareness?

STANDARDS INTEGRATION:

Science:

NGSS 3-5-ETS1-1: Define a simple design problem reflecting a need or a want that includes specified criteria for success and constraints on materials, time, or cost.

NGSS 4-ESS3-1: Obtain and combine information to describe that energy and fuels are derived from natural resources and their uses affect the environment.

Mathematics:

CCSS.MATH.CONTENT.3.MD.A.1: Solve problems involving measurement and estimation of intervals of time, liquid volumes, and masses of objects.

CCSS.MATH.CONTENT.3.NF.A.3: Explain equivalence of fractions in special cases and compare fractions by reasoning about their size.

Language Arts:

CCSS.ELA-LITERACY.W.3.1: Write opinion pieces on topics or texts, supporting a point of view with reasons.

CCSS.ELA-LITERACY.W.3.2: Write informative or explanatory texts to examine a topic and convey ideas and information clearly.

Social Studies:
Examine the impact of recycling on local communities and the environment.

Source for standard: National Governors Association Center for Best Practices & Council of Chief State School Officers, 2010a; National Governors Association Center for Best Practices & Council of Chief State School Officers, 2010b; NGSS Lead States, 2013.

Figure 11.4: Example elementary grades challenge using the challenge-based framework template.

continued →

ENGINEERING DESIGN PROCESS:

Teacher Actions and Support	Student Actions and Behavior
Ask: Introduce the concept of waste management and recycling. Provide resources and materials about recycling processes and environmental impact. Facilitate a brainstorming session on potential recycling initiatives.	*Ask:* Identify the problem of school waste and pose relevant questions. Engage with provided resources to understand recycling principles. Participate actively in brainstorming sessions.
Imagine: Encourage students to research different types of recycling programs and innovative waste management techniques. Support students in developing initial sketches and ideas for their recycling program. Organize guest speakers or virtual field trips to recycling centers.	*Imagine:* Conduct research on recycling techniques and solutions. Develop and share initial sketches and ideas with peers. Interact with guest speakers and explore real-world examples.
Plan: Guide students in creating detailed blueprints for their recycling program, including bin placement, types of recyclables, and educational materials. Provide templates and tools for project planning and management. Review and provide feedback on student plans, ensuring feasibility and sustainability.	*Plan:* Create detailed blueprints for the recycling program. Utilize provided templates and tools for planning. Incorporate feedback to refine and finalize plans.
Create: Assist students in procuring materials and setting up their recycling stations. Monitor progress and offer troubleshooting support as needed. Facilitate regular check-ins and progress reports.	*Create:* Implement the recycling program, setting up bins and educational posters according to the plan. Maintain the program, documenting progress and challenges. Report regularly on the status of the project.
Improve: Encourage students to evaluate the performance of their recycling program and identify areas for improvement. Support iterative cycles of testing and refinement. Provide opportunities for students to present their findings and reflect on their learning process.	*Improve:* Evaluate the program's performance and suggest improvements. Engage in iterative testing and refinement. Present findings and reflect on the project's impact and learning outcomes.

HABITS OF THINKING:

Teacher Actions and Support	Student Actions and Behavior
Habit 1: *Cultivate diverse curiosity* *Provide varied resources:* Curate a wide array of resources, including articles, videos, and interactive tools about different recycling methods, sustainability practices, and their global benefits. *Encourage exploratory projects:* Assign exploratory projects where students investigate different recycling systems used in various countries or communities.	**Habit 1:** *Cultivate diverse curiosity* *Engage with resources:* Actively engage with the provided resources, conducting further research to deepen understanding. *Participate in exploratory projects:* Take initiative in exploring different recycling methods, conducting experiments, and presenting findings.

Facilitate expert interactions: Organize virtual meetings or field trips with environmental scientists, recycling plant managers, and community leaders to provide diverse perspectives on recycling practices. *Create inquiry-based learning opportunities:* Design activities that prompt students to ask questions, explore various hypotheses, and investigate the outcomes of different recycling methods.	*Interact with experts:* Participate actively in discussions with experts, asking insightful questions and integrating learned knowledge into the project. *Adopt inquiry-based learning:* Show enthusiasm in exploring different aspects of recycling, formulating questions, and seeking answers through investigation.
Habit 2: *Take risks*	**Habit 2:** *Take risks*
Foster a safe environment: Establish a classroom culture where making mistakes is viewed as a valuable part of the learning process. *Encourage experimentation:* Prompt students to try innovative and unconventional recycling solutions, providing support and guidance throughout their experiments. *Offer constructive feedback:* Provide timely and constructive feedback that focuses on the learning process rather than just the outcomes. *Model risk taking:* Share examples from your own experiences where taking risks led to valuable learning, demonstrating vulnerability and resilience.	*Experiment with new approaches:* Show willingness to try new and potentially unconventional recycling methods, even if they might fail. *Reflect on failures:* Reflect on what didn't work and why, learning from these experiences to refine future efforts. *Seek feedback:* Actively seek feedback from peers and teachers to improve their projects. *Demonstrate resilience:* Persist through setbacks, demonstrating resilience and a growth mindset.
Habit 4: *Foster creativity and innovation*	**Habit 4:** *Foster creativity and innovation*
Encourage original thinking: Challenge students to think outside the box and come up with unique solutions to recycling challenges. *Provide creative tools:* Supply students with diverse materials and tools that inspire creativity, such as design software, recyclable materials for prototyping, and brainstorming templates. *Facilitate brainstorming sessions:* Conduct regular brainstorming sessions where students can share and refine their innovative ideas collaboratively. *Recognize and celebrate creativity:* Acknowledge and celebrate creative solutions, showcasing student work in the classroom and school community.	*Develop original ideas:* Generate and develop innovative ideas for the recycling program, thinking creatively about how to reduce waste. *Use creative tools:* Utilize provided materials and tools to design and prototype unique recycling solutions. *Collaborate on ideas:* Participate actively in brainstorming sessions, contributing to and building on peers' ideas. *Showcase innovation:* Present creative solutions confidently, explaining the thought process and innovation behind the ideas.

ASSESSMENTS:

Final presentation: Students will present their recycling program, including design, implementation process, and outcomes, to the class.

Written report: Students will submit a comprehensive report detailing the project's goals, methods, challenges, results, and reflections.

Peer assessment: Facilitate a structured peer-review process where students assess each other's contributions and teamwork.

Self-assessment: Students will complete a self-assessment reflecting on their learning, participation, and the project's impact.

TEACHER REFLECTION: WHAT DID I DO SUCCESSFULLY? WHAT WILL I DO DIFFERENTLY NEXT TIME?

Plan for resource procurement well in advance. Consider creating a partnership with local businesses or community organizations to secure materials.

Structured milestones: Implement more structured milestones and checkpoints throughout the project to help students manage their time and tasks better. Provide additional guidance and scaffolding for students who need more support in self-regulation.

Group dynamics: Address group dynamics early by incorporating team-building activities at the beginning of the project. Regularly monitor and support group interactions to ensure all students are contributing equally.

STUDENT GOAL:
Develop a solar-powered water purification system to provide clean drinking water to a local community.

ESSENTIAL QUESTION:
How can we design a solar-powered water purification system that is both effective and sustainable?

STANDARDS INTEGRATION:

Science:
MS-ETS1-1: Define the criteria and constraints of a design problem with sufficient precision to ensure a successful solution, taking into account relevant scientific principles and potential impacts on people and the natural environment that may limit possible solutions.
MS-PS1-6: Undertake a design project to construct, test, and modify a device that either releases or absorbs thermal energy by chemical processes.

Mathematics:
CCSS.MATH.CONTENT.8.EE.C.8: Analyze and solve pairs of simultaneous linear equations.
CCSS.MATH.CONTENT.8.SP.A.4: Understand that patterns of association can also be seen in bivariate categorical data by displaying frequencies and relative frequencies in a two-way table.

Language Arts:
CCSS.ELA-LITERACY.W.8.1: Write arguments to support claims with clear reasons and relevant evidence.
CCSS.ELA-LITERACY.SL.8.5: Include multimedia components and visual displays in presentations to clarify claims and findings and emphasize salient points.

Social Studies:
D2.GEO.5.6-8: Analyze the combinations of cultural and environmental characteristics that make places both similar to and different from other places.

ENGINEERING DESIGN PROCESS:

Teacher Actions and Support	Student Actions and Behavior
Ask: Introduce the issue of clean water scarcity. Provide resources on solar purification systems. Facilitate discussions to identify potential design challenges and criteria.	*Ask:* Engage with resources to understand the problem. Participate actively in discussions. Identify key challenges and criteria.
Imagine: Encourage research on existing solar water purification technologies. Guide brainstorming sessions to develop creative solutions. Invite guest speakers from relevant fields.	*Imagine:* Conduct research on various solar purification methods. Develop initial ideas and sketches. Interact with guest speakers and ask insightful questions.
Plan: Assist in creating detailed blueprints. Provide project management tools. Review and provide feedback on student plans.	*Plan:* Create detailed blueprints and timelines. Use provided tools for project planning. Incorporate feedback to refine plans.
Create: Facilitate procurement of materials. Monitor progress and provide troubleshooting support. Organize regular check-ins.	*Create:* Implement the design according to the plan. Document progress and address challenges. Report regularly on the status of the project.
Improve: Encourage evaluation of the system's performance. Support iterative cycles of testing and refinement. Provide opportunities for presenting findings.	*Improve:* Evaluate the system's effectiveness. Engage in iterative testing and refinement. Present findings and reflect on the learning process.

Integrate the Challenge-Based Framework and the Habits of Thinking

HABITS OF THINKING:

Teacher Actions and Support	Student Actions and Behavior
Habit 5: Practice self-regulation	*Habit 5:* Practice self-regulation
Teach students how to break down the project into manageable tasks. Provide tools such as calendars, checklists, and progress trackers. Conduct regular check-ins to help students stay on track. Encourage setting-specific, achievable goals for each phase of the project.	Use calendars and checklists to manage time and tasks effectively. Monitor progress using provided tools. Set and revise personal goals regularly. Reflect on progress during regular check-ins and adjust plans as necessary. Manage time effectively by following provided timelines and checklists. Monitor own progress and adjust work habits as needed to stay on schedule.
Habit 6: Transfer learning	*Habit 6:* Transfer learning
Facilitate discussions on how concepts from different fields apply to the project. Provide examples of how knowledge from previous lessons can be applied. Encourage students to make connections between what they are learning in this project and other areas of study.	Identify and apply relevant knowledge from different subjects to the project. Discuss and document connections between this project and other learning experiences. Use interdisciplinary knowledge to develop and refine project ideas.
Habit 8: Evaluate evidence	*Habit 8:* Evaluate evidence
Teach students how to critically assess the reliability and validity of sources. Provide tools and criteria for evaluating data and information. Facilitate group discussions on the quality of evidence collected. Encourage the use of evidence-based reasoning in project decisions.	Critically evaluate the quality and relevance of data and information. Use provided tools and criteria to assess sources. Discuss and justify project decisions based on evidence. Reflect on the evidence used and its impact on project outcomes.
Habit 9: Embrace lifelong learning and perseverance	*Habit 9:* Embrace lifelong learning and perseveranc
Encourage a growth mindset by highlighting the value of learning from mistakes. Provide opportunities for students to reflect on their learning and progress. Celebrate perseverance and incremental progress. Share stories and examples of perseverance in scientific research and technological innovation. Provide opportunities for students to reflect on their designs and learn from setbacks.	Demonstrate resilience by persisting through challenges in the project. Reflect on setbacks and use them as learning opportunities. Show a commitment to improving the solar energy system design based on feedback and testing results. Reflect on personal growth and learning throughout the project. Celebrate small successes and learn from setbacks. Set long-term learning goals inspired by project experiences.

ASSESSMENTS:

Final presentation: Students will present their solar water purification project, including design, implementation process, and outcomes, to the class.

Written report: Students will submit a comprehensive report detailing the project's goals, methods, challenges, results, and reflections.

Peer assessment: Students will assess each other's contributions and teamwork in a structured peer review process.

Self-assessment: Students will complete a self-assessment reflecting on their learning, participation, and the project's impact.

TEACHER REFLECTION: WHAT DID I DO SUCCESSFULLY? WHAT WILL I DO DIFFERENTLY NEXT TIME?

Students did well on this project and demonstrated many of the habits of thinking.

Lead a debrief session focused on the collaborative aspects of the project.

Facilitate a discussion on the broader implications of the project's findings and their relevance to real-world issues.

Source for standard: National Governors Association Center for Best Practices & Council of Chief State School Officers, 2010a; National Governors Association Center for Best Practices & Council of Chief State School Officers, 2010b; NGSS Lead States, 2013.

Figure 11.5: Example secondary grades challenge using the challenge-based framework template.

As we deepen our exploration of the challenge-based framework and its interwoven habits of thinking, it's imperative to reemphasize the significance of their integration. The confluence of the framework with these habits marks a transformative shift in educational paradigms, fostering learners who are not just consumers of information but architects of knowledge and innovation.

At each educational level, the integration of habits into the challenge-based framework needs to be deliberate and mindful of the students' developmental stages. Here are some key points for educators to consider.

- **Elementary school level:** Cultivate curiosity and creativity. At this stage, students are naturally curious and imaginative. Encourage exploration and creative thinking by integrating habit 1, cultivate diverse curiosity, and habit 4, create and innovate. Provide opportunities for students to ask questions, explore their environment, and come up with creative solutions. Use tangible, hands-on projects that allow students to see the direct impact of their work. This not only engages them but also helps them make connections between their actions and learning outcomes. Create a supportive and safe environment where students feel comfortable taking risks and making mistakes. This nurtures their confidence and willingness to try new things.

- **Middle school level:** Focus on developing analytical skills. As students' cognitive abilities grow, integrate habit 7, ask questions, and habit 8, evaluate evidence. Encourage them to think critically and analyze the information they gather. Focus on collaborative projects that require students to work together, communicate effectively, and build on each other's ideas. This fosters teamwork and enhances problem-solving skills. Connect projects to real-world issues that are relevant to students' lives. This makes learning more meaningful and helps students see the importance of their work.

- **High school level:** Encourage higher-order thinking. For older students, integrate higher-order habits such as habit 6, transfer learning, and habit 9, embrace lifelong learning and perseverance. Challenge them to apply their knowledge in new and diverse contexts and to see learning as a continuous journey. Encourage students to take on more independent projects where they can explore their interests in depth. Provide guidance but allow them the autonomy to direct their learning. Incorporate regular reflection activities where students assess their progress, identify areas for improvement, and set future goals. This promotes self-awareness and a growth mindset.

In conclusion, integrating habits of thinking into the challenge-based framework is the cornerstone of cultivating lifelong learners who are equipped to tackle the complexities of the modern world with confidence and competence. As educators, your role is pivotal in guiding and supporting students through this transformative journey, creating an environment where they can thrive and excel. The examples and templates provided serve as a practical guide to help you bring this powerful framework to life in your classroom, fostering a new generation of thinkers, innovators, and problem solvers.

Be mindful of the developmental readiness of your students, selecting and emphasizing habits that resonate most with their stage of growth. Encourage reflection at every step, as it solidifies learning and provides insights into how students can continuously develop and apply each habit. This reflective practice is what transforms the framework from a theoretical model to a living framework, dynamically evolving with each group of learners.

Remember, the strength of the framework lies in its flexibility and its capacity to grow alongside your students. It is a framework that invites adaptation, encourages resilience, and above all, champions the integration of habits that will equip your students with the skills they need to thrive in a rapidly changing world.

Concluding Thoughts

The challenge-based framework stands as a testament to the enduring power of education to transform lives. It goes beyond traditional boundaries, fostering an environment where students do not just learn about the world but learn to change it. Integrating the habits of thinking into this framework is the cornerstone of its success, instilling in students the qualities that define innovators and leaders.

As educators, the journey through the challenge-based framework offers you a chance to mentor a new generation capable of thinking critically, collaborating effectively, and engaging with their communities. By embedding these habits into your teaching practice, you are not only imparting knowledge but also empowering your students to build a future that is thoughtful, inclusive, and forward thinking.

Remember, the most profound impacts of the challenge-based framework may not be immediately measurable. They will manifest as students, equipped with the habits of thinking, step confidently into complexity and embrace challenges as opportunities. This is the legacy of the challenge-based framework—a legacy of empowerment, innovation, and hope for the future.

Let the framework and its habits be your compass and your students the explorers. Together, navigate the terrain of learning, discovery, and growth. The challenges of tomorrow await the well-prepared minds of today—minds that you are shaping.

Challenge-Based Framework Template

STUDENT GOAL:
ESSENTIAL QUESTION:

STANDARDS INTEGRATION:

ENGINEERING DESIGN PROCESS:

Teacher Actions and Support	Student Actions and Behavior
Ask:	*Ask:*
Imagine:	*Imagine:*
Plan:	*Plan:*

Renaissance Thinking in the Classroom © 2025 Solution Tree Press • SolutionTree.com
Visit **go.SolutionTree.com/instruction** to download this free reproducible.

Create:

Create:

Improve:

Improve:

HABITS OF THINKING:

Teacher Actions and Support	Student Actions and Behavior
Habit 1: Cultivate diverse curiosity	**Habit 1:** Cultivate diverse curiosity
Habit 2: Take risks	**Habit 2:** Take risks
Habit 3: Use humor	**Habit 3:** Use humor
Habit 4: Create and innovate	**Habit 4:** Create and innovate

Habit 5: Self-regulate	**Habit 5:** Self-regulate
Habit 6: Transfer learning	**Habit 6:** Transfer learning
Habit 7: Ask questions	**Habit 7:** Ask questions
Habit 8: Evaluate evidence	**Habit 8:** Evaluate evidence
Habit 9: Embrace lifelong learning and perseverance	**Habit 9:** Embrace lifelong learning and perseverance

ASSESSMENTS:

TEACHER REFLECTION: WHAT DID I DO SUCCESSFULLY? WHAT WILL I DO DIFFERENTLY NEXT TIME?

Chapter 12

Integrate Academic Standards

Welcome to chapter 12, where we navigate the convergence of established academic standards with the challenge-based framework. This chapter serves as a pivotal point in our exploration, merging the rigor of traditional benchmarks with the dynamic and innovative approach of the framework to craft a more engaging and meaningful educational experience.

The challenge-based framework, with its roots deeply embedded in a philosophy that seeks to awaken the natural inquisitiveness of learners, stands in contrast to conventional teaching models. Where traditional methods may lean on external incentives or deterrents while the framework taps into the innate motivations that drive students to learn, question, and engage with their learning environment. Inquiry lies at the heart of the framework, celebrating the process of discovery as an educational journey rather than a mere destination.

This chapter demonstrates how educators can cultivate a classroom in which they construct inquiries that align with academic standards while also sparking students' curiosity and deepening their understanding of diverse subject matter. Emphasizing learner autonomy, the chapter underscores the importance of providing students with the agency to steer their own learning. We delve into strategies for creating student-led learning experiences that allow for personal investment and foster a sense of independence that transcends the classroom while still meeting more conventional benchmarks that are a part of many school curricula. You will discover tools and insights to integrate academic standards into the framework effectively. You will also encounter real-world examples and practical advice on crafting lessons that meet educational benchmarks while engaging students and preparing them for the complexities of life beyond the classroom. By the end of this chapter, you will have a robust understanding of methods for designing educational experiences that respect the integrity of academic standards while harnessing the vibrant, challenging, and interconnected nature of our contemporary world. Prepare to embark on a journey that will reshape your approach to teaching and learning within the challenge-based framework.

Balance Academic Standards and Challenges

When introducing the challenge-based framework into the curriculum, educators often grapple with the intricate task of intertwining academic standards with meaningful challenges. On the surface, it may seem straightforward to weave every standard into a challenge; however, the dynamics of effective instructional planning reveal a more layered relationship. This layered relationship means that while some standards can be seamlessly integrated into challenge-based activities, others may require a more traditional instructional approach first to establish a strong foundational understanding.

One of the primary reasons for this complexity is the positioning of standards within a coherence map, scope and sequence, or learning progression. Standards are often strategically placed to build on one another, ensuring a logical and developmental progression of knowledge and skills. This structured approach can sometimes make it challenging to incorporate specific standards into a fluid, challenge-based framework immediately.

For instance, consider a coherence map that outlines the progression of mathematical skills from basic arithmetic to more advanced algebraic concepts. While it may be possible to integrate problem solving and real-world applications at various points, certain foundational skills require direct instruction before students can tackle more complex, interdisciplinary challenges. This phased approach ensures that students have the necessary background to engage deeply with the material.

Similarly, the scope and sequence of a curriculum often dictate the order in which standards are taught, ensuring that students build on prior knowledge systematically. This sequencing can sometimes make it challenging to align with the flexible and dynamic nature of challenge-based learning, requiring educators to strategically plan when and how to introduce challenges that align with the current stage of the curriculum.

Learning progressions further complicate this integration, as they are designed to track the development of student understanding over time. Each step in the progression builds on the previous one, making it essential to ensure that students have mastered earlier concepts before moving on to more complex ideas. This developmental approach necessitates a careful balance between direct instruction and challenge-based learning, ensuring that students are adequately prepared for each new challenge.

Given these considerations, it's clear that integrating academic standards into challenge-based learning is not always straightforward. Educators must navigate the complexities of coherence maps, scope and sequence, and learning progressions to ensure that students receive a comprehensive and coherent education. By strategically combining direct instruction with challenge-based learning, educators can create a harmonious blend that meets educational benchmarks while engaging students in meaningful and relevant challenges.

A strength of the challenge-based framework is its ability to contextualize learning, taking abstract concepts and grounding them in tangible, relatable situations. But not every standard lends itself seamlessly to this context-driven methodology. Some standards, by their very nature, require a foundation that's best built through traditional methods.

Take, for instance, the learning of grammar rules. Before they plunge into crafting compelling essays or engaging speeches, students must understand the basics of sentence structure and punctuation. Here, direct instruction, repetitive exercises, or even rote learning might be the most effective route. Once students have a foundational grasp, they can apply these rules to real-world challenges, such as editing a magazine article or scripting a podcast episode.

It's also worth noting that challenges can serve as capstones to a series of traditionally taught standards. Instead of seeing the two methods as competing philosophies, view them instead as complementary tools in the educational tool kit. After all, the objective isn't solely to embrace challenges at the expense of traditional methods but to craft a learning journey that's both rigorous and engaging.

This balance is vital. While direct instruction plays a crucial role in establishing foundational knowledge and meeting standards, it is not the sole avenue for learning. Challenge-based experiences also serve as a platform for students to apply and deepen their understanding of these standards in real-world contexts. Educators, by skillfully combining direct instruction with challenge-based learning, ensure that students not only meet but also exceed the benchmarks set by academic standards. This approach cultivates a learning environment where standards are not just taught but experienced, enabling students to harness critical thinking and problem-solving skills inherent in challenges. Thus, the integration of standards into challenges enhances the learning experience, making it both rigorous and relevant, and fully prepares students for the complexities of practical application. The goal is a harmonious blend where conforming to learning standards provides the structure, and challenges infuse the work with inspiration and real-world relevance. For instance, a standard might require students to understand the concept of supply and demand in economics. In practice, this could involve direct instruction on the fundamental principles followed by a challenge where students simulate running a business within a classroom marketplace. Here, they apply their knowledge to make pricing and production decisions, reflecting on the effects of supply and demand in real time. This not only solidifies their understanding of the economic standard but also engages them with the practical applications that bring the concept to life.

Following are some ways to find this harmonious blend in an integration of academic standards and the challenge-based framework. Key ways to harmoniously integrate academic standards into the challenge-based framework include leveraging content-neutral standards, using multimodal integration, infusing direct instruction, and navigating the complex terrain of misfit standards. I discuss these strategies in detail in the following sections.

Leverage Content-Neutral Standards

When you set out to leverage content-neutral standards within your curriculum, you're tapping into skills that apply broadly across disciplines. Consider the Common Core State Standards for English language arts, which emphasize skills like crafting well-reasoned arguments. For example, standard CCSS.ELA-LITERACY.CCRA.W.1 pushes students beyond rote learning to develop arguments supporting claims with clear reasoning and evidence (Common Core State Standards Initiative, 2024).

Imagine you're guiding students as they launch a podcast series on the ethical implications of AI. The previously noted standard focusing on crafting arguments becomes your anchor. You'll instruct your students to articulate their thoughts clearly, beginning perhaps with AI's role in healthcare, scrutinizing its potential to both heal and harm. Progressing through the series, your students might analyze how AI could reshape job markets, eventually advocating for or against specific regulations.

You start this educational journey by ensuring students grasp the essentials of argumentation—the structure of a compelling argument, the integration of credible evidence, and the importance of coherently linking claims to conclusions. Equip them with research skills to delve deeply into their topics. Teach them to draft their arguments, critique the work of their peers, and refine their positions. In orchestrating this project, you not only adhere to the educational standards but also cultivate a profound, critical engagement with pressing societal issues, thereby enriching the learning experience with relevance and depth.

Use Multimodal Integration

To effectively implement multimodal integration in your teaching practice, you should intertwine various learning modalities that cater to diverse student needs, aligning them with relevant standards. Such an approach enriches learning by engaging different senses and providing multiple avenues for students to explore and understand concepts.

Let's consider an integrated challenge that marries the Next Generation Science Standards (NGSS) with the Common Core State Standards (CCSS) for mathematics. Picture your students engaging in a project where they design an eco-friendly urban park. Under the guidance of NGSS standard HS-ESS3–4, students critically evaluate the environmental impact of their designs, proposing innovative features such as rainwater harvesting systems and solar-powered lighting. Simultaneously, the mathematics CCSS standard CCSS.MATH.CONTENT.HSA.CED.A.2 comes into play as they create and solve equations to calculate the efficiency of these features.

For practical guidance, begin by introducing the relevant science concepts and mathematical principles separately. Once students grasp these foundations, encourage them to brainstorm how these principles manifest in an urban park setting. Provide resources such as digital simulation tools for testing their models and creating visual representations of their parks. Finally, facilitate a presentation or a pitch session where students present their eco-park designs to peers or community stakeholders, highlighting the interdisciplinary nature of their project and its real-world application. This method not only solidifies their grasp of the academic standards but also fosters skills such as environmental stewardship, problem solving, and community engagement.

Infuse Direct Instruction

Infusing direct instruction into your teaching strategy is about seamlessly incorporating structured, teacher-led sessions that lay the groundwork for the application of complex concepts. This methodology is particularly effective when approaching sophisticated academic standards, like the CCSS for mathematics, which require a strong foundational understanding before students can successfully apply these concepts to real-world scenarios.

Take the standard CCSS.MATH.CONTENT.HSA.REI.B.4, which focuses on solving quadratic equations. Let's envision a scenario where you challenge your students to calculate the trajectory of a satellite launch. The path of the satellite, dictated by the laws of physics, can be modeled by a quadratic equation. Before students begin to tackle this challenge, provide them with direct instruction on the methods of solving quadratic equations. This focused lesson could include step-by-step walkthroughs, problem solving with different equations, and personalized support to ensure that each student grasps the concept.

With this foundational knowledge secured, students are now prepared to engage with the challenge. Guide them as they apply their newly acquired skills to formulate and solve a quadratic equation that models the satellite's path. Encourage collaboration and iteration, facilitating an environment where students feel comfortable experimenting and learning from their mistakes. As they refine their calculations, they will not only deepen their understanding of the mathematics involved but also experience the satisfaction of applying their classroom learning to a task that mirrors a real-world scientific endeavor.

Through this strategic combination of direct instruction and hands-on application, you provide students with a robust educational experience that honors the rigors of academic standards while also igniting their passion and curiosity through real-world relevance.

Navigate the Complex Terrain of Misfit Standards

In the vast landscape of academic standards, educators are faced with the daunting task of discerning which fit seamlessly within the challenge-based framework and which might feel like square pegs in round holes. The journey of integrating standards into challenges is filled with its own set of pitfalls, and recognizing the telltale signs of a misfit is crucial for ensuring meaningful learning experiences.

There are certain standards that thrive on repetition. These aren't merely about rote learning but pertain to mastering skills through repeated practice. Think about the methodical process of learning musical scales on a piano or the drills associated with handwriting. While challenges can provide context, the sheer repetitiveness these standards demand might be diluted within the framework of a broader challenge. The following points illustrate specific situations where targeted instruction is essential to ensure the mastery of skills.

- **The tangibility factor:** Some skills are so specific and tangible that they risk being overshadowed in a wider challenge. Examples include mastering the technique to make a precise surgical knot or understanding the calibration of laboratory equipment. These highly specialized skills require targeted instruction, ensuring that their tangible nuances aren't lost amidst broader objectives.

- **The direct instruction dilemma:** Not all concepts are things students can organically discover or explore. There are times when the direct transfer of knowledge is not just efficient but also essential. Consider the understanding of certain mathematical theorems or the historical context behind a major event. Such standards might require a focused chunk of direct instruction, ensuring that students have a robust foundational grasp before they venture into related challenges.

One way to teach skills that require direct instruction while also offering the creativity inherent in the framework is to carefully parse the steps that make up a skill. Take the activity of storytelling, for instance, and the desire to integrate the subtle intricacies of poetic meter. The depth and precision demanded by poetic meter can easily get lost in the expansive nature of storytelling. When making storytelling a challenge activity through the framework, it's tempting to weave everything under the umbrella of a single challenge. Doing so, however, might make the outcome appear forced, reducing the impact of both the challenge and the standard. In these instances, it's better to first delve into the different concepts involved in storytelling in isolation, allowing students to grasp their nuances. Once a foundation is built, guide students to incorporate their understanding into the broader challenge, ensuring both depth and context.

Chunk Within Challenges to Create a Tapestry of Interwoven Learning

The concept of chunking when including standards in challenges is comparable to assembling a jigsaw puzzle. Each standard represents a piece of the puzzle, and while each piece has its own shape and place, it's only when combined with the others that the full picture becomes clear. In practical terms, this means breaking down a complex standard into specific, achievable learning objectives. For instance, if a standard involves understanding ecological systems, start by exploring the water cycle, then move to energy flow in ecosystems, and finally examine the relationships within food webs. As students master each chunk, they begin to see how these elements interact in the broader context of ecology, leading to a comprehensive understanding of environmental science. This approach not only makes learning manageable and less overwhelming but also allows for the integration of these chunks into a cohesive unit that reflects the interconnectedness of real-world systems.

To delve deeper into the concept of chunking in action, consider, for example, when you task your students with composing a persuasive essay on renewable energy, they will be actively engaging with standards related to research, writing, and critical analysis. This visualization exercise illustrates the overlap of skills in action: (1) students gather information (CCSS.ELA-LITERACY.W.8.8), (2) they also learn to organize their arguments coherently (CCSS.ELA-LITERACY.W.8.4), and (3) they demonstrate how to achieve different educational goals through a single, well-structured activity.

Furthermore, learning naturally progresses from one stage to the next. A project in which students explore the history of their hometown might start with source analysis and evolve into creating a cohesive presentation. This reflects how one standard feeds into another when engaging in academic standards becomes part of a natural path to working through a challenge.

Collaboration, too, brings its own set of benefits. A project like designing a sustainable community garden allows different students to work on distinct aspects of the challenge—like biology or budgeting—aligned with respective standards. When students combine their work, the collective output is much richer than what they could achieve individually.

These examples and strategies are not merely exercises but serve as a foundation for creating an educational experience that is dynamic, interconnected, and reflective of real-world complexity. They provide a road map to navigate the multifaceted terrain of learning standards, ensuring that your students are not only meeting educational benchmarks but also acquiring a depth of knowledge and skills that will serve them beyond the classroom.

The following list outlines key concepts to guide integrating standards into challenge-based learning.

- **Overlapping objectives:** Every educator knows that the process of learning isn't linear. Multiple skills often overlap and reinforce each other. Consider a student who's crafting an essay for a challenge. They aren't merely writing; they're researching, analyzing sources, organizing thoughts, and crafting an argument. Each of these tasks align with distinct standards. For instance, the CCSS for English language arts ask students to gather and evaluate information (CCSS.ELA-LITERACY.W.8.8) and to produce clear and coherent writing (CCSS.ELA-LITERACY.W.8.4).
  - *Example*—A challenge might require students to draft a persuasive piece on renewable energy sources. As they embark on this task, they will organically address the aforementioned standards, finding relevant sources and shaping their findings into a compelling narrative.

- **Natural progressions:** Often, mastery of one standard can lead directly to the next. Within challenges, these progressions allow for a fluid, layered learning experience.
  - *Example*—Students working on a project about the history of their hometown might begin by analyzing primary source documents (aligned with a standard on source analysis). This could seamlessly transition into synthesizing this information into a presentation or report, connecting to another standard on effective communication.

- **Collaborative advantages:** One of the many strengths of challenges is their potential for group work. Different students can tackle different standards within the same overarching challenge, later synthesizing their findings.
  - *Example*—In a challenge on designing a sustainable community garden, one student might focus on soil and plant research, aligning with a biology standard, while another dives into budgeting and resource allocation, tapping into a mathematics standard. When they come together to finalize their garden plan, both sets of knowledge are essential, showcasing the interplay of diverse standards.

Incorporating chunking into your instructional strategies supporting challenge-based learning not only allows for multifaceted, rich learning experiences but can enhance the digestibility and retention of complex material. Here's how you can apply this method: begin by identifying the overarching concept or skill you wish to teach through the challenge-based framework. Break it down into smaller, more manageable units that students can sequentially understand and master. Each chunk should build on the previous one, gradually increasing in complexity and encouraging students to synthesize information as they progress.

For instance, if the goal is to understand the causes of the American Revolution, start with the political context, then move to specific events, and finally discuss the outcomes and long-term implications. After these iterative steps, you can design an actual challenge with an essential question that ties everything together. For example, you might pose the question, "How did the political and economic conditions of the 18th century lead to the American Revolution, and what were its lasting impacts?" This challenge encourages students to synthesize the chunks of knowledge they've acquired and apply them to a comprehensive, real-world scenario. This approach helps students construct a comprehensive narrative in a sequential fashion.

In essence, chunking within challenges is about seeing the forest for the trees. It's about understanding that while each standard plays a crucial role in shaping a student's knowledge, their true power lies in their collective application. When educators embrace the interconnected nature of standards, they can craft challenges that are not only comprehensive but also deeply meaningful, ensuring that learning is both broad and deep. When educators begin to use the challenge-based framework, they should consider several key factors to get started and organized effectively.

- **Identify relevant standards:** Begin by determining which academic standards you need to address. This ensures that the challenge-based activities align with curriculum requirements and educational benchmarks.

- **Understand student interests:** Engage with students to understand their interests and passions. This helps in designing challenges that are engaging and relevant to them, fostering a deeper connection to the material.

- **Formulate essential questions:** Develop essential questions that are open ended, thought provoking, and aligned with both the standards and student interests. These questions will drive the inquiry process and give direction to the challenge.

- **Chunk the standards:** Break down the identified standards into smaller, manageable chunks. Plan how to address each chunk within the context of the challenge. This might involve direct instruction, exploratory activities, or collaborative tasks.

- **Design the challenge:** Create a comprehensive challenge that integrates the chunks of standards. Structure the challenge in a way that allows students to progressively build on their knowledge and skills.

- **Plan assessment strategies:** Determine how you will assess student understanding and progress throughout the challenge. This might include formative assessments, self-reflections, peer reviews, and summative evaluations.

- **Prepare resources and supports:** Gather the necessary resources and supports that students will need to successfully engage with the challenge. This might include access to research materials and technology, and guidance on specific skills.

By addressing these factors, you can effectively organize and implement the challenge-based framework, creating a structured yet flexible learning environment that encourages deep, meaningful engagement with the material.

The Harmonious Intersection of Challenge and Standard

As we delve deeper into the challenge-based framework, it becomes evident that the integration of academic standards with meaningful, real-world challenges is not only precise but also more intuitive and open-ended. To truly harness the power of this framework, educators must skillfully balance, chunk, and blend standards into their instructional practices.

This section provides detailed strategies and concrete examples to guide you through this intricate process. Let's explore how to bring this balance to life in your classroom.

When introducing the challenge-based framework into the curriculum, educators often grapple with the intricate task of intertwining academic standards with meaningful challenges. On the surface, it may seem straightforward to weave every standard into a challenge; however, the dynamics of effective education reveal a more layered relationship. This layered relationship means that while some standards can be seamlessly integrated into challenge-based activities, others may require a more traditional instructional approach first to establish a strong foundational understanding. For instance, before students can effectively engage in a complex challenge, they may need to master certain fundamental skills or knowledge through direct instruction and practice. Only then can these elements be integrated into broader, real-world challenges to enhance and apply their learning.

The following offers an example of the process of designing a high school challenge-based learning project combining both science and social studies. The project objective is to understand climate change and its impact.

1. **Identify relevant standards:** Use NGSS (2013) science standard HS-ESS3-5. Analyze geoscience data and the results from global climate models to make an evidence-based forecast of the current rate of global or regional climate change and associated future impacts to Earth's systems. Use CCSS (2010a) social studies standard (CCSS.ELA-LITERACY.RH.11-12.7: Integrate and evaluate multiple sources of information presented in diverse formats and media, for example, visually or quantitatively) in order to address a question or solve a problem.

2. **Understand student interests:** Survey students to gauge their interest in environmental issues and current events related to climate change. Identify any personal connections they might have, such as local environmental concerns or family members working in related fields.

3. **Formulate essential questions:** Ask students "How is climate change affecting our planet, and what can we do to mitigate its impacts?" or "What are the socioeconomic implications of climate change in different regions of the world?"

4. **Chunk the standards:** The following is an example of how to parse the standards between learning topics and activities.
    - Understand geoscience data and how it is collected.
    - Analyze results from global climate models.
    - Forecast the impacts of climate change on Earth's systems.
    - Identify and evaluate multiple sources of information about climate change.
    - Integrate information from various media formats.
    - Develop solutions or responses to the impacts of climate change.

5. **Design the challenge:** Build the challenge into the challenge-based framework, which includes the following components.
    - *Student goal*—Develop a comprehensive climate action plan for their local community.

> *Essential question*—"How can our community address the impacts of climate change effectively?"

6. **Integrate standards:** Ensure the project addresses both the science and social studies standards through interdisciplinary learning.

    > **Engineering design process:** Take the following steps.
    >   i. *Ask*—Students research and identify the specific impacts of climate change on their local community.
    >   ii. *Imagine*—Students brainstorm potential solutions to mitigate the impacts of climate change locally.
    >   iii. *Plan*—Students develop a detailed plan outlining their proposed solutions.
    >   iv. *Create*—Students implement their plans, creating models, presentations, or campaigns.
    >   v. *Improve*—Students reflect on their work, receive feedback, and refine their plans.

7. **Plan assessment strategies:** Use formative assessments through regular check-ins and feedback sessions. Use summative assessments based on the final presentation, project report, and community impact.

8. **Prepare resources and supports:** Provide access to scientific journals, climate models, and local environmental data. Offer tools for creating presentations and prototypes. Arrange guest speakers or field trips to local environmental organizations.

By following these steps, you can effectively integrate standards into the challenge-based framework. This project example demonstrates how to chunk standards, design comprehensive challenges, and integrate interdisciplinary learning. It provides a clear road map for creating engaging, meaningful educational experiences that not only meet academic benchmarks but also prepare students for real-world challenges.

Concluding Thoughts

This chapter has charted a path through the rich landscape of challenge-based learning, with a focus on integrating traditional academic standards. As educators, you are now equipped with strategies to weave these standards into vibrant, real-world challenges that engage and inspire your students. This chapter has provided the framework for creating learning experiences that are not only intellectually rigorous but also imbued with the relevance and adaptability necessary for students to thrive in an unpredictable future. By balancing the structure of standards with the dynamism of challenges, you are preparing students to be inquisitive, knowledgeable, and capable problem solvers. The journey of education is indeed a balancing act—a thoughtful and intentional fusion of stability and innovation that prepares our students to dance gracefully into their futures.

Chapter 13

Integrate 21st Century Skills

Navigating the global educational landscape of the 21st century demands an agile approach adaptive to the perpetual shifts in technology, sociopolitical changes, and economic dynamics. As educators, leaders, and lifelong learners, we're tasked with the duty to not just keep pace with this transformation but also to be the vanguard of it. This begins with our understanding of what truly constitutes holistic education.

Traditional academic subjects like mathematics, literature, and the sciences lay the groundwork. They furnish students with a wealth of knowledge that has been accumulated over centuries. This fundamental knowledge forms the backbone of our educational systems and remains irreplaceable. Educational standards encapsulate these foundational skills, and they serve as critical benchmarks for learning. Academic standards articulate the essential knowledge and skills students need to be proficient in a subject area. For example, standards in mathematics not only require understanding numerical operations but also call for problem-solving and logical reasoning skills. In literature, standards go beyond comprehension to include critical thinking and textual analysis. Similarly, science standards encompass the methodical inquiry and understanding of scientific concepts and phenomena.

While these standards lay the foundation for essential academic competencies, they also implicitly address broader cognitive skills. They foster analytical thinking, adaptability, and creativity—abilities that are pivotal for success in the 21st century. Consequently, the true strength of these standards lies not only in the content knowledge they represent but also in the fundamental skills they nurture, which are applicable across a spectrum of real-world contexts. Thus, as you teach these subjects, you inherently bolster students' capacity to engage with complex problems and prepare them to navigate the evolving challenges of the future. However, in the context of today's fast-paced and globally connected world, this isn't enough.

Enter the concept of 21st century skills. These are abilities that students need to thrive in our modern, interconnected society, encompassing everything from digital literacy and critical thinking to global awareness and effective communication.

As we pivot to the core tenets of 21st century skills in this chapter, we delve into the capabilities crucial for students' success in a complex, rapidly evolving world. Skills such as digital literacy, critical thinking, global awareness, and effective communication are not just beneficial but essential for navigating the digital era. For example, Joke Voogt and Natalie Pareja Roblin's (2012) seminal research underscores the importance of these competencies, highlighting their increasing relevance in our interconnected society.

This chapter focuses on digital literacy as a key 21st century skill. It's not merely about using technology but understanding how it shapes communication, learning, and access to information. In the context of the challenge-based framework, digital literacy becomes a conduit for more profound engagement, allowing students to research real-world problems, collaborate with peers globally, and create solutions that are technologically adept and socially responsible.

As you progress through the chapter, you will discover strategies to embed problem solving into your teaching practice, explore its intersection with other core skills, and examine how integrating this competency can transform the learning environment. By the chapter's end, you will have a clearer vision of how to prepare students for the challenges and opportunities of the future, ensuring they are not just consumers of technology but also innovative creators and critical thinkers.

Dissect the Intersection of 21st Century Skills and Habits of Thinking

Why shift focus to 21st century skills now, especially when I've previously emphasized the transformative power of the habits of thinking? The habits of thinking are deep-seated dispositions that shape the very lens through which we perceive, interact with, and influence the world—they are the enduring intellectual traits that drive us to question, reflect, and engage purposefully with our surroundings. Twenty-first century skills, however, are tools—the practical abilities and know-how that enable us to interact effectively with today's challenges. Think of them as the modern-day equivalents of being able to light a fire or build shelter in prehistoric times. They're the skills we need to navigate the unique complexities and seize the unprecedented opportunities of the contemporary era. The distinction between 21st century skills and academic standards lies in their application and scope. Academic standards are specific, content-focused goals set by educational authorities that outline what students should know and be able to do at various stages of their education. These standards often represent the minimum requirements and are the benchmarks that measure educational attainment.

Twenty-first century skills, in contrast, are less about specific content and more about general capabilities that prepare students for a rapidly changing world. These skills—such as critical thinking, collaboration, and digital literacy—are broader and more dynamic. They transcend traditional academic disciplines and are applicable in various contexts, both within and beyond the classroom. While academic standards may evolve slowly, 21st century skills are agile, continuously adapting to the demands of the global economy, societal shifts, and technological advancements. These skills enable students to apply their knowledge in practical and often innovative ways, preparing them for life and work in ways that traditional standards alone may not.

However, one should not consider 21st century skills and habits of thinking as an either-or binary. In fact, the interplay between the two—the habits and the skills—is where the magic happens. That is, the habits of thinking provide the mindset—the why and the what of learning—while the 21st century skills provide the means—the how. Academic standards fit into the educational ecosystem as the foundation on which both 21st century skills and habits of thinking are built. They outline the essential knowledge and subject-specific skills students are expected to acquire. In essence, standards represent the "what" of education, the critical content that students must understand, while 21st century skills and habits of thinking together represent the "how" and "why"—the application and purpose of this knowledge.

By merging 21st century skills with the habits of thinking, we're ensuring students aren't just thinkers but doers, visionaries who are also adept at executing their visions. The profound habits of thinking lay the fertile ground, and the 21st century skills plant the seeds. While the habits of thinking constitute an underlying philosophical approach, providing a mindset for deeper engagement and reflection, the challenge-based framework is a more structured, actionable framework. It offers a concrete method for applying these habits to real-world challenges. The challenge-based framework, therefore, becomes the vehicle through which habits of thinking transform into action. In this context, 21st century skills serve as the tools that students use within the challenge-based framework to address and solve challenges, turning their reflective thoughts into tangible outcomes. While the habits of thinking encourage questioning and reflection, the challenge-based framework provides a pathway for applying those thoughts through 21st century skills to achieve solutions, essentially moving from thought to action. This explanation delineates the relationship between the conceptual (habits of thinking), the practical (21st century skills), and the methodological (challenge-based framework), illustrating how each contributes to a holistic educational approach.

The overlap between the 21st century skills and habits of thinking provides a rich tapestry that captures the entirety of what modern education should encompass. They are the warp and the weft of the tapestry, each enhancing and empowering the other. To delve deeper into this relationship, let's unravel the intersections between these critical 21st century skills and habits.

- **Critical thinking and problem solving:** At the core of this skill lies the essence of analysis and the drive to decipher complex issues. When mirrored with habit 8, evaluate evidence, it becomes evident that both are instrumental in teaching students to question assumptions, analyze sources, and assess information with an eagle-eyed scrutiny. It's not merely about understanding facts but discerning their validity and relevance. A student analyzing a historical event not only identifies the causes and effects but also critically assesses the credibility of their sources, distinguishing between fact and opinion to draw a reasoned conclusion about the event's significance.

- **Collaboration:** This isn't just about working together but also about co-creating and co-innovating. When juxtaposed with habit 2, taking risks, collaboration takes on a deeper significance, highlighting the beauty of collective risk taking, pushing boundaries, and achieving breakthroughs as a unified force. During a science fair project, a group of students decides to explore a complex chemical reaction that hasn't been covered in class yet. They pool their knowledge, experiment together, and learn from trial and error, leading to a successful demonstration of the reaction.

- **Communication:** Competency in expressing oneself is pivotal in the 21st century. This skill is heightened when enhanced by habit 3, using humor. It underscores the power of wit, satire, and humor as potent tools in communication, enabling students to get their point across memorably and effectively, while also navigating complex emotions. In a presentation about literary devices, a student incorporates humor by creating satirical examples of irony found in modern pop culture, engaging the audience and making the concepts more memorable.

- **Creativity and innovation:** These are essential traits in a world where standard solutions often fall short. They parallel habit 4, create and innovate, and emphasize not just generating ideas but also challenging the status quo, making connections between seemingly disparate concepts, and weaving them into something novel. In an art class, students create an installation piece that recycles materials. They combine unconventional items like plastic bottles and old electronics to construct a model city, reflecting on sustainability.

- **Digital literacy:** As the digital realm becomes our second habitat, mastering its intricacies is non-negotiable. But mere proficiency isn't enough; it also requires responsibility and discipline. Here, habit 5, self-regulation, comes into play, ensuring that students approach digital spaces mindfully, practicing self-control and understanding the implications of their online actions. Students create a blog as part of a class project, curating content responsibly. They practice citing sources accurately, commenting thoughtfully on their peers' posts, and reflecting on the digital footprint their blog leaves.

- **Cultural and global awareness:** In our global village, understanding the world beyond one's immediate surroundings is paramount. Habit 1, cultivating diverse curiosity, complements this skill beautifully, urging students to be inherently curious about global narratives, traditions, and challenges, and fostering a deep-rooted respect and appreciation for the tapestry of human experience. During a unit on global food security, students explore agricultural practices around the world, showing genuine interest in diverse farming methods and discussing how they can address local and global food challenges.

- **Emotional and social intelligence:** Beyond IQ, today's world demands EQ, or emotional intelligence. Recognizing, interpreting, and responding to emotions, both one's own and those of others, are crucial. This skill is deepened when paired with habit 9, embracing lifelong learning and perseverance. As individuals grow and evolve, their capacity for empathy, resilience, and meaningful relationship-building becomes an essential cornerstone of their development. A student council mediator facilitates a resolution between conflicting parties, demonstrating empathy and resilience as they work through the disagreement, showing growth in their leadership and interpersonal skills.

The preceding skills are embedded into the habits of thinking. This integration is evident in how each skill aligns with and enhances a specific habit, showing that the development of 21st century skills connects with fostering the habits of thinking. These 21st century skills derive from established educational frameworks such as the Partnership for 21st Century Learning (2024), which outlines the essential skills needed for success in today's world. Research by Trilling and Fadel (2009) further supports the identification and integration of these skills within modern educational practices.

Link 21st Century Skills to the Challenge-Based Framework

The challenge-based framework nurtures students holistically by fusing academic content with real-world skills and habits of thinking. Here's a deeper dive into how the elements of the challenge-based framework can amplify the development of 21st century skills.

- **Critical thinking and problem solving:**
    - *Strategy*—Develop essential questions that drive deep analysis.
    - *Example*—Pose a question such as, "How can our community transition to sustainable energy practices?"
    - *Implementation*—Guide students to research various energy sources, evaluate their environmental impact, and propose viable solutions. Encourage them to use critical thinking to assess the credibility of their sources and develop well-reasoned arguments.
    - *Tools*—Use digital databases for research, collaborative platforms for discussion, and presentation software for sharing findings.
- **Collaboration:**
    - *Strategy*—Use the engineering design process.
    - *Example*—Challenge students to create a community art project that reflects local needs and desires.
    - *Implementation*—Facilitate stages of empathizing, defining, ideating, prototyping, and testing within student groups. Promote collaborative risk taking and collective problem solving.
    - *Tools*—Utilize collaborative tools such as Google Docs, shared digital whiteboards, and project management software to streamline teamwork.
- **Communication:**
    - *Strategy*—Enhance projects with digital storytelling.
    - *Example*—Have students produce a local history documentary.
    - *Implementation*—Teach students how to research, design, and present their findings using digital storytelling techniques. Focus on clear, effective communication and the integration of multimedia elements.
    - *Tools*—Use video editing software, digital cameras, and online presentation platforms.

- **Digital literacy:**
  - *Strategy*—Integrate technology into research and presentation.
  - *Example*—Have students create a blog as part of a class project.
  - *Implementation*—Instruct students on responsible digital content creation, including citation practices, respectful online interactions, and digital footprint management.
  - *Tools*—Employ blogging platforms, content management systems, and online collaborative spaces.
- **Cultural and global awareness:**
  - *Strategy*—Explore global issues through interdisciplinary projects.
  - *Example*—Conduct a project on global food scarcity.
  - *Implementation*—Encourage students to investigate agricultural practices worldwide, considering cultural, economic, and geopolitical factors. Foster discussions that promote cultural sensitivity and global awareness.
  - *Tools*—Use global databases, video conferencing tools for international collaboration, and mapping software for visualizing data.
- **Emotional and social intelligence:**
  - *Strategy*—Facilitate projects that involve social interaction and reflection.
  - *Example*—Engage students in redesigning urban spaces
  - *Implementation*—Incorporate activities that require students to practice patience, resilience, and respect. Encourage reflective practices to help students process their emotional and social learning.
  - *Tools*—Implement reflection journals, peer feedback systems, and SEL platforms.

Consider the following actionable strategies.

- **Design challenges with intentional skill integration:** Begin with the end in mind by identifying the 21st century skills you want to develop through each challenge. Design essential questions and project tasks that naturally require these skills.
- **Leverage technology for skill development:** Incorporate digital tools that enhance collaboration, communication, and research. Familiarize students with various digital platforms that support project-based learning.
- **Foster reflective practices:** Encourage students to reflect on their learning processes and their skill development. Use journals, peer reviews, and self-assessments to help students become aware of their growth.
- **Create real-world connections:** Link challenges to real-world issues that resonate with students. This not only makes learning more relevant but also motivates students to apply their skills in meaningful ways.
- **Facilitate cross-disciplinary projects:** Design challenges that integrate multiple subject areas, showing students how 21st century skills apply across different contexts and content areas.

- **Support collaborative learning environments:** Use collaborative tools and strategies to create an environment where students can learn from each other, share ideas, and co-create solutions.

By embedding these strategies into the challenge-based framework, you can ensure that students are not only learning academic content but also developing essential 21st-century skills that will serve them well beyond the classroom.

Differentiate Grade-Level Examples Across Core Disciplines

As students progress through their schooling, their exposure to and interaction with the core disciplines should evolve in complexity. By tailoring challenges to grade levels, you can ensure age-appropriate, stimulating, and progressive learning experiences. This approach not only aligns with academic standards but also facilitates the acquisition of 21st century skills through the challenge-based framework. These skills, such as critical thinking, collaboration, digital literacy, and global awareness, are integrated into each challenge, ensuring that students develop the competencies necessary for success in the modern world.

Challenges in Elementary School Grades

At the elementary level, the emphasis on 21st century skills includes nurturing creativity, introducing basic digital tools, and sparking curiosity about the world. These foundational skills are vital for young learners to engage effectively with the content and to build a base for more complex skills as they advance.

Let's expand through an example of using mathematics in creating a classroom store.

- **Challenge description:** In this challenge, students will apply basic arithmetic in a real-world context by setting up and managing a classroom store. They will handle tasks such as pricing items, making purchases, and even tracking sales. This interactive project not only teaches fundamental mathematics concepts such as addition, subtraction, and currency manipulation but also introduces students to basic economic principles.

- **Combining habits and skills:** This challenge merges 21st century skills with habits of thinking by requiring students to use critical thinking for problem solving in a practical setting. They will evaluate evidence (habit 8) by checking the accuracy of their mathematics operations and collaborate with classmates, even when doing so may require them to take on new perspectives, to operate the store efficiently (habit 2, take risks).

- **Detailed guidance:** Introduce the concept of currency and basic arithmetic operations to the students. Allow students to create their own mock items to sell, pricing them using the mathematics skills they have learned. Students then buy and sell items using classroom currency, practicing their arithmetic in each transaction. Throughout the activity, guide students to reflect on their process, encouraging them to think about how they arrived at their solutions and how they might improve their operations.

Other challenges suitable for this grade band could include the following.

- **Science:** Life cycle of a butterfly—Students track and document the stages of caterpillar metamorphosis, using digital tools to record observations.

- **Language arts:** My first storybook—Pupils create a digital or physical book with their own stories, fostering creativity and narrative skills.
- **Social studies:** Festivals around the world—Students investigate different cultural celebrations, developing global awareness through interactive activities and multimedia presentations.

These challenges develop 21st century skills by providing practical, hands-on learning experiences that are engaging and educationally meaningful. They are structured to spark interest and cater to the natural curiosity of young students, laying the groundwork for more advanced skills in higher grades.

Challenges in Middle School Grades

For middle school grades, where students are more capable of handling complex tasks and abstract thinking, challenges can be crafted to promote deeper inquiry and interdisciplinary learning. Let's use a project focused on clean water as a science example for these grades.

- **Challenge description:** Middle school students are often passionate about global issues and are at an age where they can understand and tackle more substantive problems. In the clean water project, students explore the pressing issue of water pollution and its global implications.
- **Combining habits and skills:** Students must employ their investigative skills to identify the causes of water pollution in their local area or in a part of the world they study. They conduct research using digital databases to gather data and analyze findings. This process requires them to apply critical thinking and problem-solving skills as they evaluate sources (mirroring habit 8). Collaboration is crucial as students work in groups to brainstorm potential solutions, share tasks, and synthesize information (aligned with habit 2), ensuring that everyone contributes to the discussion and project development.
- **Detailed guidance:** Begin by introducing the topic of water pollution, including its sources, impacts, and current solutions. Assign students to small groups and have each group select a specific aspect of water pollution to research. Teach students how to conduct research using digital tools, emphasizing the evaluation of sources for credibility and relevance. Guide students through the brainstorming process to develop potential solutions to the issue they've researched. Culminate the project with a presentation or a written report where groups share their findings and proposed solutions with the class or community stakeholders, practicing their communication and presentation skills.

Other challenges for middle school students might include the following.

- **Mathematics:** Design your dream park—Students use geometry and measurement to create a scale drawing of a park, practicing spatial awareness and design principles.
- **Language arts:** Podcast series on literary heroes—Students produce a podcast discussing characters from literature, enhancing oral communication and critical analysis.
- **Social studies:** The rise and fall of ancient civilizations—In this group project, students use research and presentation tools to explore and share about ancient societies, understanding historical dynamics and cultural evolution.

These challenges are more rigorous than those in elementary school, suitable for the developmental stage of middle school students. They combine academic standards with 21st century skills, providing a well-rounded, engaging learning experience that prepares students for secondary education and beyond.

Challenges in High School Grades

In high school, the capacity for independent thought and tackling global issues becomes central to student development. Let's take a detailed look at the "Climate Change Summit" challenge as a science example.

- **Challenge description:** This challenge engages students with one of the most pressing global issues of our time: climate change. High school students, with a more sophisticated understanding of the world and access to advanced research tools, are perfectly poised to engage in this in-depth exploration.

- **Combining habits and skills:** Students will need to employ critical thinking and problem-solving skills to understand the multifaceted aspects of climate change, including its scientific basis, social implications, and the economics of sustainable practices. They will research using digital databases, engage with climate models, and collaborate to synthesize their findings into comprehensive presentations, embodying habits 2 and 8 as they venture into complex problem solving.

- **Detailed guidance:** Introduce the students to the concept of climate change, including its scientific underpinnings, the controversies, and the current state of global policies and practices. Divide the class into research teams, each focusing on a different aspect of climate change: causes, effects, mitigation strategies, policy implications, and more. Facilitate training sessions on how to use digital research tools, data analysis software, and presentation platforms. Guide the students through the process of organizing a mock summit where each team presents their findings and engages in debate and discussion about the best courses of action. Wrap up the challenge with reflective sessions where students evaluate their own learning and the potential real-world impact of the proposed solutions.

Other challenges that high school students could engage with might include the following.

- **Mathematics:** City traffic optimization—Students apply calculus and statistics to real-world scenarios, proposing innovative solutions to reduce local traffic congestion.

- **Language arts:** Digital literary magazine—Students get hands-on experience with digital publishing by curating and editing a school literary magazine that showcases student work.

- **Social studies:** Community oral history project—This project connects students with local history by compiling interviews and stories into a digital archive.

Each of these challenges is purposefully multidisciplinary, requiring students to draw on a range of skills and knowledge bases. These projects not only align with academic standards but also prepare students for the complexities of the modern world, ensuring they leave high school ready to contribute to society as knowledgeable, skilled, and engaged citizens.

Concluding Thoughts

Navigating the ever-evolving intricacies of the 21st century demands more than just rote knowledge or mere skills—it calls for a mindset that can adapt, discern, and innovate despite uncertainty. This is where the harmonious interplay of 21st century skills and the habits of thinking emerge as a pivotal force.

Consider the 21st century skills as a robust tool kit filled with multifaceted instruments, each tailored for specific tasks. From critical thinking that unravels puzzles to communication that bridges divides, these tools are indispensable. But having tools isn't enough. Enter the habits of thinking. They act as the compass, offering direction and perspective, ensuring that we use our tools with wisdom, purpose, and foresight. In uncharted territories, while our skills help us forge ahead, our habits ensure we're headed in the right direction.

The challenge-based framework doesn't just serve as a pedagogical method; it embodies a philosophy. It believes in the potency of learning that's rooted in real life, transcends textbook confines, and resonates with global realities. By placing students in the heart of genuine challenges, it nudges them to employ their skills and habits in tandem, mirroring the multifaceted demands of the outside world.

As educators, our goal isn't merely to produce students who excel at tests. We strive to sculpt learners who view the world with curiosity, connect dots across disciplines, and approach challenges with an innovator's zeal and a thinker's depth. In intertwining 21st century skills with habits of thinking and anchoring them within the challenge-based framework, we foster the development of such holistic learners.

In our quest to prepare students for tomorrow, it's imperative to provide them with more than just knowledge. We must equip them with the ability to apply this knowledge meaningfully, to think critically, to innovate, and to understand the vast, diverse world they inhabit. In doing so, we're not just educating; we're shaping thinkers, innovators, and, most importantly, aware global citizens ready to make their mark.

Chapter 14

Engage Teacher Collaboration

From the bustling workshops of the Renaissance where artists, craftspeople, philosophers, and scholars exchanged ideas, to contemporary classrooms, the essence of collaboration remains a potent force. During the Renaissance era, under the golden roofs of Florence or within the vibrant courts of Venice, collaborative spirit was not a mere happenstance. It was the norm. In Renaissance Florence, the workshop, or *bottega*, was a crucible of collaboration, where masters, apprentices, and artisans converged to produce works of art and innovation (Goldthwaite, 2009).

Imagine a setting where Botticelli discusses hues with a local dye maker, or where Machiavelli engages in a deep discourse with thinkers of his time at a Florentine café. These individuals weren't isolated experts working in vacuums; they thrived on collective wisdom. Their shared passion, disagreements, and mutual respect paved the way for innovations and works of great beauty that still resonate with us today.

Similarly, in our contemporary educational settings, such collaborative endeavors have not lost their value. While the canvas has changed from sunlit piazzas to technology-equipped classrooms, the essence of collaboration has remained the same. The walls of classrooms today can reverberate with the same cooperative spirit, where educators come together, each bringing their expertise to the table, discussing, brainstorming, and crafting lessons that echo the interdisciplinary nature of the challenge-based framework. Just as the Renaissance visionaries built on each other's ideas to shape the epoch of human history, educators today have the potential to build on collective knowledge, methods, and experiences to maximize and redefine learning experiences for their students. When channeled efficiently, the magic of cohesive collaboration among educators can be the cornerstone for an educational renaissance in our age, ensuring that learning isn't just impactful, but truly transformative.

Teacher collaboration is crucial to binding the threads of learning through the tapestry that is the challenge-based framework. The framework relies heavily on the cooperative efforts of educators to brainstorm, design, and execute challenges that are authentic, interdisciplinary, and reflective of real-world complexities. It necessitates a fusion of diverse perspectives and expertise, which only a community of engaged and communicative educators can provide. Teachers might co-create curriculum units that blend science with technology or intertwine mathematics with the arts. In doing so, they mirror the collaborative spirit of the Renaissance, not only by bridging various disciplines but by cultivating an environment where the exchange of ideas is valued and where each teacher's expertise is seen as a critical component of the collective goal.

In this chapter, we delve into the dynamics of effective teacher collaboration within the challenge-based framework. You will discover how educators can unite their strengths and address the multifaceted nature of teaching and learning. We will explore how such partnerships can lead to the development of rich, immersive challenges that prepare students for a world where collaborative skills are not optional but essential. This chapter also offers practical strategies for fostering strong collaborative relationships among teachers, discusses the impact of these collaborations on student outcomes, and examines how they form the cornerstone of a thriving learning community. In the Concluding Thoughts section at the end of the chapter, you can reflect on collaborative teacher efforts, and you will understand that just as the Renaissance artists and thinkers advanced human achievement through cooperation, so too can educators propel the advancement of education through a shared commitment to the collective intelligence that the challenge-based framework supports.

Create a Canvas of Collaboration

The challenge-based framework is like a vast canvas, and collaboration among educators is like artists pooling their unique colors, brush strokes, and techniques to create a holistic masterpiece. Among the many facets that make this collective artistry truly shine, two stand out prominently: interdisciplinary synergy and the pooling of resources.

Interdisciplinary synergy refers to the intricate interconnectedness of subjects. As teachers collaborate, they bring with them a wealth of expertise from their respective disciplines. The beauty of this lies not just in the melding of different subjects but in the way they can amplify and enrich one another. Imagine a classroom where a history lesson on the Industrial Revolution seamlessly transitions into a science experiment about steam engines. Or consider the profundity when a geometric theorem from a mathematics class becomes the cornerstone for analyzing the structure of a poem in a literature session. Such instances of interdisciplinary resonance elevate student engagement and foster a more profound understanding of concepts, as they're viewed from multifaceted lenses. Indeed, when teachers with diverse expertise collaborate, they create a dynamic learning environment where each can contribute their unique perspective and knowledge. For instance, a history teacher and a science teacher might collaborate to create a comprehensive unit on the Industrial Revolution. The history teacher provides context on the era, the social changes, and the economic forces at play, while the science teacher guides students through the mechanics and science of steam engines, which were pivotal to that era.

Here's how such collaboration could unfold.

- **Sharing knowledge:**
  - → The history teacher might start the unit with a discussion of the historical context, after which the science teacher could introduce the principles of steam power.
  - → The teachers plan a session together, discussing the key points that each will cover, ensuring that their lessons complement each other.

- **Integrating schedules:**
  - → The teachers coordinate their lesson plans and schedules. They might dedicate a week where both history and science lessons focus on the Industrial Revolution, allowing students to make connections between the classes.
  - → They agree on joint classroom activities, perhaps scheduling a lab day right after a history lecture for immediate application of the concepts learned.

- **Collaborative teaching:**
  - → The teachers might conduct a joint class where they discuss the history of steam power alongside a live demonstration of a steam engine.
  - → Students could work on a project where they build their own simple steam engines, integrating historical understanding with scientific inquiry.

By planning and executing such collaborative lessons, teachers can break down disciplinary silos, providing a holistic educational experience that reflects the true nature of understanding in the real world. This approach not only enhances the learning process but also models the kind of teamwork and interdisciplinary thinking that students will need in their future careers and lives.

Alongside this interdisciplinary synergy emerges the creation of rich resource pools. The world of education is vast, and every educator, through their journey, amasses a collection of strategies, tools, and methods. When teachers collaborate within the challenge-based framework, there is an organic, open exchange. It's reminiscent of scholars in an academic agora, where every idea is a valuable contribution, every strategy a potential game changer, and every resource a new tool for enlightenment. From innovative teaching methodologies that one educator might have tried and tested, to unique assessment techniques another might have stumbled on in their research—all these resources, when shared, become integral pieces of a larger educational mosaic. This pooling of knowledge not only broadens the horizon for each educator but also enriches the learning experience for students, making education not just a process but a dynamic, evolving journey.

To cultivate a communal resource pool, teachers initially need to establish a shared digital platform—such as Google Drive or a learning management system—where they can upload, categorize, and retrieve various educational materials. This space should be meticulously organized, with clear labels for different subjects and resource types, and it should be accessible to all educators involved. Each teacher would contribute their own materials, such as lesson plans, project templates, or assessment tools, adhering to a common format for consistency and ease of use.

Regular collaboration meetings are essential, not only to discuss and enrich the resource pool but also to identify any resource gaps and coordinate collective efforts to fill them. When a teacher introduces novel tools or strategies to others, they should provide training sessions to ensure all educators can leverage these resources effectively. An essential part of this collaborative effort includes a feedback mechanism, where educators can evaluate the utility of shared materials and offer insights for refinement.

Encouragement and acknowledgment of active contribution and utilization of the resource pool can reinforce a culture of sharing and continuous professional development. This approach ensures that the resource pool remains vibrant, current, and reflective of the collective expertise within the teaching community, thus enhancing the educational journey for both educators and students.

In essence, as teachers come together within the framework of the challenge-based framework, they aren't merely working side by side; they're weaving a tapestry of knowledge, experiences, and skills, destined to shape the future of holistic education. For practical guidance, it's essential to establish a culture within the school that values and encourages the sharing of individual expertise.

Here's how you might foster such an environment.

- **Cultivate a culture of sharing:** Begin by ensuring there's clear communication from school leadership that values the sharing of skills and knowledge. Highlighting this need and these values in staff meetings can raise awareness and set expectations.

- **Implement regular collaboration meetings:** Schedule dedicated time for regular collaborative meetings where teachers can discuss potential partnerships, share ideas, and plan interdisciplinary lessons. These should be structured yet flexible enough to allow for spontaneous creativity and sharing.

- **Create a skills inventory:** Develop a faculty-wide inventory where teachers can list their skills, areas of interest, and expertise. This registry can be a resource for finding potential collaborations and understanding the wealth of knowledge present within the staff.

- **Organize show-and-tell sessions:** Host periodic show-and-tell events for teachers. In these sessions, staff can present something they're passionate about, whether it's related to their subject area or an outside interest that could enrich the classroom experience.

- **Facilitate peer observations:** Encourage teachers to observe each other's classes, not as an evaluation, but to gain insight into different teaching styles and methods that they could incorporate into their own practice.

- **Provide professional development workshops:** Offer workshops that focus on collaboration and sharing in the educational environment. These can provide teachers with strategies for effective sharing and communication of their unique skills.

- **Incentivize collaboration:** Recognize and reward teachers who actively participate in collaborative efforts, whether through acknowledgment in staff meetings, a spot on the school newsletter, or even a small incentive.

By introducing these practical steps, you create an environment that not only recognizes the value of each teacher's individual skills but also actively promotes the sharing and integration of these skills to enrich the educational offerings of the school.

Patrick Lencioni (2002), a well-respected expert in organizational health and the author of several influential books on leadership and teamwork, presents a powerful model for team development in his seminal work, *The Five Dysfunctions of a Team*. This framework identifies and offers ways to address five core dysfunctions that can impede team success: (1) absence of trust, (2) fear of conflict, (3) lack of commitment, (4) avoidance of accountability, and (5) inattention to results. Applying Lencioni's insights to educational environments, particularly within the challenge-based framework, can significantly enhance collaboration and effectiveness among educators.

Lencioni's (2002) framework is highly relevant to the challenge-based framework because it provides a structured approach to fostering a cohesive, collaborative culture among educators. This collaborative culture is essential for the successful implementation of the challenge-based framework, which relies on teamwork and shared goals. Here's a more in-depth look at how to address each of Lencioni's five dysfunctions within the context of the challenge-based framework to support and enhance its goals.

1. **Build trust:** Trust is like the primer on canvas; it is the foundation of any effective team and crucial for the functioning of every subsequent layer. In an environment where the challenge-based framework is used, educators must trust one another to share ideas openly without fear of judgment. This can be achieved by engaging in team-building activities that allow for vulnerabilities to be shared and bonds to be formed. Schools can host regular team-building activities, retreats to focus on strengthening relationships, and open forums, which are collaborative discussions that serve as a platform for communication, shared learning, and problem solving. Open forums may include such topics as curriculum development and educational research. By fostering a safe and supportive environment, educators can build the trust necessary to engage fully in collaborative problem solving and innovation.

2. **Encourage healthy conflict:** Healthy conflict is crucial for making the best decisions. Within the challenge-based framework, educators need to feel comfortable engaging in constructive debates about teaching strategies, student needs, and challenge designs. Encouraging debate and open discussion in collaboration sessions, and addressing conflicting ideas through structured discussions, can lead to more robust solutions and innovation. Remember that every teacher has a unique role to play, bringing a wealth of knowledge and experience. Workshops and seminars can help each educator understand their specific contribution and, equally importantly, recognize and value the contributions of their peers. Just as a beautiful mosaic is incomplete without its individual pieces, so too is the learning environment.

3. **Foster commitment:** Cultivate a sense of shared ownership among team members. When decisions are made, ensure that every voice has been heard

so that all members can commit to the action plan. Establish clear goals and ensure that every educator understands how these contribute to the overall mission of the challenge-based framework. This shared commitment helps align efforts and drives collective success.

4. **Hold one another accountable:** Create an environment where peers feel comfortable holding each other accountable. This can involve setting shared goals, regularly checking in on progress, and implementing peer reviews of teaching strategies and classroom management techniques. By maintaining accountability, the team ensures that everyone contributes to the success of the challenge-based framework.

5. **Focus on achieving results:** Keep the team focused on achieving its goals by establishing clear metrics for success that everyone understands and agrees on. Celebrate the wins and analyze the losses together, learning and growing as a cohesive unit. This focus on results helps maintain momentum and ensures that the team continuously strives for improvement.

By addressing the dysfunctions with these positive actions, educators can create a more cohesive and effective team environment, which is essential for the successful implementation of the challenge-based framework. Lencioni's (2002) framework not only illuminates common barriers to team success but also provides actionable strategies for overcoming them, thereby enhancing the collaborative efforts necessary for the challenge-based framework to thrive.

In dealing with interpersonal issues that could hinder the sharing of knowledge for interdisciplinary learning, consider these strategies.

- Address any power dynamics or hierarchies that may exist. Ensure that all educators feel their contributions are equally valued.
- Provide training on conflict resolution and communication skills to help navigate the complexities of interpersonal dynamics.
- Implement regular check-ins where teachers can discuss not just their successes but also their challenges and receive support from their peers.
- Encourage mentorship programs where more experienced teachers can share their expertise and guidance with newer colleagues in a structured way.

In the following example, we explore and highlight how teachers can collaborate across disciplines using the challenge-based framework to guide students in understanding and solving local environmental issues. The project centers on the essential question, "How can our community reduce its carbon footprint?" The challenge-based framework template facilitates teacher collaboration, highlighting the integration of various subjects and the collective effort required to lead students through this complex, real-world problem.

By rigorously applying the challenge-based template, this project exemplifies how teachers can lead students through a collaborative, interdisciplinary approach to solving real-world problems. The integration of curricular standards and the fostering of 21st century skills through habits of thinking prepare students to become proactive, informed citizens. Figure 14.1 provides an example of the completed template with an emphasis on teacher collaboration.

STUDENT GOAL:
Develop and implement a campaign that effectively reduces the school community's carbon footprint.

ESSENTIAL QUESTION:
How can our community reduce its carbon footprint effectively and sustainably?

STANDARDS INTEGRATION:

Science:
Environmental systems, energy consumption, and sustainability principles

Mathematics:
Data collection, analysis, and interpretation

Language arts:
Persuasive writing and communication strategies

Art:
Visual design for campaign materials and messaging

ENGINEERING DESIGN PROCESS:

Teacher Actions and Support	Student Actions and Behavior
Ask	*Ask*
Identify specific aspects of the community's carbon footprint to address. *Teacher collaboration:* Science teachers facilitate discussions on environmental systems and data collection. Mathematics teachers assist in developing surveys and data analysis tools.	Engage actively with each engineering design process step, asking questions throughout the process.
Imagine	*Imagine*
Brainstorm possible interventions for carbon reduction. *Teacher collaboration:* Art teachers lead creative brainstorming sessions to generate campaign ideas. Language arts teachers guide persuasive techniques to engage the community.	Contribute ideas during brainstorming sessions.
Plan	*Plan*
Design a detailed campaign incorporating the brainstormed ideas. *Teacher collaboration:* All teachers collaboratively help students outline steps, assign roles, and develop timelines. Language arts teachers assist with crafting compelling messages.	Collaborate with peers from different disciplines.
Create	*Create*
Implement the campaign within the school community. *Teacher collaboration:* Teachers oversee different components, such as science teachers guiding data-driven decisions, mathematics teachers assisting with quantitative assessments, and art teachers helping with visual design.	Participate in the execution and implementation of the campaign.

Figure 14.1: Use the challenge-based framework and teacher collaboration to develop and implement a carbon footprint reduction campaign in a school community.

continued →

Improve Reflect on the campaign's impact and iterate to enhance effectiveness. *Teacher collaboration:* Teachers lead reflection sessions to assess outcomes, gather feedback, and plan for improvements. Summary of teacher collaborative actions: • Facilitate engineering design process steps. • Provide resources and expert knowledge. • Scaffold learning experiences tailored to each discipline. • Guide interdisciplinary collaboration and integration.	*Improve* Examine carbon-emissions data from school systems once campaign is underway, compare to earlier carbon-emissions data, and search for ways to continue reducing carbon emissions.

HABITS OF THINKING:

Teacher Actions and Support	Student Actions and Behavior
Habit 1: Cultivate diverse curiosity Teachers model inquisitive behavior, encouraging students to explore various environmental issues and potential solutions.	*Habit 1:* Cultivate diverse curiosity
Habit 2: Take risks Teachers support innovative campaign strategies, fostering a safe environment for experimentation.	*Habit 2:* Take risks
Habit 3: Use humor Teachers incorporate humor in communication, making the campaign engaging and relatable.	*Habit 3:* Use humor
Habit 4: Create and innovate Teachers promote creative thinking in design and messaging.	*Habit 4:* Create and innovate
Habit 5: Self-regulate Teachers guide students in setting goals and managing timelines, fostering self-discipline.	*Habit 5:* Self-regulate

ASSESSMENTS:

Formative assessment: Ongoing observations of student engagement with the engineering design process, feedback during brainstorming and planning stages.

Summative assessment: Evaluation based on the campaign's outcomes, including measurable impact on the community's carbon footprint.

TEACHER REFLECTION: WHAT DID I DO SUCCESSFULLY? WHAT WILL I DO DIFFERENTLY NEXT TIME?

Reflect on the project's successes and areas for improvement. Discuss lessons learned and potential changes for future projects. Teachers facilitate reflective discussions with students and document insights for continuous improvement.

By rigorously applying the challenge-based template, this project exemplifies how teachers can lead students through a collaborative, interdisciplinary approach to solving real-world problems. Integrating curricular standards and fostering of 21st century skills through habits of thinking prepare students to become proactive, informed citizens.

To highlight the importance of collaboration in implementing the challenge-based frame, I need to emphasize how collaborative practices among educators can enhance the effectiveness of this approach. The following strategies focus on fostering a collaborative culture that supports interdisciplinary learning and the development of 21st century skills.

- **Channels of communication:** Like the flowing rivers connecting distant lands, open channels of communication connect varied pedagogies. Encourage an ongoing dialogue between educators by institutionalizing regular departmental meetings, initiating cross-subject discussion sessions, and establishing platforms for feedback. Such measures ensure that ideas don't remain siloed and that there's a constant exchange of pedagogical wisdom.

- **Joint professional odyssey:** Shared professional development isn't merely about learning together but evolving together. Organizing joint workshops or training sessions on the challenge-based framework not only aligns teaching methodologies but also solidifies the bond between educators as they share insights, challenges, and successes.

- **Celebrate and reflect:** As in any journey, the collaborative quest will present both achievements and challenges. It's crucial to pause and celebrate team successes, be it the successful integration of a challenge-based framework lesson or a breakthrough in inter-departmental collaboration. Equally vital is the act of reflection, where challenges are not viewed as setbacks but as opportunities to learn, adapt, and grow.

Bridging educational research with the principles we've discussed, we see a clear parallel: research consistently shows that teacher collaboration correlates with improved teaching performance and higher student achievement. A study by Matthew Ronfeldt, Susanna Owens Farmer, Kiel McQueen, and Jason A. Grissom (2015) found that teachers' performance improves in environments characterized by high-quality collaboration. Similarly, a review by Yvonne L. Goddard, Roger D. Goddard, and Megan Tschannen-Moran (2007) revealed a positive correlation between teacher collaboration and student achievement. These findings underscore the universal truth that teamwork, underpinned by trust and common goals, is pivotal to success across fields. A harmonious, collaborative environment leads to enhanced outcomes, highlighting the importance of fostering such dynamics within educational settings.

In the context of the challenge-based framework, collaboration's role is magnified. For the challenge-based framework to flourish and be as dynamic as intended, collaboration is not a mere option: it's imperative. The bedrock of its triumphant execution lies not just in working side by side but in genuinely interlacing the individual strengths, strategies, and insights that each educator brings to the educational tableau.

Educators work through their differences by focusing on their shared goal: enhancing student learning through interdisciplinary collaboration. They overcome interpersonal conflicts by committing to open communication, mutual respect, and a willingness to adapt their methods. This process not only enriches the educational experience for students but also models the importance of collaboration, critical thinking, and adaptability, thus seamlessly integrating the principles of effective teamwork with the core tenets of the challenge-based framework.

Use Interdisciplinary Projects to Combine Curricula

To further develop interdisciplinary projects through teacher collaboration, let's expand with a narrative that weaves in practical, actionable guidelines.

Interdisciplinary projects, when anchored by the robust support of teacher collaboration, transform the educational landscape into a dynamic arena where the fusion of subjects provides students with a comprehensive understanding of complex concepts. For such collaboration to be effective, it must be intentional and systematic.

Begin with shared goals, where teachers from different disciplines come together to identify the objectives they collectively want to achieve. Establishing these shared goals not only provides direction but also fosters a sense of unity and purpose. This process of identification can involve collaborative discussions where teachers explore the overlaps in their curriculum and agree on a common theme or essential question to guide the project. For example, they might decide to focus on a theme like sustainability, where each discipline contributes its perspective on environmental issues.

Next, schedule regular interdisciplinary planning sessions. These sessions are crucial for educators to codesign projects, align their curricula, and integrate various disciplinary standards. It's during these gatherings that teachers can pool their knowledge, share pedagogical resources, and strategize on how to guide students through the learning process in a cohesive manner. These sessions should be structured to allow for the thorough mapping of the project, ensuring that all relevant standards and learning objectives are addressed.

- Encourage open lines of communication. Facilitate communication through a designated digital platform where ongoing conversations can occur, obstacles can be addressed, and triumphs can be celebrated. Clear communication channels ensure that every educator is on the same page and can contribute actively to the project's development. Platforms like Google Classroom, Slack, or Microsoft Teams can be effective tools for maintaining this communication.

- Designate a project lead for coordination. While collaboration is a joint effort, having a project lead can streamline the process, ensuring tasks are completed, timelines are met, and the project's vision remains clear. The lead acts as a facilitator, allowing for a balanced contribution from all teachers involved. This role is critical for maintaining momentum and ensuring accountability throughout the project.

- Implement reflective practice. After each interdisciplinary project, hold a debriefing session. This reflection allows for an honest discussion about what worked well, what challenges arose, and how to improve future collaborations. It is an opportunity to iterate on the process, refining the approach for better outcomes in subsequent projects. These sessions should focus on both the process and the student outcomes, providing insights that can inform future interdisciplinary endeavors.

By embedding these generalizable guidelines into the fabric of teacher collaboration, the interdisciplinary projects not only thrive but also become transformative experiences for both students and educators. The synergy created through such collaboration not only prepares students for the integrated nature of real-world problems but also mirrors the collaborative efforts they will likely encounter in their future endeavors.

To illustrate how to structure interdisciplinary projects and the benefits they offer, here are a few detailed examples.

- **Art and science:** Geometry in nature
    - *Objective*—Understand and appreciate the patterns and shapes that occur naturally in the environment.
    - *Approach*—Students could begin by exploring the symmetry in leaves, the fractal patterns in ferns, or the spirals in sunflowers, linking them to mathematical concepts. Subsequently, they could create art projects to represent these patterns, integrating their scientific observations with artistic expression.
    - *Benefits*—Such a project helps students see the beauty in nature through a scientific lens and understand art as a reflection of the natural world.
- **Literature and history:** Diving into the cultural context of novels
    - *Objective*—Delve deeper into the historical and cultural backdrop of literary works, enriching comprehension and empathy.
    - *Approach*—Choose a historical novel, like *The Great Gatsby* or *Things Fall Apart*. While the literature class focuses on character development, themes, and narrative techniques, the history class can dive into the Roaring Twenties' socioeconomic dynamics or precolonial West African societies, respectively. Students could even role-play, reenacting scenes from the novel, but with added context based on their historical understanding.
    - *Benefits*—Such an intertwined approach not only deepens students' appreciation of the narrative but also instills a profound understanding of the societal norms, pressures, and events that shaped the characters and their decisions.
- **Extension ideas:**
    - *Mathematics and music*—Explore the mathematical patterns in musical rhythms, scales, and harmonies.
    - *Geography and culinary arts*—Investigate the origins of various cuisines and how geographical factors influence dietary choices.
    - *Economics and environmental science:*—Analyze the economic implications of environmental policies and how economies adapt to ecological constraints.

By fostering such interdisciplinary collaborations, educators ensure that students are not learning in silos. Instead, they're encouraged to draw connections, develop a multidimensional perspective, and appreciate the rich tapestry of knowledge that our world offers. These projects are more than just academic exercises; they are journeys into the interwoven narratives of our world, igniting curiosity and deepening understanding.

Sustain Collaboration Through Regular Check-Ins

Regular check-ins play a pivotal role in ensuring the smooth and effective implementation of the challenge-based framework. These consistent interactions offer educators an avenue to sync up, share insights, discuss challenges, and collaboratively refine their teaching approaches. Let's delve deeper into how to effectively structure and leverage these check-ins through purpose-driven formal meetings, informal coffee chats, and feedback loops.

Purpose-Driven Formal Meetings

In the quest for a harmonious implementation of the challenge-based framework, purpose-driven formal meetings are essential. These meetings, occurring weekly or biweekly, should reflect the current phase of the academic cycle, allowing educators to remain aligned with both the immediate and long-term goals of their collaborative projects. These meetings should include the following.

- **Setting the agenda:** Before the meeting, circulate a clear agenda that provides a scaffold for discussion. This agenda may celebrate recent successes, encouraging a positive tone from the outset. It should also leave space to identify challenges, providing a forum to openly address issues without judgment. The agenda should stimulate brainstorming sessions, where educators, free from the constraints of formal instruction, can explore creative solutions to pedagogical challenges. Additionally, allocate time for strategic planning, ensuring upcoming projects are thoroughly prepared with assigned roles and responsibilities.

- **Utilizing collaborative tools:** To harness the full potential of collaborative efforts, employ digital tools that foster effective communication and organization. Platforms such as Google Docs offer a shared space where team members can easily access meeting minutes, ideas, and resources and edit in real time. Trello, or similar project management tools, can help track the progress of various tasks, visualize workflows, and assign deadlines, ensuring that every member of the team is informed and accountable.

- **Integrating guest speakers:** Periodically infusing new perspectives can be incredibly beneficial, which is where guest speakers come into play. These experts can introduce fresh pedagogical approaches, share industry insights, or offer guidance on educational technology. Such sessions not only serve as professional development but can reinvigorate the team's commitment to collaboration and innovation.

By meticulously structuring these formal meetings, you can maintain the momentum necessary for successful interdisciplinary collaboration, keeping the team focused on shared objectives and continually enhancing their collective practice.

Informal Coffee Chats

Informal coffee chats complement the more structured nature of formal meetings, providing a casual setting that can often lead to breakthroughs in collaborative efforts. Here's how to make the most of these gatherings.

- **Choosing the right setting:** Ambiance matters. Opt for the teacher's lounge or a cozy corner in a local café where conversations can flow naturally and without the formality of a classroom or office. A change in environment can stimulate creativity and make teachers feel more at ease to share openly.

- **Scheduling with flexibility:** Coffee chats should be regular but not rigidly scheduled, allowing for spontaneity. Whether it's weekly catch-ups or monthly reflections, the key is consistency without the pressure of mandatory attendance. This flexibility respects teachers' varying schedules and maintains an atmosphere of willingness rather than obligation.

- **Guiding the conversation:** While there's no strict agenda, guide the conversation to ensure it's productive. Start with prompts like recent classroom successes, innovative teaching methods, or even broader educational trends. However, leave room for organic discussion that might veer into shared hobbies or interests—these moments can be surprisingly pertinent to building team rapport.

- **Fostering camaraderie:** Use these chats to deepen relationships. When teachers share not only their professional challenges but also personal victories or anecdotes, it humanizes the team and strengthens bonds. This camaraderie is essential when teachers return to the more structured environment of the classroom or a project meeting, as it fosters a sense of unity and mutual support.

Through these informal coffee chats, teachers can find themselves part of a supportive community, where the exchange of ideas is just as valuable as the exchange of empathy and encouragement. This informal setting is where barriers are broken down, and the seeds of innovation are sown.

Feedback Loops

Feedback loops are crucial for ensuring that collaborative efforts remain productive and goal oriented. Let's elaborate on how to implement them effectively within an educational framework.

- **Sustaining feedback loops through peer observations:** Cultivate a culture where peer observations are normal and welcomed as opportunities for growth rather than critiques. By observing one another's teaching, educators can gain new insights and ideas, and offer constructive feedback from an informed perspective. Following these observations, feedback sessions should be structured to encourage reflective practice, highlighting strengths and areas for development in a supportive manner. This practice can lead to significant professional growth as teachers see their own practices through the eyes of their peers.

- **Leveraging shared digital forums:** In the digital age, platforms like Slack or Microsoft Teams are invaluable for creating ongoing, asynchronous discussions. These forums can act as a repository for shared resources, a space for quick problem-solving queries, and a venue for continuous dialogue. By integrating these platforms into daily practice, teachers can maintain a constant loop of communication, ensuring that ideas and feedback flow freely beyond the constraints of physical meetings and classroom walls.

- **Accessing continual professional development:** Professional growth is an ongoing journey. Regular training sessions keep teachers current with the latest developments in the challenge-based framework, allowing them to refine their practices and stay aligned with the most recent educational research. Training should be hands-on whenever possible, enabling educators to directly apply new knowledge in a supportive environment.

- **Providing interactive workshops:** Workshops offer a sandbox environment where teachers can simulate challenge-based framework implementations, receive peer feedback, and collaboratively refine their teaching strategies. These sessions should encourage experimentation and creativity, allowing educators to practice new methods in a low-risk setting before bringing them to the classroom.

By embedding these feedback loops and professional development strategies into the school culture, educators can continually refine their practice. This leads to a dynamic teaching environment where educators are empowered to innovate, collaborate, and grow together, driving forward the success of the challenge-based framework and the educational growth of their students.

Integrating the strategies throughout this section into the regular operations of teaching teams ensures a robust collaboration that enriches the challenge-based framework. Through these efforts, educators create a synergistic environment where ongoing communication, mutual learning, and shared responsibility lay the groundwork for an enriching learning experience for students. In essence, regular check-ins, whether formal or informal, act as the lifeblood of the collaborative teaching ecosystem. By ensuring consistent communication, fostering a culture of mutual respect and feedback, and providing avenues for continual learning, educators are better equipped to navigate the intricacies of the challenge-based framework and maximize its potential for student success.

Share Digital Platforms to Amplify Collaborative Potential

In our digital age, the power of shared digital platforms has revolutionized collaboration. For educators navigating the challenge-based framework, these platforms serve as invaluable repositories of knowledge, brainstorming spaces, and iterative feedback mechanisms. Let's break down the expansive benefits and best practices of leveraging platforms like Google Drive and Microsoft Teams for educational collaboration.

Centralized Repository

Creating a centralized repository for educational resources and collaborative efforts is essential for enhancing the efficiency and effectiveness of teacher collaboration. This repository should serve as a comprehensive, organized, and easily accessible digital space where educators can store, share, and manage their resources, lesson plans, and collaborative projects. Here are key components to consider when establishing a centralized repository.

- **Organized structure for ease of access:** Create a structured digital repository on platforms like Google Drive, with clearly designated folders for different subjects, grade levels, or specific challenge-based framework challenges. This organization is crucial to ensure that all materials are easily accessible to every educator involved, fostering an environment of shared resources.
- **Version control for collaborative integrity:** Use the version history feature to maintain the integrity of collaborative documents. *Version history* is a feature in

collaborative document editing platforms that allows users to view and revert to previous versions of the document, tracking changes made by different contributors over time. It allows educators to track changes, see who has contributed what, and revert to previous versions if needed, ensuring that the collaborative process is transparent and accountable.

By implementing these components, a centralized repository can become a dynamic hub for educational collaboration, promoting the sharing of best practices, innovative ideas, and effective teaching strategies. This not only saves time and effort but also ensures consistency and quality in educational delivery, ultimately benefiting both educators and students.

Feedback Forums

Establishing dedicated feedback forums is essential for fostering a collaborative and responsive educational environment. These forums provide structured spaces where educators can engage in meaningful discussions, share experiences, and collectively refine their teaching practices. By utilizing digital platforms, feedback forums can facilitate real-time communication and ensure that all voices are heard in the decision-making process. Here are key elements to consider when setting up feedback forums.

- **Creating channels for targeted discussions:** On platforms like Microsoft Teams, create channels dedicated to specific challenge-based framework challenges or subject areas. These channels become the go-to place for discussing lesson feedback, sharing teaching experiences, and troubleshooting challenges in real time. By organizing discussions into targeted channels, you can focus your team's conversations on relevant topics, making it easier to find and contribute valuable insights.

- **Utilizing polls for collective decision making:** Incorporate polls and surveys within these digital forums to efficiently collect feedback from the team. Use this feature to make democratic decisions about teaching strategies, project directions, or even to schedule meetings. Polls and surveys streamline the decision-making process by quickly gathering input from all team members, ensuring that the chosen actions reflect the collective preferences and needs of the group.

By embedding these elements into your feedback forums, you create an inclusive and efficient space for continuous improvement. This collaborative approach not only enhances the quality of teaching but also builds a stronger, more cohesive educational community. Encourage regular participation and keep the channels active to maintain a dynamic and supportive environment for all educators involved.

Shared Resource Libraries

Establishing a shared resource library is crucial for creating a collaborative and resource-rich educational environment. These libraries provide a centralized repository where educators can access and contribute a variety of teaching materials, enhancing the overall quality and consistency of the curriculum. By leveraging shared resource libraries, teachers can draw from a collective pool of knowledge, ensuring that they have access to the best possible tools and references for their instructional needs. Here are key strategies to optimize the use of shared resource libraries.

- **Curating resources for enhanced learning:** Build a shared digital library where team members can contribute various teaching resources such as articles, videos, research papers, and educational tools. A well-curated library is an asset that supports the challenge-based framework by providing a wealth of information that team members can draw on to enrich the curriculum. This collective approach to resource sharing ensures that everyone has access to high-quality materials that can enhance their teaching and support student learning.
- **Ensuring efficient retrieval through tagging:** Implement a tagging system within the shared library to organize resources effectively. Tags can be based on topics, relevance to the challenge-based framework, or the type of resource, ensuring that teachers can find what they need quickly and efficiently. This system not only saves time but also enhances the usability of the library, making it easier for educators to integrate relevant resources into their lesson plans.

By establishing a well-organized and accessible shared resource library, you create an valuable tool for continuous professional development and instructional excellence. Encourage regular contributions and updates to the library to keep it current and comprehensive. This collaborative effort will ensure that educators are always equipped with the best resources to foster student success and maintain a high standard of teaching across the curriculum.

Calendar and Scheduling

Efficient calendar and scheduling practices are essential for fostering consistent collaboration among educators. By integrating scheduling tools within digital platforms, teachers can coordinate their efforts more effectively, ensuring that everyone is on the same page and working toward common goals. This approach not only streamlines the planning process but also maximizes the use of available time, promoting a structured and productive collaborative environment. Here are key strategies to optimize calendar and scheduling practices.

- **Integrating scheduling for consistent collaboration:** Utilize the calendar features within these platforms to align team members' schedules, plan challenge-based framework project timelines, and set reminders for upcoming collaborative meetings or classroom observations. This ensures that all team members are aware of important dates and deadlines, facilitating better coordination and reducing the likelihood of scheduling conflicts.
- **Documenting meetings for transparency:** Make it a habit to document the key points discussed in meetings and share them in a central location. This practice ensures continuity and transparency, keeping all team members updated and aligned with collaborative efforts. Documenting meetings also provides a reference for future discussions, helping to track progress and decisions made.

By adopting these calendar and scheduling practices, you can create a more cohesive and efficient working environment. Regularly reviewing and updating the calendar ensures that everyone remains informed and engaged, ultimately leading to more effective collaboration and improved outcomes for both teachers and students.

Integration With Other Tools

Seamlessly integrating various digital tools can significantly enhance the efficiency and effectiveness of collaborative efforts. By connecting different applications, educators can create a streamlined workflow that supports the diverse needs of the challenge-based framework. This interconnected approach allows for smoother transitions between tasks and ensures that all necessary tools are readily accessible. Here are key strategies to optimize tool integration.

- **Streamlining workflow with connectivity:** Take advantage of the integration capabilities of digital platforms to connect with other tools like task management apps or video conferencing software, creating a seamless workflow that supports various aspects of the challenge-based framework. This integration helps to centralize tasks, communications, and resources, making it easier for educators to manage their responsibilities and collaborate effectively.

- **Utilizing collaborative document editing:** Integrate collaborative document editing tools like Google Docs or Microsoft OneNote to allow multiple educators to work on lesson plans, projects, and other documents simultaneously. This real-time collaboration capability ensures that everyone can contribute their insights and updates efficiently, fostering a more dynamic and interactive planning process.

By leveraging these integration strategies, you can create a more cohesive and efficient working environment. Regularly reviewing and optimizing the use of integrated tools ensures that collaborative efforts are streamlined, ultimately enhancing the educational experience for both teachers and students.

Security and Privacy

Maintaining robust security and privacy measures is critical when managing digital collaboration platforms. Ensuring that sensitive information is protected and only accessible to authorized individuals safeguards student data and intellectual property. Implementing strong security protocols helps to build trust among educators and stakeholders, fostering a safe and secure collaborative environment. Here are key strategies to optimize security and privacy practices.

- **Maintaining confidentiality with access controls:** Manage document permissions meticulously, ensuring that sensitive materials are only accessible to authorized personnel. This is vital to maintaining the privacy of student information and protecting the intellectual property of teachers. Regularly reviewing and updating access controls can prevent unauthorized access and ensure that all collaborative efforts are secure.

- **Implementing secure communication channels:** Use encrypted communication platforms for sharing sensitive information and conducting meetings. Ensuring that all data transmitted between educators is encrypted helps protect against unauthorized access and breaches. Additionally, educating staff on secure communication practices can further enhance overall security.

By adhering to these strategies, you can maintain a secure digital environment that protects both student and teacher data. Regular security audits and updates to protocols will help to address new threats and maintain the integrity of the collaborative platform, fostering a culture of trust and safety in the educational community.

Enrich Educator Experiences and Collaborative Insights Through Peer Observations

Peer observations, an age-old practice in education, take on new significance within the challenge-based framework, transforming from a simple classroom visitation to a robust strategy for educator development and curriculum enrichment. Here's an in-depth look at revitalizing peer observation.

Structured Framework for Peer Observation

Peer observation in the challenge-based framework is a deliberate process tailored to uncover and enhance pedagogical practices that align with the framework's goals. Begin with a preobservation meeting where the observer and the observed teacher agree on the objectives. Focus areas could include integrating challenge-based framework principles into the lesson or enhancing student engagement techniques.

Postobservation, a feedback session serves as a crucible for refining strategies. Here, both parties should engage in an open dialogue about what was observed, including strengths and areas for improvement. Discussing how the lesson aligns with the challenge-based framework's essential questions and interdisciplinary ties can provide practical insights for both teachers.

Mutual Respect and Trust in the Observation Process

In the practice of peer observation within the challenge-based framework, establishing a foundation of mutual respect and trust is not just beneficial, but imperative. Cultivate the environment to be supportive and growth focused, ensuring that the teacher being observed understands that the process is collaborative and constructive. It's critical to frame observations as opportunities for collective professional development rather than assessments or evaluations.

Interdisciplinary Integration and Collaboration

During the observation, the potential for interdisciplinary learning can shine through. Teachers observing their colleagues' lessons might notice how an exploration of geometric shapes in a mathematics class could add depth to understanding architectural styles in a history project. Alternatively, a scientific discussion on ecosystems in a biology class could enrich a literature class's exploration of environmental themes within a novel. These moments of cross-curricular connection underscore the integrative philosophy of the challenge-based framework. They illuminate how different subject areas are not siloed but are interconnected threads that, when woven together, present a comprehensive and enriched understanding of complex concepts to students.

These observations can lead to collaborative planning sessions where teachers from various disciplines come together to create integrated lessons that reflect the challenge-based framework interdisciplinary approach. They might codesign a project where students use mathematical models to understand historical population growth or employ scientific reasoning to deconstruct narratives in literature. By promoting an atmosphere of trust and openness, and actively seeking out and discussing interdisciplinary opportunities, peer observations become a catalyst for a dynamic and collaborative educational environment, reflective of the challenge-based framework's core principles.

A Repository of Best Practices

Creating a repository of best practices is a critical component of teacher collaboration within the challenge-based framework. This living library becomes a dynamic resource where educators document and share their most effective teaching strategies and classroom innovations observed during peer visits.

To construct this repository, observers should take detailed notes during observations, capturing not just what worked well but also the context in which these strategies were employed. For example, an observer may note how a peer used storytelling to solidify complex scientific concepts or implemented interactive polls during a history lesson to increase engagement.

Once documented, the observer categorizes these strategies and uploads them to a shared digital platform—such as a school intranet site, a cloud-based document folder, or a learning management system—where they are readily accessible. Teachers can then search this repository by subject, grade level, or specific challenge-based framework component, such as inquiry-based learning activities or community connection projects.

Within this system, best practices are not static; they are meant to be adapted and evolved. As such, the platform should facilitate an easy exchange of ideas and feedback. Teachers might comment on how they adapted a strategy for their classroom or suggest modifications based on different student needs.

Additionally, this repository acts as a professional development tool, providing a wealth of peer-reviewed methods that teachers can explore and integrate into their own practice. This continuous cycle of sharing, feedback, and adaptation not only fosters professional growth but also serves the core tenets of the challenge-based framework, encouraging innovation, reflective practice, and a commitment to ongoing improvement in teaching and learning.

Skill Enhancement Through Peer Learning

Peer observations serve as a platform for teachers to engage in a collaborative learning process. When educators observe their peers, they often encounter specialized skills or inventive teaching methods they can integrate into their own practice. For instance, during a peer observation, a teacher might notice a colleague using an interactive digital tool to enhance student engagement or applying a novel approach to differentiate instruction for diverse learners. Such observations spark conversations about these skills, allowing teachers to exchange knowledge and practical applications that directly benefit students. Moreover, these sessions become impromptu professional development, where educators can broaden their repertoire and refine their craft in real time, all within the supportive context of peer-to-peer learning.

Model Lessons in the Challenge-Based Framework

Model lessons are quintessential representations of the challenge-based framework in practice. They demonstrate how an educator can integrate the framework's components—such as the essential question, the challenge, and guiding activities—into a coherent and engaging lesson. Organizing observations for these model lessons allows other teachers to witness the challenge-based principles brought to life. For example, teachers might observe a lesson where students are actively engaged in solving a real-world problem, such as designing a sustainable garden for the school. This not only provides inspiration but also sets a high bar for what students can achieve through the challenge-based framework, encouraging all educators to aspire to such levels of instructional quality.

Reflective Practice With Journals

Reflection journals are a vital tool for consolidating learning and fostering professional growth following peer observations. Educators can jot down their immediate thoughts and reflections on the teaching strategies they've observed, ponder how they might adapt them to their context, and set goals for implementing new ideas. This practice not only aids in retaining new information but also encourages a deeper introspection about one's teaching philosophy and methods. The act of writing facilitates a dialogue with oneself, leading to greater clarity and purpose in teaching and learning endeavors.

Reciprocity in the Observation Cycle

A balanced observation cycle is characterized by reciprocity. It is vital that teachers who observe are also willing to be observed. This mutual openness reinforces the notion that all educators are on a continuous journey of learning and improvement. It negates any sense of hierarchy and promotes a culture where feedback and growth are valued equally by all. When teachers embrace this give-and-take, it demonstrates a commitment to collective excellence and reinforces the collaborative spirit at the heart of the challenge-based framework. It becomes a shared venture where each teacher contributes to and benefits from the collective wisdom of their peers.

By embedding these structured and reflective practices into the challenge-based framework, peer observations become a powerful tool for enhancing educational strategies and fostering a community of collaborative, innovative educators.

Catalyze Collaborative Teaching Excellence in Professional Development Workshops

In the pursuit of elevating the collaborative teaching experience within the challenge-based framework, professional development workshops are indispensable. Such workshops must be tailored specifically to the challenge-based framework, providing educators with strategies that are not only relevant but immediately applicable to their classrooms. To bridge the gap between theory and practice, these workshops should involve hands-on activities such as simulated collaborative lessons, which not only afford educators the opportunity to plan and execute a challenge-based lesson in a controlled environment but also address and troubleshoot real-world challenges in real time.

Bringing in experienced educators who have successfully implemented the challenge-based framework in their teaching can offer invaluable insights and establish a link between the framework's ideals and classroom realities. Their role in these workshops extends beyond facilitation; they act as mentors, guiding their peers through the intricacies of interdisciplinary collaboration and student-led inquiry.

Technological integration is a key aspect of these workshops, as digital platforms like Google Workspace or Microsoft Teams can significantly enhance the collaborative process. Educators should be trained not just in the basic use of these tools but in ways to integrate them effectively into collaborative lesson planning and execution. Additionally, the workshops can serve as an incubator for developing a shared repository of resources, including curated readings, lesson templates, and more.

Feedback, both from peers and workshop facilitators, is a critical component of these sessions. It fosters a culture of continuous professional growth and allows educators to refine their collaborative strategies. Following the workshops, the establishment of online support groups and regular refresher courses can ensure that the collaborative momentum is sustained. These groups also serve as networking platforms, fostering a community of practice among educators.

The workshops' success can be gauged through feedback forms and by tracking the implementation of the strategies discussed. Continuous engagement with workshop participants can help identify best practices and areas for improvement in future sessions. Ultimately, these workshops are not isolated events but ongoing, integral elements of an educator's professional journey, aligning with and enhancing the collaborative ethos of the challenge-based framework.

Overcoming the Hurdles in Teacher Collaboration

As with any grand endeavor, the collaborative journey in the challenge-based framework is not without its hurdles. However, recognizing these hurdles and proactively addressing them with care ensures that they become stepping stones to reinforcing the collaborative process. The following list outlines some possible hurdles as well as ways to address them.

- **Diverse teaching philosophies:** In the challenge-based framework, each teacher brings their unique pedagogical approach to a project. To harmonize these philosophies, educators can conduct sessions to collaboratively define how each of their strengths and teaching styles can contribute to a challenge-based framework initiative. For example, while one teacher may excel in facilitating group discussions, another might be adept at integrating technology. Through dialogue and workshops, they can learn how best to integrate these approaches, ensuring that each project stage from the "ask" to the "improve" phase in the framework leverages their collective strengths.

- **Time constraints:** Teachers often face the reality of tight schedules, which can pose a challenge to collaborative planning. To address this, school leadership might institute scheduled collaborative planning periods, freeing educators from other duties to focus on challenge-based framework projects. For instance, a planning period could be dedicated to designing a cross-curricular challenge, allowing a history teacher and a science teacher to jointly devise a lesson on the impact of technological advancements on historical events.

- **Resource allocation:** Another hurdle is ensuring that there are adequate resources—both material and time—for teachers to engage with the challenge-based framework effectively. Administrators must ensure that educators have access to the tools necessary to implement the challenge-based framework, such as digital resources, physical materials for prototypes, or spaces conducive to collaboration. Regular audits of resource needs and clear communication channels for requesting additional support can help manage this aspect.

- **Technological fluency:** In an era where digital tools are integral to implementing initiatives like the challenge-based framework, a gap in technological skills can be a significant hurdle. Professional development focused on technology integration in the classroom, as well as ongoing support from IT specialists, can empower teachers to effectively use digital tools. This is crucial for activities such as developing digital student portfolios or using online collaborative platforms for projects.

- **Interpersonal dynamics:** Finally, the varying interpersonal dynamics among staff can affect collaboration. To mitigate this, team-building exercises that foster understanding and empathy can be beneficial. This step is crucial in ensuring that when teachers collaborate on a framework project, they do so with a sense of camaraderie and a shared purpose.

By proactively addressing these hurdles, teachers can more effectively work together within the challenge-based framework. This ensures that the resultant student learning experiences are as enriching and multifaceted as the framework intends.

As educators steer the ship of education into the renaissance waters, anchoring their journey on the pillars of collaboration will be indispensable. The shared ethos, combined efforts, and mutual support can ensure that every student gets a holistic, interconnected, and profound learning experience, reminiscent of the interdisciplinary brilliance of the Renaissance era.

Concluding Thoughts

In conclusion, as we journey through the landscape of collaborative teaching within the challenge-based framework, it is evident that the road, while sometimes bumpy, leads to a destination rich with educational rewards. By embracing diverse teaching philosophies, effectively managing time, allocating resources wisely, enhancing technological fluency, and navigating interpersonal dynamics with empathy, educators can create a symphony of collaborative effort that resonates with the spirit of innovation and inquiry that the challenge-based framework embodies. It is this collective endeavor that will pave the way for our students to emerge not only as learners of today but as the informed, creative, and adaptable thinkers of tomorrow.

Chapter 15

Engage Student Collaboration

As you guide your students through learning with the challenge-based framework, you're cultivating a generation of collaborators, critical thinkers, and innovators. Think of your classroom as a modern-day Florentine workshop, where the exchange of ideas is not just encouraged but is the bedrock of learning.

In this chapter, you'll learn to harness student collaboration to foster a dynamic educational experience. You will explore strategies to weave together diverse insights and facilitate an environment where feedback is a tool for growth and refinement of ideas. This chapter includes practical examples, real-world scenarios, and techniques to integrate student collaboration into the challenge-based framework. It also covers differentiated strategies for different grade levels, ensuring that the collaborative approach is tailored to meet the developmental and academic needs of your students. Encourage your students to step into the roles of inquirers, explorers, and innovators. Urge them to ask probing questions that lead to deeper understanding, to apply theories to tangible challenges outside the classroom, and to synthesize knowledge across disciplines to create new solutions. It is through these active roles that challenge-based learning transforms from a framework to a lively, intellectual incubator. The Concluding Thoughts section offers a chance to reflect on the various elements of engaging students in collaboration.

As you engage with the challenge-based framework with a focus on student collaboration, remember that your role extends beyond instruction. You are a facilitator of the very skills that define our age: adaptability, teamwork, and interconnectivity. Through the lessons, projects, and discussions you'll facilitate, you're not only preparing students for a complex future but also inviting them to actively shape it. Let this chapter be your guide to creating a classroom that mirrors the collaborative spirit of the past, tailored for the innovators of the future.

Find the Essence of Student Collaboration in the Challenge-Based Framework

In the challenge-based framework, student collaboration coalesces individual strengths, fueling a deeper educational journey. Here's an example, using the scenario of the sustainable urban garden project. A student with a proclivity for botany might contribute knowledge about the types of plants suitable for urban gardens, contributing to the biological diversity of the project. Another student, with a keen eye for design, would plan the layout, ensuring that the garden is not only functional but also visually pleasing. Meanwhile, a third student, mindful of sustainability, might research and propose water conservation techniques. This synergy enables students to see beyond their singular views, fostering an environment where learning is a shared experience.

Through this process, students are not merely engaging with the curriculum, they are actively applying it. They learn to appreciate the value of different perspectives, and in negotiating their ideas with others, they develop critical life skills such as communication, compromise, and project management. The act of collaboration thus extends beyond completing a task; it becomes a medium for students to engage critically with content, apply their learning in real-world contexts, and develop soft skills essential for their future.

Teacher collaboration is instrumental in modeling this process. Educators who collaborate demonstrate the power of collective effort. They show that uniting diverse areas of expertise leads to enriched, multifaceted learning experiences. When teachers work together, they exemplify the practice of sharing knowledge, challenging assumptions, and building on each other's strengths. This sets the stage for students, guiding them on how to work in teams, listen actively, and value each contribution. In essence, teacher collaboration is the blueprint that students follow, underscoring the message that the whole is greater than the sum of its parts.

In isolation, each student's contribution might have been valuable but limited. However, in collaboration, their combined expertise culminates in a solution that is comprehensive, innovative, and grounded in diverse knowledge. Such is the power of student collaboration within the framework—a testament to the adage that the whole is often greater than the sum of its parts.

Use the Nine Habits of Thinking to Fuel Effective Student Collaboration

The synergy between the nine habits of thinking and collaboration in the challenge-based framework isn't merely coincidental: it's profoundly intentional. As students immerse themselves in collaborative endeavors, these habits emerge not just as individual cognitive processes but as collective forces that drive, enrich, and refine their collaborative output. Let's dissect this interplay further by examining it in each habit.

1. **Cultivate diverse curiosity:** The very essence of the challenge-based framework is to pose multifaceted real-world challenges. Thus, the solutions sought naturally cater to diverse interests and curiosities. In such an environment, every student's unique curiosity becomes an asset. As each student dives deep into their sphere of interest, the collaborative output gains depth and dimension, offering solutions that are holistic and well-rounded.

2. **Take risks:** The collaborative nature of the challenge-based framework provides students with a collective safety buffer. While one student might hesitate to voice a radical idea, the encouragement and support of peers can embolden them to venture outside their comfort zones. Thus, the group becomes a crucible for experimentation, allowing for the melding of conservative and radical ideas alike.

3. **Use humor:** Shared moments of levity can dissolve tensions and foster camaraderie. As students navigate the complexities of real-world challenges, light-heartedness can serve as a bonding agent, creating a conducive environment for free-flowing ideas and removing inhibitions.

4. **Create and innovate:** As the saying goes, "Two heads are better than one." In a collaborative setting within the challenge-based framework, diverse perspectives converge, leading to a kaleidoscope of ideas. This mosaic of thought becomes a breeding ground for innovation, with each contribution amplifying the group's creative potential.

5. **Self-regulate:** Collaboration isn't always seamless. Differences in opinion, approach, or work ethic can arise. Here, the ability to self-regulate, to remain cognizant of one's emotions, reactions, and their impact on the group, becomes paramount. A group that can self-regulate can navigate challenges with maturity and grace, ensuring that the focus remains on the task at hand.

6. **Transfer learning:** The beauty of the framework lies in its interdisciplinary approach. When students collaborate, they become conduits for knowledge transfer, contributing insights from diverse disciplines. This confluence of knowledge sparks connections that might otherwise remain unseen, leading to solutions that are both innovative and holistic.

7. **Ask questions:** In a collaborative setup, the questioning doesn't remain a solitary pursuit. Every query becomes a springboard, launching deeper discussions, challenges, and refinements. The continuous volley of questions and answers ensures that ideas are constantly refined, evolving into well thought-out solutions.

8. **Evaluate evidence:** Diverse perspectives naturally lead to varied interpretations of evidence. In a collaborative environment, these interpretations are laid bare, debated, scrutinized, and refined. This collective evaluation ensures that the group's conclusions are not just informed but are also well-rounded and robust.

9. **Embrace lifelong learning and perseverance:** Tackling real-world challenges is no mean feat. As students navigate the intricacies of these challenges, they inevitably face hurdles. However, the collective nature of the challenge-based framework ensures that no student faces these challenges alone. The group

becomes a beacon of mutual support, teaching each member the values of persistence, resilience, and the continuous quest for knowledge.

In sum, the interplay between the nine habits of thinking and student collaboration within the challenge-based framework is like a well-orchestrated symphony, where each habit amplifies the others, creating a harmonious, impactful, and transformative learning experience.

Differentiate Strategies for Helping Students Collaborate

The integration of collaboration within the challenge-based framework necessitates educators be aware of the unique developmental and academic needs of students across different grade bands. A one-size-fits-all approach would fall short; instead, differentiated strategies that cater to the evolving cognitive capacities and interests of students are key. Following is a look into collaboration strategies across grade bands, complete with examples across subjects.

Elementary School Students

In the elementary grades, group activities that blend learning with interaction foster collaboration. Students can utilize storyboarding in mathematics to visually solve problems together, promoting discussion on different methods to reach a solution. In science, mind mapping becomes a team effort as students collectively expand on the central theme of ecosystems, with each student contributing their ideas to the map. Social studies classes become collaborative when groups brainstorm the multifaceted roles of community helpers, integrating each other's thoughts to present a more comprehensive picture. Language arts classes are enhanced by role-playing, where students work in teams to bring stories to life, understanding character dynamics through interactive narratives.

Middle School Students

For middle school students, cross-subject group projects facilitate a deeper connection between different fields of study. In mathematics, collaborative design of a dream park brings together geometric calculations and historical or cultural research, requiring students to harmonize their findings. Science classes encourage joint efforts to research and then advocate through writing or digital presentations about environmental concerns, combining scientific investigation with communicative skills. Social studies classes integrate scientific exploration as students create inventions for ancient civilizations, thereby blending historical context with scientific application. Language arts discussions evolve into collaborative analysis, as book clubs explore the setting of novels and relate them to actual geographical and historical facts.

High School Students

As students reach high school, the stakes of collaborative projects increase to reflect real-world complexities. Statistical analysis of public transport systems in mathematics requires collective brainstorming and negotiation to formulate proposals. The study of genetics in science leads to ethical debates, blending scientific knowledge with persuasive argumentation skills. In social studies, researching global economic policies leads to the creation of mock summits, combining the analytical rigor of mathematics with the nuanced understanding of global interrelations. Literature classes tackle scientific topics through discussions about the feasibility of the worlds depicted in dystopian novels, intertwining narrative analysis with scientific reasoning.

Across all grade levels, technology platforms like Padlet, Trello, or Google Docs serve as virtual spaces for students to plan and execute projects, ensuring continuous dialogue and peer review. These collaborative exercises are instrumental in developing students' ability to work together, think critically, and approach problems from multiple perspectives within the challenge-based framework.

A Real-World Inspired Classroom Scenario

The classroom, a microcosm of the larger world, can beautifully reflect the power and possibilities of collaboration when educators like Ms. Anderson infuse lessons with real-world relevance. Let's delve deeper into such a scenario to understand the intricate dynamics and transformative potential of such an approach.

In Ms. Anderson's seventh-grade class, collaboration became the cornerstone of the renewable energy project. Initially, students engaged in group brainstorming sessions using collaborative tools like Padlet, where they shared ideas, posed questions, and collectively outlined their project goals. Each group was assigned a specific aspect of renewable energy to research, such as solar power, wind turbines, or hydroelectricity.

As they delved deeper into their research, students collaborated on Google Docs to compile their findings, analyze data, and draft proposals for implementing renewable energy solutions within their school or local community. Through peer-feedback sessions facilitated by Ms. Anderson, students refined their ideas, addressed potential challenges, and honed their persuasive arguments.

The interdisciplinary nature of the project encouraged students to explore connections between science, mathematics, humanities, and technology. For instance, while investigating the scientific principles behind solar energy, students applied mathematical concepts to calculate the potential energy output of solar panels. They also examined the historical and environmental contexts of renewable energy adoption, drawing parallels between past movements and contemporary initiatives.

In addition to digital collaboration, Ms. Anderson organized hands-on activities to deepen students' understanding of renewable energy concepts. Students worked in teams to design and construct miniature models of renewable energy systems using recyclable materials, fostering creativity, problem solving, and teamwork.

Near the culmination of the project, students presented their proposals to a panel of guest experts, including local environmental activists, engineers, and policymakers. This real-world audience provided authentic feedback, validating students' efforts and inspiring them to advocate for sustainable solutions beyond the classroom.

Overall, Ms. Anderson's collaborative approach to the renewable energy project empowered students to take ownership of their learning, cultivate essential 21st century skills, and become active agents of change in their communities. Through meaningful collaboration, students not only acquired knowledge but also developed the critical thinking and collaboration skills necessary to tackle complex challenges in the world around them.

On announcing the project, she witnessed a palpable surge of excitement in the room. Students eagerly formed groups, each voluntarily gravitating toward a specific form of renewable energy that piqued their interest—solar, wind, hydro, geothermal, and biomass. The diversity in choice was a testament to the range of curiosities and the scope of the challenge.

To ensure holistic research, Ms. Anderson provided guiding questions: What are the mechanics of this energy form? What are its benefits and limitations? How would it be implemented in our town, considering the local geography and resources?

As the days progressed, the classroom buzzed with activity. Students were engrossed in discussions, debating feasibility, sketching designs, or immersed in virtual simulations.

The solar team, for example, discussed the optimal locations for solar panels in their town, considering factors like sunlight duration and building structures. The wind energy enthusiasts delved into wind patterns, even reaching out to local meteorologists for insights. They toyed with the idea of community-owned wind farms and their potential outputs. Meanwhile, the hydro group explored local water bodies, speculating about hydroelectric plants and their environmental impacts.

The culmination of students' research was an interconnected web—a visual representation of how these renewable sources could interact and symbiotically power their town. The web highlighted the synergies between energy sources, showcasing, for instance, how excess solar energy during sunny days could be stored and used to supplement wind energy on less windy days.

Presenting their findings to their peers and invited local experts, the students received constructive feedback, which further refined their understanding. This real-world scenario became a vivid demonstration of not just the complexities of renewable energy but also the profound outcomes of collaborative endeavor.

The success of Ms. Anderson's project resonated beyond the classroom walls. It inspired students to engage in community discussions, fostered a deeper appreciation for sustainable practices, and most importantly, instilled in them a belief in the power of collective problem solving.

Challenges to Student Collaboration in the Challenge-Based Framework

In the landscape of collaborative challenge-based framework implementation, several challenges emerge, each intersecting with strategies informed by the nine habits of thinking. Equitable participation is paramount, as highlighted by Elizabeth G. Cohen and Rachel A. Lotan (1997), who underscore the risk of some students dominating group work while others remain passive. Addressing this challenge involves fostering the habit of asking questions, which encourages all students, including the more reticent ones, to actively contribute, thereby promoting balanced participation (Wilen, 2001).

Another significant challenge is managing group dynamics, as emphasized by research from David Johnson and Roger Johnson (2009), which stresses the importance of positive interdependence and individual accountability. To mitigate conflicts and foster harmony, educators can draw from the habits of self-regulation and using humor, cultivating emotionally intelligent interactions infused with light-heartedness (Brackett, Reyes, Rivers, Elbertson, & Salovey, 2011).

Maintaining the interdisciplinary essence of the challenge-based framework presents another hurdle. Mark H. Nichols and Karen Cator (2008) highlight the strength of the framework's interdisciplinary nature but also caution against collaborations becoming unidimensional. Encouraging the habit of transfer learning ensures that students continuously seek connections across subjects, preserving the multifaceted essence of the challenge-based framework (Perkins & Salomon, 1988).

Navigating diverse skill sets within collaborative settings is essential for effectiveness (Dillenbourg, 1999). Harnessing these diverse competencies constructively becomes easier by promoting the habit of creating and innovating, which encourages students to recognize and utilize their peers' strengths to foster collective creativity and innovation.

Furthermore, ensuring both depth and breadth in collaborative endeavors is crucial. Collaboration can sometimes lead to either superficial coverage or an overly narrowed focus (Barron, 2000). Striking the right balance requires guided exploration informed by the habits of evaluating evidence and embracing lifelong learning and perseverance. This approach encourages students to delve deeply into topics while maintaining a broad perspective, resulting in comprehensive and well-rounded solutions (Zimmerman, 2002).

In sum, integrating research-backed strategies with the nine habits of thinking can provide educators the road map to navigate the labyrinth of challenges inherent in using the challenge-based framework, enriching the collaborative experience for students.

Concluding Thoughts

In the grand tapestry of education, the challenge-based framework serves as a vibrant thread, intricately weaving the essence of real-world problem solving with student collaboration. But beyond the confines of a classroom, this approach resonates with an even deeper importance. As we steer through an era dominated by globalization, the digital revolution, and intercultural dialogues, nurturing collaboration isn't merely a pedagogical choice; it's a foundational necessity.

The landscape of the 21st century calls for individuals who can seamlessly collaborate, merge ideas across disciplines, and devise groundbreaking solutions to the globe's pressing challenges. By incorporating the nine habits of thinking within the challenge-based framework, educators transform from mere conduits of information to catalysts, igniting the spark in the next generation of collaborative pioneers.

These pioneers, armed with the synergistic power of the challenge-based framework and the nine habits, are poised to break traditional paradigms. Their propensity to harbor diverse curiosity, scrutinize evidence, and continuously champion lifelong learning distinguishes them as global pathfinders. As they tackle the multifarious challenges of tomorrow, they'll not only seek resolutions but craft pathways in unison.

In summation, our direction is evident. As educators and guardians of the future, our responsibility transcends standard teaching. By fervently intertwining collaboration within the challenge-based framework and fostering these holistic habits of thinking, we're laying the foundation for a cooperative future, led by the pioneers we mentor today.

Epilogue

Renaissance Reimagined

As educators, you are positioned to transform the educational landscape by rekindling the spirit of inquiry and wonder akin to the polymaths of the past. This book serves as a practical guide, offering a detailed map to instill multifaceted inquiry in today's students, rather than merely romanticizing the Renaissance. Classrooms must evolve beyond the traditional confines of four walls and a chalkboard. They need to become dynamic spaces of discovery and imagination, where students are not just passive recipients of information but active participants in the learning process. In these transformed spaces, the wisdom of the past cultivates the minds of today.

The polymaths we have noted throughout the book exemplify the integration of diverse fields of knowledge. These polymaths navigated between arts and sciences, theory and practice, and in doing so, they laid the foundation for a holistic educational approach. By adopting similar methods, students can learn to think broadly and deeply, combining insights from multiple disciplines to solve complex problems. In modern classrooms, this means fostering an environment where interdisciplinary learning is the norm. Encourage students to blend insights from various subjects.

By emulating the habits of these historical figures, students can develop a versatile skill set that prepares them for the complexities of contemporary life. They can learn to see connections where others may see only silos, to innovate by drawing on a wide array of knowledge, and to approach problems with a mindset that values both rigorous analysis and creative thinking. The framework presented here rests on nine deliberate habits of thought, serving as a blueprint for transformative teaching and learning. These habits are interconnected, reinforcing and enhancing the others and forming a comprehensive approach to education that addresses the multifaceted challenges of modern learning environments.

By integrating these nine habits into your teaching practice, you create a dynamic and supportive learning environment that prepares students for the complexities of the contemporary world. Together, these habits offer a robust approach that empowers students to become thoughtful, innovative, and resilient individuals. However, these habits must be embedded within a structured educational design. The challenge-based framework emphasizes real-world issues and cross-disciplinary learning, providing the infrastructure for these habits to flourish.

The future of education lies beyond textbooks and syllabi. It is an expansive horizon where disciplines blur, creating limitless learning opportunities. This transformative vision lies with educators who ignite curiosity, leaders who pave the way for innovation, and stakeholders who champion the cause.

Imagine a world where the spirit of the Renaissance is a palpable energy in every classroom, inspiring students to become inventors, artists, and visionaries. In this world, lessons spark curiosity and wonder, preparing students for a dynamic future. Absorb the insights, internalize the frameworks, and act on them. Collaborate to sculpt this vision, ensuring every generation bears the hallmark of a new-age Renaissance. Every student is a beacon of infinite potential, painting their unique masterpiece on the world's canvas.

As you conclude this book, recognize that this is the beginning of a profound journey. The vision of Renaissance thinking in the classroom is about inspiring transformation, lighting a fire in students and educators to usher in an educational renaissance.

References and Resources

Altieri, M. A., & Nicholls, C. I. (2020). Agroecology: Challenges and opportunities for farming in the Anthropocene. *International Journal of Agriculture and Natural Resources, 47*(3), 204–215.

Aronson, J., & Dee, T. (2012). Stereotype threat in the real world. In M. Inzlicht & T. Schmader (Eds.), *Stereotype threat: Theory, process, and application* p. 264–279). New York: Oxford University Press.

Bandura, A. (1982). Self-efficacy mechanism in human agency. *American Psychologist, 37*(2), 122.

Barron, B. (2000). Achieving coordination in collaborative problem-solving groups. *Journal of the Learning Sciences, 9*(4), 403–436.

Berk, R. A. (2000). Does humor in course tests reduce anxiety and improve performance? *College Teaching, 48*(4), 151–158.

Bishop, S. R., Lau, M., Shapiro, S., Carlson, L., Anderson, N. D., Carmody, J., ... & Devins, G. (2004). Mindfulness: A proposed operational definition. *Clinical psychology: Science and practice, 11*(3), 230.

Boix Mansilla, V., Miller, W. C., & Gardner, H. (2000). On disciplinary lenses and interdisciplinary work. In S. Wineburg & P. Grossman (Eds.), *Interdisciplinary curriculum: Challenges to implementation* p. 17–38). New York: Teachers College Press.

Boix Mansilla, V., Miller, W. C., & Gardner, H. (2009). On disciplinary lenses and interdisciplinary work. In S. N. Durlauf & L. E. Blume (Eds.), *The new Palgrave dictionary of economics* (2nd ed.). New York: Palgrave Macmillan.

Bolkan, S., Griffin, D. J., & Goodboy, A. K. (2018). Humor in the classroom: The effects of integrated humor on student learning. *Communication Education, 67*(2), 144–164.

Brackett, M. A., Reyes, M. R., Rivers, S. E., Elbertson, N. A., & Salovey, P. (2011). Classroom emotional climate, teacher affiliation, and student conduct. *Journal of Classroom Interaction, 46*(1), 27–36.

Bransford, J. D., Brown, A. L., & Cocking, R. R. (2000). How people learn: *Brain, mind, experience, and school*. Washington, DC: National Academies Press.

Brundiers, K., & Wiek, A. (2017). Beyond interpersonal competence: Teaching and learning professional skills in sustainability. *Education Sciences, 7*(1), Article 39. https://doi.org/10.3390/educsci7010039

Brundiers, K., Wiek, A., & Kay, B. (2013). The role of transacademic interface managers in transformational sustainability research and education. *Sustainability, 5*(11), 4614–4636.

Chi, M. T. H., Adams, J., Bogusch, E. B., Bruchok, C., Kang, S., Lancaster, M., et al. (2018). Translating the ICAP theory of cognitive engagement into practice. *Cognitive Science, 42*(6), 1777–1832.

Chi, M. T. H., & Wylie, R. (2014). The ICAP framework: Linking cognitive engagement to active learning outcomes. *Educational Psychologist, 49*(4), 219–243.

Cohen, E. G., & Lotan, R. A. (Eds.). (1997). *Working for equity in heterogeneous classrooms: Sociological theory in practice*. New York: Teachers College Press.

Common Core State Standards Initiative. (2024). *English language arts standards*. Accessed at https://www.thecorestandards.org/ELA-Literacy/ on June 24, 2024.

Conzemius, A. E., & O'Neill, J. (2014). *The handbook for SMART school teams: Revitalizing best practices for collaboration* (2nd ed.). Bloomington, IN: Solution Tree Press.

Costa, A. L., & Kallick, B. (Eds.). (2009). *Habits of mind across the curriculum: Practical and creative strategies for teachers*. Arlington, VA: ASCD.

Cowan, N. (2012). *Working memory capacity*. London: Psychology Press.

Davidson, R. J. and Schuyler, B. S. (2015) Neuroscience of happiness. In J. F. Helliwell, R. Laryard, & J. Sachs (Eds.), *World Happiness Report 2015* p. 82–105). New York: Sustainable Development Solutions Network.

Deans for Impact. (2015). *The science of learning*. Austin, TX: Author.

Désert, M., Gonçalves, G., & Leyens, J. P. (2013). Public speaking: Stereotype threat and control. *International Journal of Social Psychology, 28*(2), 169–181.

Deslauriers, L., McCarty, L. S., Miller, K., Callaghan, K., & Kestin, G. (2019). Measuring actual learning versus feeling of learning in response to being actively engaged in the classroom. *Proceedings of the National Academy of Sciences, 116*(39), 19251–19257.

Dewey, J. (1938). *Experience and education*. Bridgewater, MA: Kappa Delta Phi.

Dillenbourg, P. (Ed.). (1999). *Collaborative learning: Cognitive and computational approaches*. New York: Pergamon.

Duckworth, A. L., & Carlson, S. M. (2013). Self-regulation and school success. In B. W. Sokol, F. M. E. Grouzet, & U. Müller (Eds.), *Self-regulation and autonomy: Social and developmental dimensions of human conduct* (pp. 208–230). New York: Cambridge University Press.

Duke, A. (2018). *Thinking in bets: Making smarter decisions when you don't have all the facts*. New York: Portfolio.

Dunbar, N. E., Banas, J. A., Rodriguez, D., Liu, S. J., & Abra, G. (2012). Humor use in power-differentiated interactions. *Humor, 25*(4), 469–489.

Eskreis-Winkler, L., & Fishbach, A. (2019). Not learning from failure—The greatest failure of all. *Psychological Science, 30*(12), 1733–1744.

Fisher, D., & Frey, N. (2008). *Improving adolescent literacy: Content area strategies at work* (2nd ed.). Upper Saddle River, NJ: Merrill/Prentice Hall.

Forgas, J. P. (1995). Mood and judgment: The affect infusion model (AIM). *Psychological Bulletin, 117*(1), 39.

Forgas, J. P. (2017). Can sadness be good for you? *Australian Psychologist, 52*(1), 3–13.

Fredrickson, B. L. (2001). The role of positive emotions in positive psychology: The broaden-and-build theory of positive emotions. *American Psychologist, 56*(3), 218–226.

Frumos, F. V., Leonte, R., Candel, O. S., Ciochină-Carasevici, L., Ghiațău, R., & Onu, C. (2024). The relationship between university students' goal orientation and academic achievement. The mediating role of motivational components and the moderating role of achievement emotions. *Frontiers in Psychology, 14*, 1296346.

Gentner, D. (1983). Structure-mapping: A theoretical framework for analogy. *Cognitive Science, 7*(2), 155–170.

Gentner, D. (2003). Why we're so smart. In D. Gentner & S. Goldin-Meadow (Eds.), *Language in mind: Advances in the study of language and thought* (pp. 195–235). Cambridge, MA: MIT Press.

Goddard, Y. L., Goddard, R. D., & Tschannen-Moran, M. (2007). A theoretical and empirical investigation of teacher collaboration for school improvement and student achievement in public elementary schools. *Teachers College Record, 109*(4), 877–896.

Goldthwaite, R. A. (2009). *The economy of Renaissance Florence*. Baltimore: Johns Hopkins University Press.

Hattie, J., & Donoghue, G. M. (2016). Learning strategies: A synthesis and conceptual model. *Science of Learning, 1*(16013).

Haystead, M. W. (2009). *Meta-analytic synthesis of studies conducted at Marzano Research Laboratory on instructional strategies*. Englewood, CO: Marzano Research Laboratory.

Holyoak, K. J., & Thagard, P. (1995). *Mental leaps: Analogy in creative thought*. Cambridge, MA: MIT Press.

Howard, D. J., Gengler, C., & Jain, A. (1995). What's in a name? A complimentary means of persuasion. *Journal of Consumer Research, 22*(2), 200–211.

Johnson, D. W., & Johnson, R. T. (2009). An educational psychology success story: Social interdependence theory and cooperative learning. *Educational Researcher, 38*(5), 365–379.

Kane, M. J., Brown, L. H., McVay, J. C., Silvia, P. J., Myin-Germeys, I., & Kwapil, T. R. (2007). For whom the mind wanders, and when: An experience-sampling study of working memory and executive control in daily life. *Psychological Science, 18*(7), 614–621.

Kirschner, P. A., Sweller, J., & Clark, R. E. (2006). Why minimal guidance during instruction does not work: An analysis of the failure of constructivist, discovery, problem-based, experiential, and inquiry-based teaching. *Educational Psychologist, 41*(2), 75–86.

Kornell, N., & Bjork, R. A. (2007). The promise and perils of self-regulated study. *Psychonomic Bulletin & Review, 14*(2), 219–224.

Kornell, N., Hays, M. J., & Bjork, R. A. (2009). Unsuccessful retrieval attempts enhance subsequent learning. *Journal of Experimental Psychology: Learning, Memory, and Cognition, 35*(4), 989.

Koutstaal, W., Kedrick, K., & Gonzalez-Brito, J. (2022). Capturing, clarifying, and consolidating the curiosity-creativity connection. *Scientific Reports, 12*(1), 15300.

Kriegbaum, K., Kofoed, P., & Thomsen, D. (2018). Motivation matters: A study on the impact of motivation on academic performance. *International Journal of Learning, Teaching and Educational Research, 17*(5).

Kross, E., & Ayduk, O. (2011). Making meaning out of negative experiences by self-distancing. *Current Directions in Psychological Science, 20*(3), 187–191.

Lencioni, P. (2002). *The five dysfunctions of a team: A leadership fable* (20th anniversary ed.). San Francisco: Jossey-Bass.

Leyden, K. M., Goldberg, A., & Michelbach, P. (2011). Understanding the pursuit of happiness in ten major cities. *Urban Affairs Review, 47*(6), 861–888.

Lovins, A. B., Ürge-Vorsatz, D., Mundaca, L., Kammen, D. M., & Glassman, J. W. (2019). Recalibrating climate prospects. *Environmental Research Letters, 14*(12), 120201.

Lurie, N., Saville, M., Hatchett, R., & Halton, J. (2020). Developing COVID-19 vaccines at pandemic speed. *New England Journal of Medicine, 382*(21), 1969–1973. https://doi.org/10.1056/NEJMp2005630

Martens, R. (2000). *Kepler's philosophy and the new astronomy*. Princeton, NJ: Princeton University Press.

Martin, R. A. (2019). Humor. In M. W. Gallagher & S. J. Lopez (Eds.), *Positive psychological assessment: A handbook of models and measures* (2nd ed., pp. 305–316). Washington, DC: American Psychological Association.

Marzano, R. J., Pickering, D. J., Arredondo, D. E., Blackburn, G. J., Brandt, R. S., & Moffett, C. A. (1992). *Dimensions of learning*. Arlington, VA: ASCD.

Marzano, R. J., Pickering, D., & Pollock, J. E. (2001). *Classroom instruction that works: Research-based strategies for increasing student achievement*. Arlington, VA: ASCD.

Matheson, H. E., Kenett, Y. N., Gerver, C., & Beaty, R. E. (2023). Representing creative thought: A representational similarity analysis of creative idea generation and evaluation. *Neuropsychologia, 187*, 108587.

McCrae, R. R., & Costa, P. T., Jr. (1997). Personality trait structure as a human universal. *American Psychologist, 52*(5), 509.

McGraw, A. P., Warren, C., & Kan, C. (2015). Humorous complaining. *Journal of Consumer Research, 41*(5), 1153–1171.

Miller, M., & Boix Mansilla, V. (2004). *Thinking across perspectives and disciplines*. Accessed at https://scholar.harvard.edu/sites/scholar.harvard.edu/files/boix-mansilla/files/thinkingacross.pdf on June 21, 2024.

Monk, R. (1996). *Bertrand Russell: The spirit of solitude 1872–1921*. New York: Free Press.

National Council for the Social Studies. (n.d.). National curriculum standards for social studies. Accessed at https://www.socialstudies.org/standards/national-curriculum-standards-social-studies-introduction on July 9, 2024.

National Governors Association Center for Best Practices & Council of Chief State School Officers. (2010a). *Common Core State Standards for English language arts and literacy in history/social studies, science, and technical subjects*. Washington, DC: Authors. Accessed at https://corestandards.org/wp-content/uploads/2023/09/ELA_Standards1.pdf on July 9, 2024.

National Governors Association Center for Best Practices & Council of Chief State School Officers. (2010b). *Common Core State Standards for mathematics*. Washington, DC: Authors. Accessed at https://corestandards.org/wp-content/uploads/2023/09/Math_Standards1.pdf on July 9, 2024.

National Research Council, Division of Behavioral, Committee on National Statistics, Board on Behavioral, Sensory Sciences, & Committee to Review the Scientific Evidence on the Polygraph. (2003). *The polygraph and lie detection*. Washington, DC: National Academies Press.

Nichols, M. H., & Cator, K. (2008). *Challenge based learning: Take action and make a difference* [White paper]. Cupertino, CA: Apple. Accessed at https://www.challengebasedlearning.org/wp-content/uploads/2019/03/CBL_Paper_2008.pdf on May 15, 2024.

NGSS Lead States. (2013). *Next Generation Science Standards: For states, by states*. Washington, DC: National Academies Press.

Panorama Education. (2024). *Social-emotional learning assessment*. Accessed at http://panoromaed.com on June 21, 2024.

Partnership for 21st Century Skills. (2024). *P21 Resources*. Accessed at www.battelleforkids.org/insights/p21-resources on June 21, 2024.

Pedretti, C. (1964). *Leonardo da Vinci on painting: A lost book (libro A) reassembled from the Codex Vaticanus Urbinas 1270 and from the Codex Leicester by Carlo Pedretti* (Vol. 3). Oakland: University of California Press.

Pedretti, C. (1978). *The Codex Atlanticus of Leonardo da Vinci: A catalogue of its newly restored sheets*. New York: Harcourt, Brace, Jovanovich.

Pekrun, R., Goetz, T., Titz, W., & Perry, R. P. (2002). Academic emotions in students' self-regulated learning and achievement: A program of qualitative and quantitative research. *Educational Psychologist, 37*(2), 91–105.

Perkins, D. N., & Salomon, G. (1988). Teaching for transfer. *Educational Leadership, 46*(1), 22–32.

Pittinsky, T. L., Shih, M., & Ambady, N. (2000). Will a category cue affect you? Category cues, positive stereotypes and reviewer recall for applicants. *Social Psychology of Education, 4*(1), 53–65.

Project Vesta. (2024). *Vesta*. Accessed at http://vesta.earth on June 21, 2014.

Rahwan, I., Cebrian, M., Obradovich, N., Bongard, J., Bonnefon, J.-F., Breazeal, C., et al. (2019). Machine behaviour. *Nature, 568*(7753), 477–486. https://doi.org/10.1038/s41586-019-1138-y

Raichle, M. E., MacLeod, A. M., Snyder, A. Z., Powers, W. J., Gusnard, D. A., & Shulman, G. L. (2001). A default mode of brain function. *PNAS, 98*(2), 676–682.

Reschly, A. L., Huebner, E. S., Appleton, J. J., & Antaramian, S. (2008). Engagement as flourishing: The contribution of positive emotions and coping to adolescents' engagement at school and with learning. *Psychology in the Schools, 45*(5), 419–431.

Ritchie, S. J., & Tucker-Drob, E. M. (2018). How much does education improve intelligence? A meta-analysis. *Psychological Science, 29*(8), 1358–1369.

Robson, D. A., Allen, M. S., & Howard, S. J. (2020). Self-regulation in childhood as a predictor of future outcomes: A meta-analytic review. *Psychological Bulletin, 146*(4), 324.

Ronfeldt, M., Farmer, S. O., McQueen, K., & Grissom, J. A. (2015). Teacher collaboration in instructional teams and student achievement. *American Educational Research Journal, 52*(3), 475–514.

Sagan, C. (1996). *The demon haunted world: Science as a candle in the dark.* New York: Ballantine Books.

Savage, B. M., Lujan, H. L., Thipparthi, R. R., & DiCarlo, S. E. (2017). Humor, laughter, learning, and health! A brief review. *Advances in Physiology Education, 41*(3), 341–347.

Schunk, D. H., & Zimmerman, B. J. (2012). Self-regulation and learning. In I. B. Weiner, G. E. Miller, & W. M. Reynolds (Eds.), *Handbook of psychology (Vol. 7): Educational psychology* (2nd ed., pp. 59–78). New York: Wiley.

Smallwood, J., & Schooler, J. W. (2015). The science of mind wandering: Empirically navigating the stream of consciousness. *Annual Review of Psychology, 66*, 487–518.

Sriraman, B. (2004). The characteristics of mathematical creativity. *The Mathematics Educator, 14*(1), 19–34.

St-Amand, J., Smith, J., & Goulet, M. (2024). Is teacher humor an asset in classroom management? Examining its association with students' well-being, sense of school belonging, and engagement. *Current Psychology, 43*(3), 2499–2514.

Surowiecki, J. (2004). *The wisdom of crowds: Why the many are smarter than the few and how collective wisdom shapes business, economies, societies, and nations.* New York: Doubleday.

Sweller, J. (1988). Cognitive load during problem solving: Effects on learning. *Cognitive Science, 12*(2), 257–285.

Thomsen, B. M. S., Kofoed, J., & Fritsch, J. (Eds.). (2021). *Affects, interfaces, events.* Vancouver, British Columbia, Canada: Imbricate! Press.

Trilling, B., & Fadel, C. (2009). *21st century skills: Learning for life in our times.* San Francisco: Jossey-Bass.

Tschannen-Moran, M., Salloum, S. J., & Goddard, R. D. (2014). Context matters: The influence of collective beliefs and shared norms. In H. Fives & M. Gregoire Gill (Eds.), *International handbook of research on teachers' beliefs* (pp. 301–316). New York: Routledge.

University of California, Office of the President. (n.d.). *SMART goals: A how to guide.* Accessed at https://www.ucop.edu/local-human-resources/_files/performance-appraisal/How%20to%20write%20SMART%20Goals%20v2.pdf on July 12, 2024.

Venville, G. J., Wallace, J., Rennie, L. J., & Malone, J. A. (2002). Curriculum integration: Eroding the high ground of science as a school subject? *Studies in Science Education, 37*(1), 43–83.

Voelkel, J. R. (1994). Kepler's analogy between light and gravitation: Understanding the influence of analogy in the scientific revolution. *Isis, 85*(2), 310–321.

Voltaire. (1919). *Voltaire in his letters; being a selection from his correspondence.* New York: Putnam. Accessed at https://archive.org/stream/cu31924026378335/cu31924026378335_djvu.txt on June 21, 2024. (Original work published 1767)

Voogt, J., & Roblin, N. P. (2012). A comparative analysis of international frameworks for 21st century competences: Implications for national curriculum policies. *Journal of Curriculum Studies, 44*, 299–321. https://doi.org/10.1080/00220272.2012.668938

Vroom, V. H., & Jago, A. G. (2007). The role of the situation in leadership. *American Psychologist, 62*(1), 17–24.

Wanzer, M. B., Frymier, A. B., & Irwin, J. (2010). An explanation of the relationship between instructor humor and student learning: Instructional humor processing theory. *Communication Education, 59*(1), 1–18.

Wiggins, G. P., & McTighe, J. (2005). *Understanding by design.* Arlington, VA: ASCD.

Wilen, W. W. (2001). Exploring myths about teacher questioning in the social studies classroom. *The Social Studies, 92*(1), 26–32.

Willingham, D. T. (2009). *Why don't students like school? A cognitive scientist answers questions about how the mind works and what it means for the classroom.* San Francisco: Jossey-Bass.

Wood, J. M., Nezworski, M. T., & Garb, H. N. (2023). Rorschach inkblots. In J. N. Stea & S. Hupp (Eds.), *Investigating clinical psychology: Pseudoscience, fringe science, and controversies* p. 45–57). New York: Routledge.

World Health Organization. (2021, November 17). *Mental health of adolescents.* Accessed at https://www.who.int/news-room/fact-sheets/detail/adolescent-mental-health on May 15, 2024.

Young, S. H. (2019). *Ultralearning: Master hard skills, outsmart the competition, and accelerate your career.* New York: Harper Business.

Zhao, Y., Lin, S., Liu, J., Zhang, J., & Yu, Q. (2021). Learning contextual factors, student engagement, and problem-solving skills: A Chinese perspective. *Social Behavior and Personality, 49*(2), 1–18.

Zimmerman, B. J. (2002). Becoming a self-regulated learner: An overview. *Theory Into Practice, 41*(2), 64–70.

Zull, J. E. (2002). *The art of changing the brain: Enriching the practice of teaching by exploring the biology of learning.* New York: Routledge.

Index

NUMBERS

21st century skills
   about, 199–200
   challenge-based framework, linking to, 203–205
   concluding thoughts, 208
   differentiating grade-level examples across core disciplines, 205–207
   intersection of and habits of thinking, dissecting, 200–203

A

accountability, 214
action plans, 95
active learning, 8, 21, 32, 112, 122
active memorization, 115.
   See also memorization
agency, 35, 37
agendas, 220
Al-Haytham, I. and creating and innovating, 83.
   See also creating and innovating
analogical thinking, 110–112
analogies with toys strategy, 81
analytic thinking and skills
   academic standards and, 199
   creativity and, 75–76
   cultivating diverse curiosity and, 86

   middle school students and, 184
   nature walks and, 41
   questioning and, 146
   risk taking and, 47, 59
   transfer learning and, 106
anchoring bias, 49.
   See also bias
anxiety and public speaking, 155–156
artificial intelligence and ethics, 3
asking questions.
   See also evaluating evidence; habits of thinking; questions
   about, 7, 125–126
   activities to nurture inquiry in students, 133–137
   concluding thoughts, 137
   encouraging insightful questions, 145–146
   habits of thinking and, 4
   Hypatia of Alexandria and, 132–133
   letting inquiry pave the way, 126–129
   student collaboration and, 233
   supplementing procedural questions, 129–132
assessments, 9, 94, 175, 196, 198
autonomic nervous system (ANS), 155–156
availability bias, 49.
   See also bias

B

background knowledge, 116
baloney detection kit, 133, 135–137
bandwagon effect, 50.
　See also bias
bansho, 130
benign violation theory, 63
bias, 48–52
bird watching, 42
breathing exercises, 156
budgeting activities, 55, 57

C

calendars and scheduling, 224
captain's log of collective intellectual voyages, 131–132
Carver, G. and self-regulation, 101–102.
　See also self-regulation
cause and effect analysis, 95
celebrations, 217
challenge-based framework.
　See also integrating the challenge-based framework and the habits of thinking
　　21st century skills and, 203–205
　　about, 7–9, 12
　　anatomy of, 166–172
　　habits of thinking and, 173–174
　　modeling lessons in, 227–228
　　student collaboration and, 232, 236–237
　　template, 10–11, 176–178
challenge-driven innovation, 78–83
"Challengers" debate forum, 135.
　See also debates and discussions
check-ins, 94, 219–222
chunking, 194–196, 197
classrooms
　　classroom discussions, 108
　　eco-friendly classrooms, 84–85
　　encouraging concentration and, 93
　　interdisciplinary learning environments and, 20–23
climate change, 2–3
coffee chats, 220–221
cognitive biases, 48–52.
　See also bias
collaboration.
　See also student collaboration; teacher collaboration
　　21st century skills and, 202, 203, 205
　　challenge-driven innovation and, 79
　　chunking within challenges and, 194
　　collaborative advantages, 195
　　collaborative goals, 167
　　collaborative practice, 37, 38
　　collaborative teaching, 211
　　incentivizing, 213
　　nurturing collaboration and community, 156–158
　　purpose-driven formal meetings and, 220
　　sustaining through regular check-ins, 219–222
commitment, 213–214

communication
　　21st century skills and, 202, 203
　　coffee chats and, 221
　　security and privacy, 225
　　teacher collaboration and, 217
community, nurturing collaboration and, 156–158
community projects, 42–43, 86
compassion, practicing self-compassion, 109–110
concentration, encouraging, 91, 93
confirmation bias, 49, 50.
　See also bias
conflict, 213
conscious breathing, 156
constructivist thinking, 112–115
content-neutral standards, 191–192.
　See also standards
coping skills, 98, 99–100
creating and innovating.
　See also habits of thinking
　　21st century skills and, 202
　　about, 6–7, 73–74
　　activities to nurture creative thinking and innovative actions in students, 83–86
　　Al-Haytham, I. and, 83
　　concluding thoughts, 86–87
　　fantasy and reality, intersection of, 74–77
　　NASA and challenge-driven innovation, 78–83
　　student collaboration and, 233
creative processes, 76
creative thinking, 5–6, 76
creativity, 21, 120, 184
critical observations, 77
critical thinking, 76, 201–202, 203
cross-disciplinary projects, 76, 204
cultivating diverse curiosity.
　See also habits of thinking
　　about, 6, 31–32
　　activities to nurture curiosity in students, 41–43
　　concluding thoughts, 43
　　curiosity and interdisciplinary learning, 21
　　elementary school students and, 184
　　Feynman, R. and, 40
　　learning dispositions and motivations, developing, 35–39
　　science of a wandering mind, looking to the, 32–35
　　student collaboration and, 233
cultural and global awareness, 202, 204
culturally relevant pedagogy, 35, 37
culturally sustaining pedagogy, 35, 37
cultures of sharing, 212
Curie, M. and evaluating evidence, 146–147.
　See also evaluating evidence
curiosity.
　See cultivating diverse curiosity
customization, 23, 24, 26–27, 76

D

data analysis projects, 143
data sets and arguments, 143–145
debates and discussions, 82, 86, 135, 144, 148

decision making, 46–47, 51
deconstruction, 80–82
default mode network (DNM), 33–35
depression, 61
detective activities, 91, 94–95, 134–135, 148
digital literacy, 161, 200, 201, 202, 204.
  See also digital tools
digital tools
  artificial intelligence and ethics, 3
  deconstruction and, 82
  feedback loops and, 221
  integration with other tools, 225
  linking 21st century skills to the challenge-based framework, 203, 204
  "My Learning Journey" activity, 161
  security and privacy, 225
  self-reflection and, 155
  sharing digital platforms to amplify collaborative potential, 222–225
  technological fluency, 229–230
direct instruction, 192–193
dysfunctions of a team, 213–214

E

eco-friendly classrooms, 84–85
economics, 54
effort, cultivating an environment for, 153–156
elaborative rehearsal, 115
elementary school students
  activities to nurture creative thinking and innovative actions in, 84–85
  activities to nurture curiosity in, 41–42
  activities to nurture evaluating evidence in, 147
  activities to nurture genuine inquiry in, 134–135
  activities to nurture learning through humor in, 69–70
  activities to nurture perseverance and lifelong learning in, 160
  activities to nurture risk taking in, 53–55
  activities to nurture self-regulation in, 102
  activities to nurture transfer learning in, 121
  differentiating grade-level examples of 21st century skills across core disciplines, 205–206
  example elementary grades challenge using the challenge-based framework template, 179–181
  humor in learning, modeling use of, 66
  student collaboration and, 234
embracing lifelong learning and perseverance.
  See also habits of thinking
  about, 7, 151–152
  activities to nurture perseverance and lifelong learning in students, 159–161
  concluding thoughts, 161
  cultivating an environment for effort, 153–156
  establishing objectives, 152–153
  nurturing collaboration and community, 156–158
  Sancho, C. and, 158–159
  student collaboration and, 233
emotional intelligence, 77, 202–203, 204

emotions, expressing, 108
engaging student collaboration.
  See student collaboration
engaging teacher collaboration.
  See teacher collaboration
engineering design process
  about, 171–172
  additional tips for educators using, 173
  challenge-based framework and, 8, 166
  challenge-based instruction and habits integration and, 175
  intersection of challenge and standard and, 198
  linking 21st century skills to the challenge-based framework, 203
environmental projects, 42–43
error analysis projects, 108
essential questions
  about, 168
  challenge-based framework and, 8, 166, 175, 196, 197
  example of moving from a student goal to, 168–169
evaluating evidence.
  See also asking questions;
  habits of thinking
  about, 7, 139–140
  activities to nurture evaluating evidence in students, 147–148
  concluding thoughts, 148–149
  Curie, M. and, 146–147
  data sets and arguments and, 143–145
  encouraging insightful questions, 145–146
  evaluating like a detective, 91, 94–95
  evidence, sources and validity of, 143
  evidence, teaching the meaning of, 140–142
  evidence evaluation checklists, 144
  scientific method in, 142–143
  student collaboration and, 233
expectations for groups, 158
experiments
  activities to nurture genuine inquiry in students, 135, 136
  activities to nurture learning through humor in students, 69
  activities to nurture risk taking in students, 54, 55
  intersection of fantasy and reality and, 76
  scientific method and, 142

F

factor investigations, 54
failure
  embracing failure, 106–110
  failure boards, 20
  NASA and challenge-driven innovation and, 79
fantasy, intersection of and reality, 74–77
feedback
  evaluating like a detective, 95
  feedback forums, 223
  feedback loops, 221–222
  incorporating positive feedback, 91, 92–93

Feynman, R. and cultivating diverse curiosity, 40.
  See also cultivating diverse curiosity
flexibility, 79
flexible seating, 21
focus sessions, 93
fostering the nine habits of thinking in
    K–12 learning.
  See also habits of thinking
    about, 19–20
    concluding thoughts, 27
    interdisciplinary learning, engaging students in,
      23–27
    interdisciplinary learning environments,
      developing, 20–23
    reproducibles for, 28–29
Franklin, B. and using humor, 67–68.
  See also using humor

G

Gentner, D., 111
goals
    challenge-based framework and, 8, 166–167
    concentration and, 93
    goal of *Renaissance Thinking in the Classroom*, 4
    "My Learning Journey" activity, 159–161
    reconnecting with purpose and, 109
    self-regulation and, 90, 91, 98–99
    SMART goals, 152–153, 167
    student goals, 166–167, 175
gradual release of responsibility, 32, 37–38
growth mindset, 21, 92
guest speakers, 220
guided practice, 37–38

H

habits of thinking.
  See also asking questions; creating and innovating;
    cultivating diverse curiosity; embracing lifelong
    learning and perseverance; evaluating evidence;
    fostering the nine habits of thinking in K–12
    learning; integrating the challenge-based
    framework and the habits of thinking; risk taking;
    self-regulation; transfer learning; using humor
    about, 5–7
    challenge-based framework and, 9,
      173–176, 179
    intersection of 21st century skills and, 200–203
    planning and documenting habits, 175
    student collaboration and, 232–234
herd mentality, 50.
  See also bias
high school students
    activities to nurture creative thinking and
      innovative actions in, 85–86
    activities to nurture curiosity in, 42–43
    activities to nurture evaluating evidence in, 148
    activities to nurture genuine inquiry in,
      135–137
    activities to nurture learning through humor in,
      70–71
    activities to nurture perseverance and lifelong
      learning in, 161
    activities to nurture risk taking in, 56–57
    activities to nurture self-regulation in, 102–103
    activities to nurture transfer learning in, 122
    differentiating grade-level examples of 21st
      century skills across core disciplines, 207
    example secondary grades challenge using the
      challenge-based framework template, 182–183
    humor in learning, modeling use of, 66
    student collaboration and, 234–235
higher-order thinking, 117, 129, 184
hindsight bias, 50.
  See also bias
honoring students' achievements, 58–59
humor.
  See using humor
Hypatia of Alexandria, 132–133.
  See also asking questions

I

identifying strengths, 25–26
identity, 36
independent practice, 37, 38
information retrieval and transfer learning,
    118–119.
  See also transfer learning
innovating.
  See creating and innovating
inquiry
    "Inquiry Incubator" module, 135–137
    inquiry lesson starters, 128
    inquiry problems, 129
    letting inquiry pave the way, 126–129
integrating 21st century skills.
  See 21st century skills
integrating academic standards.
  See standards
integrating new information with prior
    knowledge, 114
integrating schedules, 211
integrating the challenge-based framework and the
    habits of thinking.
  See also challenge-based framework;
    habits of thinking
    about, 165
    anatomy of the challenge-based framework,
      166–172
    challenge-based framework examples for
      different grade bands, 179–185
    challenge-based instruction and habits
      integration, 173–179
    concluding thoughts, 185
    reproducibles for, 186–188
interactive workshops, 222.
  See also professional development
interconnected concepts, 77
interdisciplinary learning
    about interdisciplinary thinking and learning,
      1–4
    engaging students in, 23–27
    interdisciplinary learning environments, 20–23
    interdisciplinary projects, 21, 22, 218–219
    intersection of fantasy and reality and, 76
    supporting interdisciplinary student learning,
      12–13

Index

interdisciplinary synergy, 210
interpersonal dynamics, 230
introduction
    about interdisciplinary thinking and learning, 1–4
    challenge-based framework, 7–12
    how this book is organized and how to use it, 13–14
    nine habits of thinking, 5–7
    supporting interdisciplinary student learning, 12–13
    taking inspiration for contemporary K–12 learning from polymaths throughout history, 14–15
invention journals, 85.
    See also journaling
investigations, 54

J

Jemison, M. and risk taking, 52–53.
    See also risk taking
joint professional odysseys, 217
jokes, 63, 65, 69, 70.
    See also using humor
journaling
    invention journals, 85
    nature journaling, 42
    reflection journals, 108
    reflective practice and, 228
    self-regulation and, 98, 100–101

K

kind word theory, 111

L

leaf rubbing art, 41–42
learning.
    See also embracing lifelong learning and perseverance
    intersection of fantasy and reality and, 76
    learning dispositions and motivations, developing, 35–39
    NASA and challenge-driven innovation and, 79
    real-world learning, 21
learning diaries, 94
Lovelace, A. and transfer learning, 120.
    See also transfer learning

M

McTighe, J., 105
meetings, 212, 220
memorization, 115, 118–119
mental models, 119–120
mentorship programs, 157
metacognition, 39, 91, 94
method of loci, 115
middle school students
    activities to nurture creative thinking and innovative actions in, 85
    activities to nurture curiosity in, 42
    activities to nurture evaluating evidence in, 148
    activities to nurture genuine inquiry in, 135
    activities to nurture learning through humor in, 70
    activities to nurture perseverance and lifelong learning in, 160
    activities to nurture risk taking in, 55–56
    activities to nurture self-regulation in, 102
    activities to nurture transfer learning in, 121–122
    differentiating grade-level examples of 21st century skills across core disciplines, 206–207
    example secondary grades challenge using the challenge-based framework template, 182–183
    humor in learning, modeling use of, 66
    student collaboration and, 234
mind mapping, 81
mindfulness, 93
misfit standards, 193–194.
    See also standards
mistakes, 107–108, 109
mnemonic devices, 92, 115, 118
modeling
    coping skills and, 99–100
    gradual release of responsibility and, 37
    use of humor in learning and, 65–67
modes of instruction, aligning, 91–92
motivation, 35–36
multimodal integration, 192
"My Learning Journey" activity, 159–161
Myers-Briggs Type Indicator, 48
mystery box activity, 147

N

NASA and challenge-driven innovation, 78–83
natural progressions, 194, 195
nature journaling, 42.
    See also journaling
nature photography projects, 42
nature walks, 41
norms, 158
note-taking aids, 118–119

O

objectives, 152–153, 195
Occam's razor, 133, 134, 135, 136
out-of-the-box thinking, 79

P

paraprosdokian, 65–67
patterns and big ideas strategy, 116–117
peer observations, 212, 221, 226–228
peer reviews, 108, 144
perseverance.
    See embracing lifelong learning and perseverance
persistence and self-regulation, 39
planning and self-regulation, 90
polygraph exams, 48
polymaths, taking inspiration from, 14–15
population impact activity, 56
positive behavioral interventions and supports (PBIS), 157
prior knowledge, 114, 116

probabilities, activities for, 51, 53–58.
　　See also risk taking
problem solving
　　21st century skills and, 201–202, 203
　　asking questions and, 126
　　challenge-based framework and, 8, 9, 166
　　experiential learning and, 31–32
　　habits of thinking and, 5, 6
　　interdisciplinary learning and, 3, 12
　　learning dispositions and motivations and, 35
　　NASA and challenge-driven innovation and, 78–81
　　using humor and, 70
procedural questions, 129–132
processing and visualizing, 117–118
professional development
　　catalyzing collaborative teaching excellence in, 228–229
　　collaborative environments and, 212
　　teacher collaboration and, 217, 221–222
progress tracking, 91, 93–94, 155
prototype buildings, 85
public health, 3
public speaking anxiety, 155–156
purpose, reconnecting with, 108–109
purpose-driven formal meetings, 220

Q

questions.
　　See also asking questions
　　asking peers and teachers for assistance, 158
　　challenge-based framework and, 8
　　encouraging insightful questions, 145–146
　　interdisciplinary learning environments, developing, 21
　　self-questioning, 95

R

reality, intersection of fantasy and, 74–77
real-world connections, 204
real-world learning, 21
real-world scenarios strategy, 81–82
reflections
　　challenge-based framework and, 9
　　coping skills, 100
　　encouraging insightful questions and, 145
　　evaluating like a detective, 95
　　journaling and, 101, 108
　　linking 21st century skills to the challenge-based framework, 204
　　peer observations and, 228
　　planning and documenting habits and, 175
　　progress tracking and, 94
　　recognizing and assessing probabilities and, 51
　　self-compassion and, 109
　　teacher collaboration and, 217
　　teaching self-reflection, 154–155
reproducibles for
　　challenge-based framework template, 186–188
　　reflection cycle guide, 28
　　strengths utilization guide, 29

research, 54, 57
resilience, 94–95
resistance to change, 24
resources
　　diverse learning resources, 21
　　resource allocation, 229
restorative practices, 157
results, 214
risk taking.
　　See also habits of thinking
　　about, 6, 45–46
　　activities to nurture risk taking in students, 53–58
　　concluding thoughts, 59
　　considering the odds and bias, 48–52
　　decisions as risks, understanding, 46–47
　　honoring students' achievements, 58–59
　　Jemison, M. and, 52–53
　　student collaboration and, 233
role playing, 82, 100, 144
Rorschach inkblot test, 48
Russell, B., 125

S

Sagan, C., 133
Sancho, C. and perseverance, 158–159.
　　See also embracing lifelong learning and perseverance
schedules, 211, 224
schoolwide recognition programs, 157
scientific method, 142–143
selective attending, 113–114
self-assessment tools, 94
self-awareness
　　intrapersonal skills and, 61
　　personalized goals and, 93
　　progress tracking and, 94
　　self-regulation and, 7, 95
　　wandering minds and, 34
self-compassion, 109–110
self-feedback, 93.
　　See also feedback
self-questioning, 95
self-reflection, 154–155
self-regulation.
　　See also habits of thinking
　　about, 7, 89–90
　　activities to nurture self-regulation in students, 102–103
　　Carver, G. and, 101–102
　　concluding thoughts, 103
　　evaluating students' self-regulation and offering opportunities to practice, 95–101
　　learning dispositions and motivations, developing, 35, 36, 38–39
　　self-reflection and, 154
　　student collaboration and, 233
　　student self-regulation check, 96–97
　　using strategies to promote the development of, 90–95

shared resource libraries, 223–224.
  See also digital tools
sharing ideas, giving students ways for, 130–131
sharing knowledge, 211
show-and-tell sessions, 212
skills inventories, 212
SMART goals, 152–153, 167.
  See also goals
social and emotional learning (SEL) programs, 157
social intelligence, 202–203, 204
spaced repetition, 115
standards
  about, 189–190
  balancing academic standards and challenge, 190–194
  chunking within challenges and, 194–196
  concluding thoughts, 198
  intersection of challenge and standard, 196–198
  standards integration, 8, 166, 169–171, 175
Stanford-Binet intelligence test, 48
STEM education, 7–8
stereotype boost, 36–37
stereotype threat, 36
storytelling
  activities to nurture risk taking and, 54, 56
  linking 21st century skills to the challenge-based framework and, 203
  misfit standards and, 194
  silly story prompts, 69
  story cubes, 84
  story deconstruction, 80–81
strategic categorization, 114–115
student collaboration.
  See also collaboration
  about, 231–232
  challenges to in the challenge-based framework, 236–237
  concluding thoughts, 237
  differentiating strategies for helping, 234–235
  finding the essence of in the challenge-based framework, 232
  habits of thinking and, 232–234
  real-world inspired classroom scenario, 235–236
student goals, 166–167, 175.
  See also goals
supplementing procedural questions, 129–132
systems thinking, 77

T

taking control, 90–91
taking risks.
  See risk taking
tangibility factor, 193
teacher collaboration.
  See also collaboration
  about, 209–210
  concluding thoughts, 230
  creating a canvas of collaboration, 210–214, 217–218
  digital platforms to amplify collaborative potential and, 222–225
  interdisciplinary projects and, 218–219
  overcoming hurdles in, 229–230
  peer observations and, 226–228
  professional development and, 228–229
  sustaining collaboration through regular check-ins, 219–222
  using the challenge-based framework and to develop and implement campaigns in a school community, 215–216
teacher-driven goals, 167.
  See also goals
teaching philosophies, 229
teaching self-reflection, 154–155
tech-free zones, 93
technological fluency, 229–230.
  See also digital tools
time, 24, 229
transfer learning.
  See also habits of thinking
  about, 7, 105–106
  activities to nurture transfer learning in students, 121–122
  analogic thinking and, 110–112
  concluding thoughts, 122–123
  constructivist thinking and, 112–115
  embracing failure, 106–110
  implementing effective transfer learning strategies, 115–120
  Lovelace, A. and, 120
  student collaboration and, 233
trust, 92, 213–214, 226

U

using humor.
  See also habits of thinking
  about, 6, 61–63
  activities to nurture learning through humor in students, 68–71
  concluding thoughts, 71
  cultivating safe environments for, 63–65
  Franklin, B. and, 67–68
  modeling use of humor in learning, 65–67
  role of in education, 64
  student collaboration and, 233

V

version history, 222–223. *See also* digital tools
visualization, 117–118
Voltaire, 48

W

wandering minds, 32–35. *See also* cultivating diverse curiosity
why and reconnecting with purpose, 109
Wiggins, G., 105
wins and reconnecting with purpose, 109

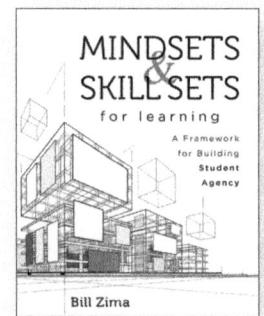

Mindsets and Skill Sets for Learning
Bill Zima
Rely on *Mindsets and Skill Sets for Learning* to help you cultivate confident thinkers who have a strong sense of agency over their lives. Use this guide to enhance your classroom culture with targeted, student-centered learning.
BKL051

Inquiring Minds Want to Learn
Erik M. Francis
Hook students into learning with inquiry and questioning. *Inquiring Minds Want to Learn* guides students down four different inquiry pathways: Foundational, Understanding, Deep, and Expertise. This book delivers detailed guidance for how to phrase and pose good questions that facilitate inquiry-based learning.
BKG102

Everyday Instructional Coaching
Nathan D. Lang-Raad
Coaching teachers in schools is integral to supporting effective teaching methods. This teaching resource provides practical instructional coaching strategies for teachers and educators.
BKF802

The New Art and Science of Teaching Mathematics
Nathan D. Lang-Raad and Robert J. Marzano
Make the most of the New Art and Science of Teaching model in math classrooms. Discover teaching resources, tools, and instructional strategies for math that will aid teachers in articulating learning targets, conducting math lessons, tracking students' learning outcomes, and more.
BKF810

Mathematics Unit Planning in a PLC at Work®, Grades PreK–2
Sarah Schuhl, Timothy D. Kanold, Jennifer Deinhart, Nathan D. Lang-Raad, Matthew R. Larson, and Nanci N. Smith
Bring a laser-like focus to the content PreK–2 students need to learn in every unit throughout the year. This unit planning resource enhances teacher collaboration through the PLC at Work process, increasing student learning in mathematics in early childhood education classrooms.
BKF964

Visit SolutionTree.com or call 800.733.6786 to order.

Global PD teams
Collaborative Learning for School Improvement

Quality team learning **from authors you trust**

Global PD Teams is the first-ever **online professional development resource designed to support your entire faculty on your learning journey.** This convenient tool offers daily access to videos, mini-courses, eBooks, articles, and more packed with insights and research-backed strategies you can use immediately.

GET STARTED
SolutionTree.com/**GlobalPDTeams**
800.733.6786